POPULISM: LATIN AMERICAN PERSPECTIVES

Also by Ronaldo Munck and published by Agenda

Rethinking Global Labour: After Neoliberalism

Social Movements in Latin America: Mapping the Mosaic

POPULISM: LATIN AMERICAN PERSPECTIVES

Edited by

RONALDO MUNCK
MARIANA MASTRÁNGELO
PABLO POZZI

agenda
publishing

First published in 2023 by Agenda Publishing

Agenda Publishing Limited
The Core
Bath Lane
Newcastle Helix
Newcastle upon Tyne
NE4 5TF
www.agendapub.com

ISBN 978-1-78821-598-5

British Library Cataloguing-in-Publication Data
A catalogue record for this book is available from the British Library

Typeset by Newgen Publishing UK
Printed and bound in the UK by CPI Group (UK) Ltd, Croydon, CR0 4YY

CONTENTS

ABBREVIATIONS AND ACRONYMS

AD	Acción Democrática (Democratic Action)
ALBA	Alternativa Bolivariana para las Américas (Bolivarian Alternative for the Americas)
AMAN	Academia Militar Agulhas Negras (Military Academy Black Eagles)
AMO	Arco Minero del Orinoco (Orinoco Mining Arch)
AMLO	Andrés Manuel López Obrador
ANEF	Asociacion Nacional de Empleados Fiscales (National Association of Fiscal Employees)
Banxico	Bank of Mexico
BCIE	Central American Bank of Economic Integration
CAFTA	Central America Free Trade Agreement
CARSI	Central American Regional Security Initiative
CBST	Central Bolivariana Socialista de Trabajadores (Socialist Bolivarian Labor Central)
CELAC	Community of Latin American and Caribbean States
CEPCH	Confederación de Empleados Particulares de Chile (Chilean Private Employees' Confederation)
CGT	Confederación General del Trabajo (General Labour Confederation)
CNDH	Comisión Nacional de Derechos Humanos (Human Rights National Commission)
CNMCIOB -BS	National Confederation of Campesino, Indigenous, and Native Women of Bolivia
COB	Central Obrera Boliviana (Bolivian Labour Central)
COFECE	Comisión Federal de Competencia Económica (Federal Commission of Economic Competence)

CONALCAM	Coordinadora Nacional por el Cambio (National Coordination for Change)
CONAMAQ	National Council of Ayllus and Markas of Qullasuyu
CONEVAL	Concejo Nacional para la Evaluación de Política Social (National Council for the Evaluation of Social Policy)
COPEI	Comité de Organización Política Electoral Independiente (Organizing Committee for Independent Electoral Politics)
COSEP	Concejo Superior de Empresa Privada (Superior Council of Private Enterprise)
CRAC	Confederación Republicana de Acción Cívica (Civic Action Republican Confederation)
CSSL	Health and Safety at Work Committees
CSUTCB	Unitary Syndical Confederation of Peasant Workers of Bolivia
CTCH	Confederación de Trabajadores de Chile (Workers' Confederation of Chile)
CTV	Confederación de Trabajadores de Venezuela (Venezuela Labor Confederation)
CUT	Central Única de Trabajadores (Sole Central of Workers)
ECLAC	Economic Commission for Latin America and the Caribbean
FGR	Fiscalía General de la República (Attorney's General Office)
FIDEG	International Foundation for the Global Economic Challenge
FIT	Frente de Izquierda y de los Trabajadores (Worker and Left Front)
FNLP	Frente Nacionalista Patria y Libertad (Fatherland and Freedom Nationalist Front)
FOCH	Federación Obrera de Chile (Labour Federation of Chile)
FP	Frente Popular (Popular Front)
FRAP	Frente de Acción Popular (Popular Action Front)
FSLN	Frente Sandinista de Liberación Nacional (Sandinista National Liberation Front)
FTAA	Free Trade Area of the Americas
GDR	German Democratic Republic
IC	Izquierda Cristiana (Christian Left)
IFE	Instituto Federal Electoral (Federal Electoral Institute)
IFT	Instituto Federal de Telecomunicaciones (National Telecommunications Institute)

IMF	International Monetary Fund
INAI	Instituto Nacional de Acceso a Información (National Institute of Transparency and Access to Information)
INEE	Instituto Nacional para Evaluaciion Educativa (National Institute for Educational Evaluation)
INEGI	Instituto Nacional de Geografía y Estadística (National Institute of Geography and Statistics)
INSABI	National Institute for Health Care and Wellbeing
LAB	Anti-Lockout Law (LAB)
LOTT	Ley Orgánica del Trabajo y de los Trabajadores (Organic Law of Work and Labour)
MAPU	Movimiento de Acción Popular Unitaria (Unitary Popular Action Movement)
MAS	Movimiento al Socialismo (Movement Towards Socialism)
MBL	Movimento Brasil Livre (Free Brazil Movement)
MIFA	Enlarged Corn Field with Fruit Trees Programme
MIR	Movimiento de Izquierda Revolucionaria (Revolutionary Left Movement)
MNR	Movimiento Nacionalista Revolucionario (Revolutionary Nationalist Movement)
MPF	Ministerio Público Federal (Federal Public Ministry)
MVR	Movimiento Quinta República (Fifth Republic Movement)
NDP	National Development Plan
NED	National Endowment for Democracy
NSM	New Social Movements
OAS	Organization of American States
OECD	Organisation for Economic Co-operation and Development
PCA	Partido Comunista Argentino (Argentine Communist Party)
PCCh	Partido Comunista de Chile (Communist Party of Chile)
PCR	Partido Comunista Revolucionario (Revolutionary Communist Party)
PDC	Partido Demócrata Cristiano (Christian Democratic Party)
PDVSA	Venezuela's petroleum corporation
PGS	Plan Guayana Socialista (Socialist Guyana Plan)
PHS	Public Health System (PHS)

PNR	Partido Nacional Revolucionario (Revolutionary National Party)
POS	Partido Obrero Socialista (Socialist Worker Party)
PPO	Public Prosecutor's Office
PRD	Partido de la Revolución Democrática (Party for a Democratic Revolution)
PRI	Partido Revolucionario Institucional (Institutional Revolutionary Party)
PSCh	Partido Socialista de Chile (Socialist Party of Chile)
PSOE	Partido Socialista Obrero Español (Spanish Socialist Workers' Party)
PSOL	Partido Socialismo y Libertad (Socialism and Freedom Party)
PT	Partido do Trabalhadores (Workers' Party)
PTB	Partido Trabalhista Brasileiro (Brazilian Labour Party)
SNA	Sociedad Nacional de Agricultura (National Society for Agriculture)
STyP	Secretaría de Trabajo y Previsión (Department of Labour and Prevision)
UOM	Unión Obrera Metalúrguca (Union of Metallurgical Workers)
UOT	Union Obrera Textil (Textile Workers' Union)
UP	Unidad Popular (Popular Unity)
USAID	US Agency for International Development
YPF	Yacimientos Petrolíferos Fiscales (Argentina's state-owned petroleum corporation)

FOREWORD

The value of this book is, above all, in its erudite restatement of the centrality of Latin America to the theorization of populism and, by implication, representation, citizenship and the state. That the region does not occupy a more important position within the sociological literature on populism, citizenship and the state, and is not used more widely as the basis for comparative social theory, is a frank mystery – and one this book sets out to challenge. The fault lies with longstanding biases in social science that mean Latin American states and societies are more frequently studied for what they fail to be, instead of what they are. There is little point imagining Latin American states will behave like European ones since they emerged from quite different social and political circumstances, have different levels of capacity, and face different dilemmas. But, instead of probing these differences analytically, Latin America so often finds itself shoehorned into social and political theories that render it, almost inevitably, failing and deviant. And even when the region offers rich, complex, multifaceted histories of important political phenomena that could serve as the starting point for wider theoretical debate – as with populism – its vital contribution is still all too easily sidelined or bolted awkwardly onto theories driven by Anglophone and European narratives. In the case of populism, this really is a huge opportunity lost, since on this particular subject, Latin America is a gift that keeps on giving, as this admirable set of studies makes abundantly clear.

All experiments in populist politics begin with grievances of citizens or subjects who think they deserve better from government. It should not come as a surprise, therefore, that one important contribution of this collection stems from the set of essays that explores populism as the expression of those grievances within the context of the Latin American left. Emphasizing the roots of populism as – at least at times – a vehicle for progressive social demands, stands in refreshing contrast to the contemporary emphasis, in the media and European scholarship especially, on populism as the expression of radical right politics and the rise of chauvinism, racism, xenophobia and extreme, and frequently gendered, law and order programmes of social control. But it is also the case that there are important manifestations of right-wing populism in Latin America, including some of the so-called "neo-populist" experiments in the 1990s, as well as the lamentable experience of Brazil under Jair Bolsonaro, where the label is frequently applied to capture behaviours and policies that are the absolute antithesis of measured, rational action and democratic accountability.

Making progress in understanding populism means moving beyond a simple left–right binary and Latin America is a good place to help scholars do exactly that. In order to explore populism in diverse national contexts, authors here take the view that it should be understood chiefly as "the construction of popular identities" (Panizza 2005), with such identities being socially and politically created and reproduced, and sometimes temporal and contested in character, rather than permanently inscribed in a single or dominant discourse. Taking this approach opens up debates about both democracy – is populism an expression of democracy or an alternative to it? – and the meaning of the term "the people".

The distinguished Chilean sociologist, Enzo Faletto (1985: 95) described Latin American populism, more than 35 years ago, as an attempt to respond to the crisis of oligarchic domination and, at the same time, "a divorce from a liberal vision of democracy". He identified the origins of populism in the ambiguities and tensions that followed the region's embrace of liberalism, starting at the end of the nineteenth century. The adoption of liberal constitutions and economies, he suggested, operated in practice as a systemic source of support for elite power; by extension, therefore, Latin America's troubled relationship with liberal democracy, which persisted for most of the twentieth century, was rooted in the limitations of liberal models of citizenship. Latin American populism emerged as a way of contesting, not only the authority of elites to speak for the nation, but also as a questioning of emergent forms of elite-managed liberal democracy. It posited that the "people" could act as an agent of social transformation and serve as the key to the construction of a new or improved social order. Of course, the people could be – and were – captured by pragmatic and adept political leaders for their own ends. But to focus only on how the electorate can be manipulated from above, is to miss the vital significance of populism as a key moment in the emergence of demands for accountability in government and more equitable citizenship in Latin America.

Latin America's history of populism, as well as the ideas and narratives that attach to it, are quite different in some key ways from its history in Europe, including in relation to its radical origins. Whatever demerits attached to populist governments once in office, they signalled the end of the complacent exercise of elite power. The result was not always the broadening of democracy, however; in many cases, in fact, the political struggles culminated in closure of popular political spaces and the introduction of authoritarian rule. This legacy, and the fear of overpromising a mobilized electorate, has profoundly shaped contemporary democracies in the region. Yet the social demands that led to populism in the first place remain central elements within popular political imaginaries, re-emerging in the moments of crisis and frustration that have been all too frequent since the restoration of democracy in the 1980s. Scholars would do well, therefore, to follow the example of the contributors to this volume who, rather than lamenting the continued appeal of populism, explore the drivers and identities encapsulated in populist movements, in the face of democracies that continue to deliver thin and partial citizenship and provide poor services to the people they are supposed to serve.

Jean Grugel
Professor of Development Politics
Director of the Interdisciplinary Centre for Global Development (IGDC)
University of York

REFERENCES

Faletto, E. 1985. "Sobre populismo y socialismo". *Opciones* 7: 90–121.
Panizza, F. 2005. *Populism and the Mirror of Democracy*. London: Verso.

INTRODUCTION

Populism is perhaps one of the most overused, yet under-analysed, terms in political discourse today. It can embrace authoritarian and nativist right-wing politicians, but also those on the left who appeal for popular support for transformation. In its dominant usage it is seen as inimical to the values of liberal democracy. Yet others see it as part of the construction of a "people"-centred project that can help us democratize democracy, to put it that way. What is clear is that much of the debate around populism has been from the perspective of the global North and the voice of the South has been largely missing.

The term "populism" today spells, for most people in the global North, something akin to racism and with dark memories of fascism lurking in the background. The "populists" who come to mind are Orbán, Le Pen, Farage or Trump, who cultivate a mass base around the needs of the "left behind" or native-born. The political elites are cast as globalizers, not from somewhere in particular, and dangerously complacent about the dangers of being swamped by mass immigration.

In Latin America the same term has had a very different resonance. It is bound up with democratization, the incorporation of the working classes, and the making of the national developmental state. Its emergence is marked by the crisis of the conservative export-oriented state in the 1930s that burst into the open after the Second World War, with the growth of an organized labour movement and the consolidation of nationalism in the new world order that emerged. This gave way to what can be called a compromise state that replaced the old oligarchic state, and in which the popular masses were both mobilized and controlled by what became known as populist state politics.

There have been many interpretations of populism in Latin America. Early studies tended to place it in terms of the modernization of society and the emergence of disposable masses, waiting to be captured by an ideology that would promote social change while maintaining the stability of the dominant order. This perspective was closely tied to the dominant modernization perspective promoted by the US following the Second World War, as it sought to dominate the postcolonial world. It was also deployed in a different way by the advocates of national development, a conservative modernization from above, led by the state. It was thus often seen as tied to the emergence of national inward-looking development strategies, that were an integral component of the postcolonial era. National industrialists would thus support these movements, as would the military in some cases due to their national developmentalist ambitions.

Classic political terminology was also deployed, including the terms of fascism and Bonapartism/Caesarism. Against the opposition between oligarchy and people deployed in the nationalist frame, they sought parallels with the rise of fascism in Germany and Italy, reading the local through European lenses, as it were. The Gramscian concept of Caesarism was perhaps more relevant as it signalled an equilibrium between classes and the emergence of a "Bonapartist" leader above classes who could "save the system from itself". Likewise, the Gramscian notion of "passive revolution" pointed towards a political transformation that left the fundamentals of the dominant order intact. There is still, maybe, a sense that these theoretical frames were somewhat forced on the recalcitrant realities of Latin America and often rode roughshod over national particularities.

This volume starts from the particular historical reality of Latin America with all the contributors being openminded about the historical record, not seeking to force it into a pre-existing mould. Of course, social and political theory can contribute to elucidating the history of "actually existing populism" but it needs to be a grounded theory that is derived from its complex history, and not imposed from outside. Our endeavour can also be framed in terms of current concerns to "decolonize the curriculum", which means we need to bring to the fore subaltern views and understandings of the world. In that way, we hope to bring the rich experience of populism in Latin America to bear on the current international debates that too often are just reduced to the North Atlantic domain.

Overall, this volume seeks to contribute to the global debate on populism from a Latin American perspective, or perspectives to be precise. The international debates on populism have tended to simplify the Latin American experience, for example positing Peronism as a form of fascism in the past, and then, more recently, calling the left governments after the year 2000 "populist", mainly because they broke with austerity politics and were thus deemed irresponsible. The various authors of this volume show how Latin America, in its rich and early experience of populism, is a valuable laboratory to take our understanding forward and to address the question of whether populism now goes beyond the dichotomy of left and right and is, indeed, a new political phenomenon.

This book presents a series of national case studies that illuminate some well-known, and some not so well-known, experiences, along with cross-cutting overview chapters that highlight the lessons to be learned from the research reported in this volume. In particular, there are general chapters on populism and the left and in relation to the politics of the right. Each chapter is set within a conceptual framework in order to both better understand contemporary Latin American politics as a new phase of progressive politics opens up and, at the same time, to enrich the international debate on populism from diverse Latin American perspectives.

Ronaldo Munck opens the volume with a broad review of the international debate on populism and in its Latin American context. It is not his purpose to produce a "Latin American" theory of populism. However, it is necessary to develop a grounded theory to underpin the subsequent sections that will more concretely outline the characteristics of "classical" and "contemporary" populism in Latin America. From the 1950s–60s structural functionalist approach, we can take a focus on the changing social patterns (and the crucial role that workers played) in the period that preceded the emergence of populism. Then, from the 1960s–70s structural dependence paradigm, we can take a systematic focus on the "compromise state" underpinning populist regimes. Subsequently, it is the figure of Ernesto Laclau that dominates, from a Gramscian phase in the 1980s–90s to a more formal discourse theoretic approach in the 2000s. While not neglecting the advances made by Laclau in creating a formal theory of populism, we might also consider his earlier Gramscian lens as best suited to our analysis of populism in the context of the various phases of capital accumulation and the social construction of capitalist hegemony in Latin America.

Marcelo Raimundo takes up the vexed question of whether Peronism in Argentina should be seen as a phenomenon of the right or left wing in politics. The question of Peronism's political orientation is, in fact, a result of the historical process. For most intellectuals in 1945 it was quite impossible to associate Peronism with the left wing of politics. Peronism was seen as demagogy, totalitarianism, or as the manifestation of fascism in Argentina. Later, some of the left came to believe that Peronism was in some way "progressive" that is, anti-imperialist and anti-oligarchic. After the 1955 coup that displaced Perón, the political narrative shifted beyond discussing the progressive aspects of Peronism, as the left steered towards a more intense debate about its role in connection with socialism. In truth, this era opened a discussion about the revolutionary or non-revolutionary character of populist movements within a considerable part of the Latin American left.

The debates in Argentina were perhaps some of the more intense, if we consider that an important part of the new left guerrilla movement that emerged in the 1960s, and gained prominence in the 1970s, identified itself with Peronism.

Igor Goicovic takes up the early development of the socialist and communist parties in Chile and shows that, from the 1930s to the mid-1950s, they shared some of the characteristics we now associate with populism. In that period, the Socialist Party in particular showed three phenomena typical of the Latin American matrix of populism: it stimulated a mass mobilization, anchored in paternalism, personalism, nationalism and the promise of immediate gratification; it contributed to the formation of heterogeneous coalitions, mainly composed of workers, but led by sectors from the middle and wealthy classes; and it promoted economic programmes based on the need for industrialization and a degree of wealth redistribution. However, this approach would have been exhausted by the mid-1950s, in the context of the criticism of the populist front experience, to be definitively overcome in the 1960s, when the Socialist Party of Chile (PSCh) fell under the influence of the Cuban Revolution. However, its demise was not absolute, since an important part of the party, both in its rank and file as well as in its leadership, remained attached to populist political practices.

Reinaldo Lindolfo Lohn and *Silvia Maria Fávero Arend* take up the history of the Workers Party (PT) in Brazil and its leader "Lula", often accused of being populist and not a true part of the left. Since the 1950s the term "populism" has referred to a situation in which there could not be a full formation of social classes endowed with awareness of their "historical role". Such a vision placed Brazilian workers as part of a "gelatinous" or "weak" civil society, dependent on an all-powerful state, dedicated to manipulation, co-optation and corruption. The term "populism" in Brazil was deployed by the liberal-conservative opposition to Getúlio Vargas in 1945, when it was a question of disqualifying the popular support for the then dictator. Around the expression populism, an image of the "people", as a mixture of the ignorant and the alienated was built, even in the academic field and within a substantial portion of the left. An image was crystallized, according to which the history of Brazil in the twentieth century was summarized as a succession of authoritarian leaders, followed by moments in which there was imperfect democracy led by devious politicians. The people could only observe the exercise of power, without the agency to alter their own destiny. Lula and the PT were to change that. But at what cost?

Victor de Oliveira Pinto Coelho turns our attention to Jair Bolsonaro who became president of Brazil in 2019 on a wave of opposition to the long-lasting Workers Party governments that had ruled since 2003. Here "Bolsonarism" is characterized as an extreme right-wing populist phenomenon, similar to that which saw the global wave of right-wing politicians that emerged from a situation of crisis of democracy. This, in turn, is directly linked to economic transformation (the rise of neoliberalism) that has been causing profound change in the labour market, increasing inequality but also creating greater expectations. When these expectations are eventually frustrated, an extreme right-wing populism can emerge. In Brazil, Bolsonarism made explicit the authoritarian agenda of the country, marked in recent history by the dictatorship of 1964–85 and the older anti-communist tradition, and updated through the anti-PT movement. The decisive role of the neo-Pentecostal churches was also key to the "culture wars" as was the xenophobia of voters from the south and southeast regions of the country in relation to the people of the northeast.

Patricia Pensado Leglise turns to Mexico and takes up the case of Andrés Manuel López Obrador (known as AMLO) who came into office in 2018 after several attempts at gaining the presidency. He took over a country characterized by deep social malaise and with serious and longstanding problems such as increasing levels of violence, low economic growth for more than 30 years, widening social inequalities, predominance of precarious jobs and low tax revenues. Many commentators have pointed to his support for the poor but this commitment lacks a discernible strategy and public policies to overcome the vicious circle of poverty. Money transfers as well as educational and economic programmes are required and, above all, there needs to be an understanding that there can be no social development without sustained economic growth and good, formal and well-paid jobs. Is AMLO's government populist (in the sense of popular) and one that is moving towards the demolition of unfair structures? Or is it conservative and incapable of laying the foundations of a mixed economy articulated by a national investment programme, a state of law and universal rights, sustained by sound, flexible and transparent public finance? This is still an open question.

Roberto López Sánchez turns our attention to Venezuela and President Hugo Chávez who came into office in 1998 and won every election until his death in 2013, when his chosen successor, Maduro, stood and won in his place. For many, Chávez was the epitome of Latin American populism, but his political trajectory is more complex. In a dizzying electoral surge in 1998, Chávez prevailed over the candidate of the traditional parties, which had taken turns in power since 1958. With a central proposal to convene an assembly to draft a new constitution, Chávez put forward a political-economic programme very close to the welfare state in a global neoliberal context. His electoral proposal announced an endorsement of the "Third Way", as formulated by British "New Labour" leader Tony Blair and others. Upon coming to power, Chávez was labelled as a "populist" leader similar to others throughout Latin America's twentieth century. But his performance in government quickly transcended traditional populist frameworks, moving closer to models of "socialist revolution" such as Cuba. Chávez reformulated the ideal of "socialist revolution" that linked the principles of national sovereignty and continental integration, dating from the War of Independence, with the more recent traditions of popular revolutionary struggle.

John Brown looks to the career of Evo Morales in Bolivia who assumed the presidency in 2006, was re-elected three times, was deposed by a right-wing coup in 2019, but then saw his party win the elections in 2021 after a period of intense social movement mobilization. The emergence of populist outsider Evo Morales at the head of the Movement Towards Socialism (MAS) was a direct response to a crisis of representation within the country's population. An exclusionary market model of democracy organized the interests of white elites into politics, while indigenous-popular voices were excluded from policymaking. A myriad of groups such as *cocaleros* (coca growers), urban labour, lowland indigenous groups and women's groups, among others, faced dual political and socioeconomic exclusion under the neoliberal-infused market model of democracy. Although each group had specific grievances, Morales successfully framed their issues under a common banner of anti-neoliberalism and called on organizations to unite in social and electoral protest against market democracy. Morales's populist framing mechanism and dual street/electoral protest tactics directly challenged the status quo and called for a reconstruction of the social order, whereby the state would act as a guarantor of societal well-being.

Pablo Dávalos examines the Correa decade (2007–17) in Ecuador, where the Constituent Assembly process of 2007–08 changed the constitutional rules of the game in a transcendental manner. This made it possible to move from the rule of law to the constitutional rule of rights and justice, and also served to create the governing party, Alianza País. With enormous political capital, the nascent government had a wide margin of manoeuvre and used the elections that endorsed the constitutional change as proposed by the Constituent Assembly to structure and define the governing party. The new Constitution reflected the need for a radical reformulation of the political system and its institutions but, at the same time, it provided the new government with the tools to ensure its own conditions of political domination. Its geographical context was also favourable to the new government. It had around it a number of governments that subscribed to, and supported, its redistribution and sovereignty proposals and that constituted a regional environment critical of the Washington Consensus. Rafael Correa became one of the most radical and implacable critics of these policy prescriptions and of the international financial institutions that promoted them.

William I. Robinson turns to a case that has divided many of those who were enthused by the overthrow of the dictator Somoza in Nicaragua in 1979 and the emergence of the Sandinistas as an independent new left in Latin America. When Nicaraguan president Daniel Ortega began a fourth consecutive term in office in January 2022, it was in the midst of a political and economic crisis that portends protracted instability in the Central American country. Since returning to office in 2007, Ortega and his wife, and vice president, Rosario Murillo, have dressed in a quasi-leftist discourse of "Christian, Socialist, and Solidarity" their programme of constructing a populist multiclass alliance under the firm hegemony of capital and Sandinista state elites. This alliance began to unravel in the second decade of the century and then collapsed entirely in the aftermath of the government's violent repression of a 2018 mass popular uprising. The repression – which, according to Amnesty International, involved excessive use of force, extrajudicial executions, control of the media and the deployment of pro-government paramilitary squads against protesters – left several hundred dead and sent tens of thousands more into exile. It is doubtful that there is anything here that can be called part of the left any longer.

Based on the case studies developed above we seek to draw some general lessons learnt that can feed into the global, and especially European, debates on populism. This very malleable political phenomenon needs to be understood, and not just condemned. Its relationship with democracy is not straightforward but the difference with liberal democracy is not sufficient to deem it beyond the pale. Above all, we need to understand populism rather than demonize it.

Barry Cannon considers the relationship between populism and what has traditionally been called the right in politics. He views populism as an academic analytical tradition rather than empirical fact, emphasizing instead the left/right dichotomy as the essential conceptual tool to help order, understand and explain political phenomena. He develops Bobbio's conception of the left/right dichotomy as a dyad, shaped by historical consensus and rupture centred on (in)equality. This distinction between left and right can be loosely mapped onto the Latin American experience in terms of the postwar "state developmentalist" or classic "populist" phase and the more recent phase of left-oriented, "pink tide" governments. These have both been contested by right-oriented administrations, viewed in the dominant literature as "neo-populist" and associated with figures such as Menem in Argentina, Collor in Brazil and, most notably, Fujimori in Peru, and a more recent radical right populism, associated primarily with Jair Bolsonaro in Brazil. Cannon's chapter reviews these instances of right-wing populism in Latin America consecutively, using a contextually sensitive approach that is equipped to appreciate their distinctions, while emphasizing what they share.

Mariana Mastrángelo and *Pablo Pozzi*, in turn, consider the relationship between populism and what has been considered the left in politics. We need to ask whether the Latin American populist movements are moving in the same direction as the left or if, rather, they are in opposition to the left. We also need to pose the question of whether the populist movements considered in this volume are, in fact, a new type of left more attuned to the politics of the twenty-first century. To do that we also need to (re)consider what we mean by the left in a Latin American context: the traditional communist tradition is not the same as the anarchist or anarcho-syndicalist tradition and they are, also, of course distinct from the theology of liberation or revolutionary nationalism. For the authors, the term "left" describes all those political movements which question capitalism as a social and economic system, which consider populist those movements that see themselves as vehicles of the people, and whose aspirations imply a progressive slant to their policies and a challenge to established elites.

Finally, *Francisco Panniza*, in an Afterword reflects on the definitional questions around populism, on the basis that they need to be clarified if we are to have a useful paradigm or lens of study. As with many of the contributors to this volume Panniza grounds his theory of populism in the history and the political economy of Latin America. He examines two waves of populism in Latin America, namely the "national popular" phase that begins, more or less, in the 1940s, and the second twenty-first-century populism he discerns after the year 2000. By discerning both the commonalities and the differences between these variants, Panizza is able to answer broader questions about the nature of populism and its relationship with development and democracy.

CHAPTER 1

POPULISM IN LATIN AMERICA: DEVELOPMENT, DEMOCRACY AND SOCIAL TRANSFORMATION

Ronaldo Munck

In both popular and academic parlance, the term "populism" has taken on a more or less uniformly negative connotation. It implies being an enemy of democracy, anti-immigrant and, most obviously, irrationally under the sway of a charismatic leader. Yet in Latin America, populism has been an integral element of the development and democratization process and plays an important role in the contemporary process of social transformation under the left-of-centre governments that have emerged since the turn of the century. Thus, we need to deconstruct the term "populism" and explore its diverse historical manifestations, to rethink its meaning and its prospects moving forward.

This introduction to a volume consisting of detailed case studies of Latin American populism, or populism in Latin America, advances in several moments. First, I will approach the burgeoning international debate on rethinking populism to distil some broad lines of investigation, that might serve to guide our research. I distinguish between a structural/socioeconomic frame for understanding populism, another where the focus is on populism as political strategy/style and, finally, one where populism is seen within an ideational or discursive frame. I also introduce the complex, and sometimes contradictory, relationship between populism and development, democracy and social transformation. A second section introduces several Latin American perspectives on populism in a broad conceptual sense. It examines the structural functionalist approach of the 1950s, the dependent development "compromise state" interpretation of the 1970s and, finally, the discourse approach and its critiques that dominated in the 1990s. We then move from the abstract to the concrete, with two stylized accounts of the classical populism of the 1930–70 period and the contemporary populism that has emerged in the 1990s and, particularly, in the context of the progressive governments post-2000. This account is set in a broadly political economy frame, with a focus on the changing patterns of capital accumulation, the role of the state and the waves of popular mobilization that have characterized Latin America since 1930.

RETHINKING POPULISM

Anyone meeting the word "populism" in the North Atlantic region will assume it has a negative connotation. It may refer, as in "economic populism", to governments that do not exercise financial prudence and just give handouts to the population to ensure their popularity. For others – as in "populist politician" – it will be seen to refer to something dark and dangerous, scapegoating minorities or foreigners to gain popularity among the native population. Those who vote for these populist politicians are seen to be affected by some form of "false consciousness" or are, simply, in need of therapy. Those who support economic populism need to be disciplined by the market and a good dose of austerity politics, that will soon bring them down to earth. For my part, I will take the issues raised by populism and populist politics as real and valid. Furthermore, I will not engage in the futile academic game of seeking out what populism "is" but, rather, I will situate populism in its concrete historical context and also its geographical one, making clear my remit is Latin America.

Simplifying the vast international literature, we can discern three main perspectives that are relevant to our enterprise. The first lens is a structural one, focused on the socioeconomic context of populism. The emphasis here is on the historical pattern of industrialization and the impact that has had on the development of social classes, and the political manifestations of class struggles. There is also a considerable focus on the emergence of new working classes and their entry into the political arena. In later years, it placed more emphasis on the "populist" nature of economic polices where any form of economic redistribution was thus dubbed, so as to disqualify it among all right-minded people. From a Latin American perspective (see next section) this approach could still be valuable in providing a grounding of political processes in terms of the social structures of accumulation.

The second perspective focuses on populism as a political strategy and/or as a political style. Quite simply, here, populism is part of a strategy for power, and diverse constructions of "the people" are an integral element of it. It may involve a charismatic figure developing a direct and unmediated relationship with the masses, but that is not always the case. In Latin America there have been salient examples where this is the case (to the extent of becoming a caricature) but the construction of a "people" for electoral and/or social movement purposes may be conducted by political parties as well. A variant of this approach, a minor one in my view, is a focus on "populist" leadership styles, where mass mobilization is fomented through conserved linguistic and dress codes seeking to portray the leader as a person "of the people". This paradigm, taken as a whole, directs our attention to state power and the way in which populism is part and parcel of the normal political process.

The third perspective is a poststructuralist one, focused on the discourse of populism, sometimes called an ideational approach. Over and above the socioeconomic and sociopolitical context in which populism emerges, it is always already constructed as an idea or a discourse. It is through this construction that "the people" and, their counterpart, "the elite" emerge. Mudde and Rovira Kaltwasser advocate a definition of populism as a "thin-centred ideology", which allows us to grasp the malleability of the concept and the way in which it can be attached to both right-wing and left-wing projects (Mudde & Rovira Kaltwasser 2017: 6). Populism, from this perspective, is never "pure" in the sense of having a given ideological content, and it is often "transitional" in the sense that it will either persist or transform itself into something else.

We can now move towards specifying our theoretical frame, by examining the relationship of populism to three distinct but interrelated problematics, namely development, democracy and social transformation. An earlier wave of populism studies in the 1970s focused very much on populism as a characteristic of backwardness. Thus, Andrzej Walicki wrote that "studies of Russian populism can help us understand some ideological patterns which emerge today in the backward areas of the contemporary world" (Walicki 1969: 92). Peter Worsley built his whole theory of populism around what he saw as the "elective affinity" between populism and the backward capitalism of what was then called the Third World (Worsley 1969). Populism is seen as a bridging ideology, as "modernization" gets underway and capitalism undermines the pre-capitalist, communalist modes of production. It is seen as a particular rural response to the onwards march of capitalism, modernity and industrialization.

The history of the Russian "populists" of the late nineteenth century is indeed relevant here, if set in the development context and not just as an ideological precursor to the concept of populism today. This was a movement, based on the social principles of the traditional Russian commune, that sought to bypass the capitalist stage of development. It was a view that the late Marx, to some extent, went along with and which led to his rejection of traditional unilinear theories of development (see Munck 2021). But, in 1895, Lenin attacked the movement in *The Economic Content of Populism* (Lenin 1969) and, incidentally, introduced the term "populist" as a term of abuse within Marxism. He reinstated a mechanical Marxist theory of development, with the emphasis on the social differentiation of the peasantry and the absolute necessity of the capitalist stage of development. Subsequent attempts to build on collectivist agrarian structures, to generate democratic development have, in this tradition, been dismissed as "neo-populist" (Blaikie 2000). Nevertheless, they persist and have even increased in importance, for example in the *buen vivir/sumak kawsay* discourse of the Andean countries.

Basically, the relationship of populism to democracy is taken for granted in the North Atlantic sphere: populism is an enemy of liberal democracy. In the 1970s, Peter Worsley was one of the few to declare categorically, against the wisdom of the age, that: "Populism as 'direct' participation is ... a dimension of the democratic and socialist tradition" (Worsley 1969: 247). The reality of "actually existing populism" (as I have called it above) is that it can, at one and the same time, promote democracy, but also lead to a degradation of democracy. It can lead to the incorporation of popular classes, previously excluded from the political process, but it can also develop authoritarian features as it seeks to remain in office. One way of describing its relationship to democracy is via Margaret Canovan's description of populism as lying in the gap between the "redemptive and pragmatic sides of politics" with modern democracy sitting at the intersection (Canovan 1999: 9). From this perspective, democracy is not (or should not be) just a pragmatic way of dealing with conflict, but should retain a redemptive aspect when taken to be part of a radical democratic project.

The commonly presented binary oppositions between "populist" and "non-populist" politicians do not actually make sense in practice, and lead to somewhat meaningless taxonomies. To go beyond this paradigm, we can take up Francisco Panizza's conclusion that the "core meaning" of the concept of populism can be defined as "a mode of identification for the construction of popular identities" (Panizza 2005: 211). As with democracy, populism can be seen as a political methodology rather than a set ideology. If we agree on this approach, we will be less torn by the binary opposition of populist/non-populist and democratic/non-democratic. As Panizza puts it, in relation to populism, "its inherent ambiguity becomes less problematic: if identities are not fixed once and for all and overall have split and overlapping identities, the same applies to the modes of identification that seek, more or less successfully, to constitute these identities" (Panizza 2005: 211). Our identities are not simple, but complex and sometimes contradictory. It follows thus that populism and democracy, like all politics, is both complex and contradictory. This opens up a fluid research agenda for the study of populism.

Finally, we need to consider the relationship between populism and social transformation: is it, in the broadest sense, regressive (conservative) or progressive? From a Marxist and a liberal perspective alike, it is easy to argue that it is a regressive phenomenon. It is an ideology that reflects backwardness and not the "forward march of history". It is explicitly opposed to liberal democracy, and it seeks to build a mythical (even racialized) "people", rather than citizens. In reality "liberal democracy" can also be seen as a myth that has only prevailed for limited periods, in specific regimes and benefitting some populations. Marxism has had its own teleological tendencies – going back to Lenin's polemics with the Russian populists – that also ignored the combined and uneven nature of development. Populism can, on the contrary, be viewed as a perfectly normal aspect of politics and as an open-ended, transitional, or mixed, response to capitalist development.

We need to accept that both Hitler and Mao were "populists" and in that sense it is, indeed, beyond left and right. We can also argue that populism is progressive for social transformation in a very specific way. As Ernesto Laclau puts it: "populism presents itself both as *subversive* of the existing state of things and as the starting point for a more or less radical *reconstruction* of a new order whenever the previous one has been shaken" (Laclau 2005: 177, emphasis in original). Populism is part of the process of social transformation, but it has no necessary end point. Here we might draw useful parallels with Karl Polanyi's analysis of social transformation as an interplay between the expansion of the free market and the protective mechanisms of society (Polanyi 2001). Commenting on the various reactions to the great crisis of the 1930s, Polanyi observed: "the discarding of the market utopia brings us face to face with the reality of society. It is the dividing line between liberalism on the one hand, and fascism and socialism on the other" (Polanyi 2001: 267). The crisis of the 1930s, and the reaction of society, could lead equally, to Hitler, Stalin or Roosevelt. Populism likewise can be seen to have no necessary class belonging, and its politics depend on how it is articulated with the various class ideologies. That insight could be a useful pillar for an engaged research agenda around populism in contemporary politics.

LATIN AMERICAN PERSPECTIVES

Latin American political theorists – not least Ernesto Laclau – have made a major contribution to the international debates around populism outlined above. To understand these theories, they need to be placed in their Latin American context. Thus, Laclau's approach needs to be situated in terms of the experience of Peronism in Argentina. More broadly, we need to place Latin America as a peripheral global region with its distinctive pattern of capital accumulation and political regimes (Munck 2013). This has tended, broadly speaking, to be more exogenous in its dynamic, compared to the more endogenous development of the core capitalist countries, and it has been characterized by a greater degree of state intervention in both economic and political terms. But, unlike sub-Saharan Africa (cf. Saul 1969), it has been integrated into the global capitalist system since colonization and there is far less of a communal economy. Thus, populism does not play a role as "national" or cohesive ideology for a rural community in the same way.

Gino Germani was a refugee from Mussolini's Italy, who took up residence in Argentina in 1934, and set about laying the basis for a "scientific" sociology. His model was the structural-functionalist approach, that was designed to underpin the modernization approach of the US to create a new colonialism after the demise of European colonialism. In his classic study *Política y Sociedad en una Época de Transición* (Germani 1965), he examined the destruction of traditional forms of consensus, and the search by the masses for another form of personal identity. Argentina's newly formed working class, as a product of industrialization and internal migration, was mobilized by General Perón, outside of the traditional working-class ideologies of socialism, syndicalism, anarchism and communism. For him, charismatic leadership and "disposable" newly mobilized urban masses, created the conditions for an amorphous authoritarian "national populism", that was the very antithesis of democracy and sailed very close to fascism.

A definitive critique of Germani's model occurred at both the empirical and theoretical level. As against his motion that Peronism was simply a populist movement mobilizing naïve masses, Murmis and Portantiero (1971) showed how the labour unions (and the "old" working class) were key drivers in creating the Peronist movement, that took an obscure colonel into the presidential office. In broader terms, Germani's theoretical frame was questionable. For one, Argentina did not possess the social data needed to "apply" the structural functionalist model and, in fact, Germani distanced himself from it when he was in Harvard in the late 1960s (see later work such as Germani 1978 and a wide-ranging appreciation of his work in Serra 2019). In terms of the model itself, Murmis describes how Germani's early class analysis "was imbued with a certain evolutionist confidence in a unidirectional process of change" (Murmis 2010: 75). Peronist populism was, from this perspective, an unfortunate detour in the "normal" evolution of class structures and ideologies.

Germani's emphasis on the way in which populism demobilized the working class was a theme picked up some time later by Francisco Weffort (1978), albeit from a Marxist perspective. Weffort emphasized the positive aspects of popular participation as a result of the populist governments in Brazil during the 1960s but, after the 1964 coup, he began to criticize the demobilizing aspects of populism and the need for proletarian autonomy. Yet he always argued that populism was more than the manipulation of the masses, and he criticized all elitist interpretations of politics. One of Weffort's most interesting contributions was the notion of populism as a "compromise state". This resulted from the incapability of the Latin American bourgeoisie to achieve hegemony in the context of the relative autonomy of the state which, through populism, substitutes for the crisis of hegemony of the dominant classes.

Another major theoretical contribution to the analysis of populism was that of Octavio Ianni (1975), which was close to the dependency paradigm that posited domination by the advanced industrial economies as the overdetermining feature of Latin American society. Ianni saw the emergence of classical Latin American populism (Perón, Árbenz, Goulart) as the product of the struggle between the urban classes and industrial centres against the agrarian oligarchies and the archaic forms of imperialism. For Ianni, we need to distinguish between a "populism from above" that promotes class harmony and eventually abandons the masses to their fates, and a "populism from below", driven by the urban masses, migrants, the lower middle class and the left, in a struggle where the masses can engage in class struggle. Populism also represents a process of secularization at the cultural level, and a modern political alliance that is congruent with the history of the working class, and not an anomaly.

Ernesto Laclau's first systematic engagement with populism in the mid-1970s began with a critique of Germani, for whom he had been a research assistant in the early 1960s. Laclau rejected the teleology of modernization theory, and the notion that populism represented merely a transitional phase. Nor did he go along with the class determination of history, as in the orthodox Marxist accounts. The thesis that Laclau puts forward is that "populism consists of the presentation of popular-democratic interpellations as a synthetic-antagonistic complex with respect to the dominant ideology" (Laclau 1977: 172–3). As with nationalism, it has no necessary class connotation, given that both a fascist project and a communist one can equally articulate it. Populism is set in the context of a crisis of hegemony when the dominant classes seek redress through an appeal to "the people". Likewise, it can be articulated by the subaltern classes, and here Laclau notes, against accepted wisdom, that "a socialist populism is not the most backward form of working-class ideology but the most advanced" (Laclau 1977: 174).

In 2005 Laclau returned to the subject of populism in a book-length study *On Populist Reason* (Laclau 2005), which went beyond his earlier work, to seek a new theory. His new definition was "that by 'populism' we do not understand a type of movement – identifiable with either a special social base or a particular ideological orientation – but a *political logic*" (Laclau 2005: 117, emphasis in original). While, in his Gramscian moment, the concept of "hegemony" had served to break with the essentialist social logic of orthodox Marxism, Laclau was now firmly in a post-Marxist discourse-centred domain. Populism is seen as a "floating signifier" that can be taken over by radically opposed ideologies and purposes. In a process of conceptual inflation (to my mind) Laclau begins to argue that "the political becomes synonymous with politics" or, more precisely that "the construction of the 'people' is the political act *par excellence*" (Laclau 2005: 154). In brief, the concept of the "people", that lies at the heart of populism, is not attached to any particular symbolic matrix.

Laclau's work has attracted a lot of attention and has been taken up by many of the global theories of populism. In the Latin American context, it was appreciated, but also heavily criticised, for what some saw as his filo-populism orientation in his open support for existing populist governments in Argentina and elsewhere. In theoretical terms, as Francisco Panizza argued, "populism cannot be understood, as Laclau claimed, in purely formal, ontological terms" (Panizza 2005: 197). Certainly, populism is about the construction of political frontiers, an articulation of the people *vis-à-vis* the elite. Populist discourses – around the sovereignty of the people – are not autonomous but draw meaning from other discourses, such as those of democracy, justice and rights. Put most simply, "if populist discourses convey meaning and values they are not an ideology" (Panizza 2005: 197).

One of the critiques of Laclau that I would like to take up here is that of Samuele Mazzolini (2020) which basically calls for a "re-Gramscianization" of his approach to populism. Whereas, in his earlier work, Laclau had equated hegemony with politics, in *On Populist Reason* he shifted to a position that "populism is the royal road to understanding something about the ontological constitution of the political as such" (Laclau 2005: 6). At best, we can say that Laclau puts populism and hegemony on the same plane. In practice, when Laclau engaged with the left-of-centre governments in Latin America, he prioritized the populist movement and the successful contesting of elections. He focussed less on the struggle for hegemony by the left, and the way in which social movements were co-opted by the "progressive governments" of the early 2000s (see Munck & Sankey 2020a). As Mazzolini puts it, "Populism can ensue in a new hegemonic order, but it is far from settled that it will. The question is what decides if it will" (Mazzolini 2020: 770).

It is not our purpose here to produce a "Latin American" theory of populism. However, it is necessary, I would argue, to have a grounded theory to underpin subsequent sections of this book that will more concretely outline the characteristics of "classical" and "contemporary" populism in Latin America. From the 1950s–60s structural functionalist approach, we can focus on the changing social patterns that preceded the emergence of populism. Then, from the 1960s–70s structural dependence paradigm, we can have a systematic focus on the "compromise state", underpinning populist regimes. Latterly, it is the figure of Ernesto Laclau that dominates, from a Gramscian phase in the 1980s–90s, to a more formal discourse theoretic approach in the 2000s. While not neglecting the advances made by Laclau in creating a formal theory of populism, I will, in practice, develop his earlier Gramscian lens. This, I would argue, is best suited to our analysis of populism, in the context of the various phases of capital accumulation and the social construction of capitalist hegemony.

CLASSICAL POPULISM

The study of populism in Latin America is of wider relevance in terms of international debates on populism insofar as "Latin America is the region with the most enduring and prevalent populist tradition" (Mudde & Rovira Kaltwasser 2017: 27). Yet Latin America is most often misunderstood as though "populism" is simply part of the region's DNA. It is remarkable how wrong international observers can get it sometimes. Thus Margaret Canovan, a major scholar of populism, can refer continuously to Peronism as a classic case of "populist dictatorship" (Canovan 1981: 138), despite Perón having won democratic elections in 1946, 1951 and 1973. I will seek to deconstruct populism in its historical context, and not simply contrast it against what it is not, namely liberal democracy. My sense is that Latin America represents a true laboratory to critically deconstruct the phenomenon of populism in all its complexity.

I start from the assumption that the emergence of a populist movement is usually related to crisis, whether it be that of the oligarchic state in the case of the classical populism of the 1940s, or of neoliberalism in the case of the left populism of the 2000s. As Arditi puts it "populism arises as the result of a crisis of representation, as a response to either the incapacity, or the refusal, of elites to respond to people's concerns" (Arditi 2010: 496). A crisis of representation creates a terrain where new identities can be forged and alliances created to articulate progressive responses to both distributive and representational demands. The crisis that created the conditions for the emergence of classical populism was the crisis of the agro-export-based oligarchic state which, by 1930, was no longer fully functional. Politically, this model of domination had begun to fracture before the 1930s world depression, but it was this international element that sealed its fate.

The agro-export economic model had served the dominant classes well from around 1870 to 1914 and the outbreak of the First World War. The Great Crash of 1929, and the depression of the 1930s, acted as a catalyst for the emergence of a new model of accumulation and political control. This was not a sharp turn – and nor did it occur everywhere – but there was a socioeconomic shift and the emergence of new political forces. The laissez-faire attitude towards the state – the "night watchman" model (overseer but not player) was no longer viable. The working class, created by capitalist development, and a growing urban middle class could no longer be excluded from politics. The ruling classes could no longer say, as a Brazilian minister once put it, that trade unions "were a matter for the police". The need to incorporate the new emerging classes, and to reaccommodate the balance between agrarian- and industrial-based dominant classes, created considerable pressure for regime change.

Argentina was, in many ways, the paradigmatic case, of a national-popular reaction to the drawn-out crises of the 1930s, known as the *década infame* (decade of infamy) there. Perón built a "populist" movement, with the active collaboration of the trade unions that were thinking in terms of a labour party. During the first period of Peronism, 1946–55, workers' share in the national income rose sharply from 41 per cent in 1946–48 to 49 per cent in 1952–55 and trade union organization took a massive step forward, even if those unions were firmly linked to the Peronist state through corporatist structures. Workers achieved a degree of "labour dignity" but they were also expected to deliver better labour productivity. National industrialists were encouraged by the state, but cordial relations were also forged with foreign capital. Above all, the developmentalist state promoted capitalist expansion, and ensured the stable reproduction of the labour force, through better education and the beginnings of a welfare state, something not considered necessary by the previous oligarchic state.

Peronism is an interesting case study, not least as interpretations of this "populist" movement range from fascist to socialist. It can also, however, be taken as a model for what Garretón *et al.* call the "statist-national-popular socio-political matrix" that would prevail from 1945 to 1975 across most of Latin America (Garretón *et al.* 2003: 176). The development model was based on inward-looking, or import substitution, industrialization. The state was very much to the fore in this model, organizing production and the management of the economy while acting as a reference point for all social demands. Social movements were incorporated through varying degrees of corporatism. The old order of an oligarchic state, and a very partial liberal democracy, was replaced by a national-popular discourse – not simply reducible to "populism" – in which the people versus oligarchy became the dominant opposition in society, articulating a "historic bloc" (in Gramscian terms) between national and popular aspirations.

While Peronism can be taken as an emblematic case of classical populism, similar political dynamics were at play in other countries, albeit in quite distinctive was. Populism in Brazil was quite different from that in Argentina. As Cardoso and Faletto put it "the populism of Vargas was a rather vague movement of people's incorporations into the nation ... It was less an economic definition of workers' rights which would imply political participation, than a political movement in favour of the 'humble'" (Cardoso & Faletto 1979: 141).

Even then, Brazilian *trabalhismo* (labourism or workerism) lacked the dynamism and radicalizing impact of Peronist trade union organizing, in terms of creating a worker identity. Vargas did promote a nationalist industrial expansion programme, particularly around the iron and steel sectors, but it could be said that this simply followed worldwide trends at the time. His "populist" successors, in particular João Goulart who came into office in 1961, did preside over a more radicalizing variant (that allowed for rural unionization for example), which led to the 1964 military coup to preserve the dominant order.

Another variant of the "compromise state" was that of "Cardenismo" in Mexico during the 1930s. Building on the historical impact of Latin America's first revolution in 1910, Lázaro Cárdenas utterly changed the course of the country's history. His main initiatives were designed to create a stable and viable regime of capital accumulation, a far-reaching agrarian reform (doubling the amount of land redistributed since the revolution) and the development of a trade union movement to organize the emerging proletariat. Cardenismo was clearly not a socialist ideology, and in many ways it served to consolidate bourgeois hegemony in Mexico after the revolution, through co-option of the subaltern masses under a vague "revolutionary" ideology. Nevertheless, as Knight points out, "Cardenismo was, in terms of its objectives, a genuinely radical movement, which promised substantial changes, that also embodied substantial popular support, albeit this was not mediated through liberal democratic forms of representation" (Knight 1994: 79). The difference between a radical movement and liberal democracy was now becoming clear after all the Eurocentric readings of Latin America.

Historians often point to the way in which not all countries in Latin America follow this same pattern, and certainly populism does not always emerge from a crisis of hegemony. In the Andean countries, for example, dependent development was based on an enclave economy, usually producing minerals, and later oil. The persistence of a strong oligarchic state meant that the middle sectors could only seek incorporation through alliances with the subaltern classes, which could set up a dangerous dynamic. Thus, in Peru, the closest to a populist movement, the APRA (Alianza Popular Revolucionaria Americana), sought to create a mass mobilization in the mid-1930s but was brutally repressed. In Ecuador, politics was dominated for a long time by Velasco Ibarra (1934–72) but his "populism" was hardly radical, consisting of a lay state with protection of religious rights, a promotion of progress, a sense of nation and a general ethos that popular participation should be allowed (see Burbano & de la Torre 1980).

Populist regimes came to an end in the 1970s, partly because the economic model they were based on ceased to be effective. There was a sense that import substitution industrialization had been "exhausted" insofar as the "easy" phase had been achieved and tariffs were becoming counterproductive. The world order had also changed, with the global disciplinary policies of the peripheral capitalist economies being driven by a disciplinary market regime. Above all, there was an emerging contradiction between "populism from above" and "populism from below". The "compromise state", that had served the dominant classes well, and acted as a shock absorber for political struggles, was no longer able to cope with the increased tempo of class conflict, in the period following the Cuban revolution of 1959. *Guevarismo*, the combative trade unions, and the land leagues were not as amenable to *transformismo* (absorption and domestication) as was the case earlier. Populism was becoming a dangerous indulgence, and class struggle was going to become much more open.

The ruling classes moved beyond the phase in which they had to rely on the "compromise state" and sought a dramatic and permanent rebalancing of class forces. This shift began in Brazil, with the 1964 coup that sought to end the "populist" political era that was verging on something more dangerous. The Chilean coup of 1973 ended a constitutional socialist regime that had also opened up space for mass mobilizations, which threatened to overflow its set boundaries. Finally, in Argentina in 1976 a decisive move was made by the military to not only end Peronist populism (that had an effective armed wing by now), but to create a new economic, political and social model. This was a model based on full integration into the global economy, a dramatic reduction of the economic role of the state and the permanent disciplining and atomization of civil society. A new era had begun in which "populism" was held to blame for poor economic performance and political instability.

CONTEMPORARY POPULISM

The new hegemonic project of the dominant classes, supported by the international financial institutions, was to create a new matrix of accumulation and political control. Market allocation would be the priority mechanism for the allocation of resources, the state would have a hugely decreased role, and the system of political representation would be greatly weakened (Garretón *et al.* 2003: 95–6). Against the primacy of politics as the organizing agent of society, the self-regulating market would become the rational regulator of society. Thus, society was fundamentally disarticulated and restructured in what was known as the "lost decade" of the 1980s. Not only did counterhegemonic projects fade away, but so did the counterhegemonic imagination. While authoritarianism went deep into society, there were still bonds of solidarity that survived – in trade unions, community groups, women's organizations, church circles and the new movements of relatives of the disappeared.

The 1990s were to see the emergence of a strange hybrid politics that was described as "neo-populist": populist in form but neoliberal in substance.

Emblematic public figures of the era included Carlos Menem (Argentina 1989–99), Alberto Fujimori (Peru 1990–2000), and Carlos Pérez (Venezuela 1989–93). These leaders, along with others in Brazil and Ecuador, came into office with the full trappings of populism as political style (and promises), but soon reverted to the now dominant economic ideology. They shared none of the structural features of classical populism, and the polices they enacted were the exact opposite of those of classical populism. It seemed that the term "neo-populism" was coined to describe what was essentially a form of *caudillismo* (leaderism) and was soon to fade away in the debates (see Viguera 1993). It did, however, have an impact on the way in which politics was perceived.

On the one hand, there were Marxists for whom this supposed death of populism would turn history back to the true path of class struggle. Thus, Jeremy Adelman boldly proclaimed the emergence of "post-populism" in Argentina, with Menem's warm embrace of neoliberalism in the 1990s, even tying Argentina's currency to the US dollar, that had "brought the country full circle – reopening the class nature of the Argentine state which Perón had sought to elide with a populist alliance" (Adelman 1994: 89). Peronism and populism had sought to draw a veil across class rule, and now this was drawn open and the class struggle would resume. More grounded voices, like Sergio Zermeño (1989), had already been forecasting the "return to the leader" as a result of the atomization and anomie caused by neoliberalism. In fact, after Menem and the collapse of neoliberalism in Argentina in 2001, the one who emerged at the head of a new hegemonic project was a representative of the left Peronism of the 1970s, namely Néstor Kirchner.

The "progressive popular" governments post-2000, were born out of the crisis of the neoliberal matrix, and the search for some kind of post-neoliberal development strategy. They were also, on the whole, part of an intense bout of class struggle and social conflict. In Argentina, in 2002, there was a semi-insurrectional, or dual power situation, for a time, while in Ecuador and Bolivia massive struggles erupted after 2000 around natural resources and indigenous uprisings. What these new governments all had in common was commitment to a form of economic nationalism, and the recovery of the category of *pueblo* (people). Thus, for example, Néstor Kirchner in Argentina "set up a discursive dividing line" (Panizza 2009: 245) between his policies and those of the previous anti-national neoliberalism of Menem and the military, to define his own economic and political project through a reframing of the national-popular politics of the 1940s. The tendency, at the time, was to see a somewhat simplistic divide between a "democratic" left and a "populist" left (e.g., Castañeda 2006), that reflected more the politics of those who proposed it than a real divide in practice.

Carlos de la Torre and Cynthia Arnson have recognized that, "the re-emergence of populism as part of the discussion [in the US] of contemporary politics in Latin America is, for the most part, a product of the regime and persona of Hugo Chávez" (de la Torre & Arnson 2013: 2). In a way that mirrored the earlier reaction to Juan Domingo Perón in Argentina, all attention on Venezuela and Chávez was focused on his supposed authoritarianism and charismatic leadership. This was certainly not liberal democracy. A new constitution created a new form of direct democracy (imperfect and uneven to be sure) that replaced the "pacted democracy" or *partidocracia* that had preceded Chávez and marginalized popular participation. With his death in 2013, Chavismo sank into a spiral of confrontation and demoralization, showing the weak side of this type of "high intensity" populist regime. However, it acted as a pole of attraction for a continent-wide left revival that, significantly, made strong discursive links with the pre-colonial history of resistance.

While I would argue that the "populist" versus "democratic" left divide is both overblown and politically motivated, we can distinguish between "populism from below" and "populism from above" modalities during the post-2000 developments. Venezuela, Bolivia and Ecuador, all saw significant levels of social activation that placed pressure on the "progressive" governments of Morales and Correa respectively. Their innovative constitutional strategies created a new, more inclusive, and participatory political order. They clashed with the social movements – particularly the environmental and indigenous ones – over the economic model that they followed. Extractivism was seen as simply the modern face of the old pre-1930 "enclave economies", even if the governments were using the income for social redistribution. The economic role of the state increased considerably in Ecuador – from 25 per cent in 2006 to 50 per cent in 2011 – signalling a partial return to the national-popular development matrix of the 1950s.

While born out of mass upheavals and social mobilization, the progressive governments of Ecuador and Bolivia (in different ways) had to face the problem of how to institutionalize their power base and create a durable hegemonic alliance. As Errejón and Guijarro note, "the allegiances created through the conflict are hard to transfer to an institutionalisation of the new correlation of forces" (Errejón & Guijarro 2016: 34). This was particularly the case in Ecuador, where Correa, with only a weak self-created party base, sought to marginalize the social movements and relied mainly on his individual charismatic persona. In Bolivia, while there was more of a "government of social movements", there was, nevertheless, increasing tension within the governing coalition that Morales sought to override through a plebiscite to run for president a third time. Belying the "populist" label to some extent, the party Morales created was able to win an election again in 2021, showing that some durable hegemonic strength had been built.

The left-of-centre governments that emerged in Argentina, Brazil and Uruguay after 2000 could be categorized as "populism from above", insofar as they have not seen the same high-intensity conflicts that characterized the Andean countries and Venezuela. Symbolically, they were far less committed to the Bolivarian project or the discourse of twenty-first-century socialism. The process whereby progressive governments came to power in Brazil and Uruguay was not shaped by mass insurrection but rather by a slow accretion of social and political forces for change. In Argentina while born from an insurrectionary movement, the neo-Peronist governments soon established their hegemony over the social movements. In all cases there was an astute construction of a national-popular coalition that could win elections. To call them "middle class populism" (Svampa 2013) or a "populist left" (Castañeda 2006) may or may not add to our understanding of these processes.

What we can say, following Grigera, is that these cases show that "the historical task of populism is institutionalisation of social conflict" (Grigera 2017: 447). Whether it is "Kirchnerism", dealing with the unemployed movement of the *piqueteros*, or "Lulismo", dealing with the landless movement, we see a pattern of co-option and domestication of contestatory movements. Unlike the situation in the Andean countries, both progressive political movements operated within the parameters of the established political system. So much so that in Brazil the once autonomous oriented Workers' Party got sucked into the pork-barrel politics of the establishment parties. In Uruguay, even more clearly, the party system prevailed, and we simply cannot refer to "populism" in the common prejudicial sense of economic profligacy and political irrationalism. Yet all these governments of the left (or centre left) reflect the political economy of populism, as a movement oriented towards redressing the imbalance of wealth in society.

From 2013 onwards, the demise of the populist-progressive governments that swept across Latin America from 2000 was often predicted, but they have proven remarkably resilient, despite considerable disenchantment. My conclusion is that the neoliberal market-driven sociopolitical matrix that prevailed in the 1980s and 1990s, has now been decisively superseded. Yet this has not led to the consolidation of a stable new hegemonic order, not least due to internal divisions. It would seem to mirror Gramsci's famous statement that "the crisis consists precisely in the fact that the old is dying and the new cannot be born" (Gramsci 1970: 276). There seems little doubt, based on our analysis here and the history of recent years, that "progressive populism" will continue to play a role. In its ongoing study we shall have to prioritize the strategic approach, while not neglecting the structural focus on socioeconomic change and the post structural emphasis on discourse construction.

REFERENCES

Adelman, J. 1994. "Post-Perónist Argentina". *New Left Review* 203(1): 65–91.

Arditi, B. 2010. "Populismo es hegemonía es política?" *Revista Constellations* 17(2): 488–97.

Blaikie, P. 2000. "Development, post-, anti-, and populist: a critical review". *Environment and Planning A* 32: 1033–50.

Burbano, F. & C. de la Torre 1980. *El populismo en el Ecuador.* Quito: ILDIS.

Canovan, M. 1981. *Populism.* London: Junction Books.

Canovan, M. 1999. "Trust the people! Populism and the two faces of democracy". *Political Studies* 47(1): 2–16.

Cardoso, F. & E. Faletto 1979. *Dependency and Development in Latin America.* Los Angeles, CA: California University Press.

Castañeda, J. 2006. "Latin America's left turn: there is more than one pink tide". *Foreign Affairs* 85(3): 28.

de la Torre, C. & C. Arnson 2013. "Introduction". In C. de la Torre & C. Arnson (eds), *Latin American Populism in the Twenty-First Century* , 15–36. Baltimore, MD: Johns Hopkins University Press.

Errejón, I. & J. Guijarro 2016. "Post-neoliberalism's difficult hegemonic consolidation: a comparative analysis of the Ecuadorean and Bolivian processes". *Latin American Perspectives* 43(91): 34–52.

Garretón, M. *et al.* 2003. *Latin America in the 21st Century: Toward a New Sociopolitical Matrix.* Miami: North South Centre Press.

Germani, G. 1965. *Política y Sociedad en una época de transición.* Buenos Aires: Paidós.

Germani, G. 1978. *Authoritarianism, Fascism and National Populism.* New Brunswick, NJ: Transaction.

Gramsci, A. 1970. *Selections from the Prison Notebooks.* London: Lawrence & Wishart.

Grigera, J. 2017. "Populism in Latin America: old and new populisms in Argentina and Brazil". *International Political Science Review* 38(4): 441–55.

Ianni, O. 1975. *La formación del Estado Populista en América Latina.* Buenos Aires: Era.

Knight, A. 1994. "Cardenismo: juggernaut or jalopy?" *Journal of Latin American Studies* 26(1): 73–107.

Laclau, E. 1977. *Politics and Ideology in Marxist Theory.* London: New Left Books.

Laclau, E. 2005. *On Populist Reason.* London: Verso.

Lenin, V. 1969. "The economic content of narodism and the criticism of it in Mr. Struve's book." In *Collected Works Volume 1*, 333–50. Moscow: Progress Publishers.

Mazzolini, S. 2020. "Populism is not hegemony: towards a re-Gramscianization of Ernesto Laclau". *Theory & Event* 23(3): 765–86.

Mudde, C. & C. Rovira Kaltwasser 2017. *Populism: A Very Short Introduction.* Oxford: Oxford University Press.

Munck, R. 2013. *Rethinking Latin America, Development, Hegemony and Social Transformation.* London: Palgrave Macmillan.

Munck, R. 2021. *Rethinking Development: Marxist Perspectives.* New York: Palgrave Macmillan.

Munck, R. & K. Sankey (eds) 2020a. "Social movements in Latin America: the progressive governments and beyond part 1". *Latin American Perspectives* 4: 44–255.

Munck, R. & K. Sankey (eds) 2020b. "Social movements in Latin America: the progressive governments and beyond part 2". *Latin American Perspectives* 5: 4–245.

Murmis, M. 2010. "Clases sociales en el primer Germani". In C. Mera & J. Rebón (eds), *Gino Germani La sociedad en cuestión Antología comentada,* 110–26. Buenos Aires: Consejo Latinoamericano de Ciencias Sociales.

Murmis, M. & J. Portantiero 1971. *Estudios sobre los orígenes del Peronismo.* Buenos Aires: Siglo XXI.

Panizza, F. 2005. "Introduction: populism and the mirror of democracy". In F. Panizza (ed.), *Populism and the Mirror of Democracy,* 3–25. London: Verso.

Panizza, F. 2009. *Contemporary Latin America Development and Democracy beyond the Washington Consensus.* London: Zed Books.

Polanyi, K. 2001. *The Great Transformation: The Social and Political Origins of Our Time.* Boston, MA: Beacon.

Serra, P. 2019. *El Populismo Argentino*. Buenos Aires: Prometeo.

Saul, J. 1969. "Africa". In G. Ionescu & E. Gellner (eds), *Populism: Its Meanings and National Characteristics*. London: Macmillan.

Svampa, M. 2013. "La década kirchnerista: populismo, clases medias y revolución pasiva". *LASA Forum* 44(4): 14–17.

Viguera, A. 1993. "Populismo" y "Neopopulismo" en América Latina. *Revista Mexicana de Sociología* 55(3): 49–66.

Walicki, A. 1969. "Russia". In G. Ionescu & E. Gellner (eds), *Populism: Its Meanings and National Characteristics* , 62–96. London: Macmillan.

Weffort, F. 1978. *O Populismo na Política Brasileria.* Rio de Janeiro: Paz e Terra.

Worsley, P. 1969. "The concept of populism". In G. Ionescu & E. Gellner (eds), *Populism: Its Meanings and National Characteristics,* 212–50. London: Macmillan.

Zermeño, S. 1989. El regreso del líder: crisis, neoliberalismo y desorden. *Revista Mexicana de Sociología* 51(4): 115.

CHAPTER 2

PERONISM IN ARGENTINA: LEFT OR RIGHT?

Marcelo Raimundo

INTRODUCTION

Populist movements usually emerge as events: no one is expecting them, but they suddenly take place. Because they directly affect established domination regimes, due to the fact that they are anti-*establishment* movements strongly supported by important sectors of the subaltern classes, both adhering and opposing sides tend to highlight their disruptive character. The former experience them as revolutions, and the latter as cursed creations of a leader with authoritarian tendencies and charismatic attributes who manages to ideologically manipulate the masses by resorting to irrational elements. Fortunately, these longstanding, deep-rooted categorizations have progressively lost their strength and have led to less emotionally and politically driven analyses. However, there is still a tendency in this direction, as seen in questions like the ones in the title of this chapter, which (as many others) seeks to analyse the Argentine case of populism in terms of whether Peronism is right wing or left wing. But is this question as posed even appropriate to better understand a phenomenon such as Peronism? A perspective anchored in a "Yes, it is"/"No, it is not" polarity can only partially ensure a critical and objective approach to explain Peronism. It is my intention to explore the conceptual potential of the idea of *simultaneity* as a *passive revolution*, in terms of the relationship between Peronism and the working class, to allow us to bring the heterogeneity of historical reality into play.

EX MACHINA ORIGIN

A prevailing tendency of sociologists, historians and political scientists, when interpreting Peronism, was to search for its permanent characteristics in its original stage. Gino Germani, an Italian sociologist who escaped fascism, was the initiator of that initial scheme, based on a structural-functionalist interpretation of a failed correspondence between socioeconomic modernization and political participation. This concept was surpassed gradually. As decades passed, an explanation anchored in its origin was seen as insufficient to describe it, either as a political identity that remained unshakable for most of the Argentinian working class or in terms of the politico-ideological evolution that occurred in the country as of the 1960s. Thus, an analysis emerged, derived from finding sociological explanations in terms of an internally migrating working class, which was young, basically anomic and ideologically unshaped – therefore, easily captured by an authoritarian, charismatic leader. This started to progressively add elements that made the peculiar dynamics of the general classification of the "national-popular movement" even clearer.

One of the reinterpretations that gained more strength was around the incorporation of new actors and new observation scales. This would make the formation of the multiclass alliance more complex – a common element in the whole populist experience – when reformulating the dynamics of the working class. Germani's interpretation was based on the heteronomous image of irrational, impressionable workers, so that the role played by trade union leaders began to emerge. Most of these leaders espoused left-wing traditions that posited conscious, class-oriented activists. For Germani (1973), the "labour old guard" had ceased being seen as a homogeneous block and, like many "new workers", a sector had come to support Perón. In his interpretation, this support was given in order to finally achieve a long list of demands. In exchange they offered their union structures and were receptive to the creation of new political organizations such as a labour party. This implied that they freed themselves – for a short period of time – of the contradictions between a political and a labour logic, which frequently tormented the left-wing labour activists, as their party's political line ran counter to the demands and struggles of the union rank and file. During a crisis, actions from a political will that understands the need to act as *collective capitalist* to ensure the system, opens a temporary process of *relative state autonomy* with regard to the contemporary model of capitalist accumulation. In Argentina's case, this allowed different labour factions to perceive a neutral state and a "permeable leader" which they could influence. Conspicuously, this happened despite the extremely repressive state of affairs enforced at the time by both military and civil governments. Facing this long-lasting reality, many leaders – syndicalists, socialists and others – were willing to listen to someone who could represent something different to the national and foreign establishment.

To follow the path of a state acting as a mediator in social struggle (instead of focusing on the hunger for power of a providential leader) contributed to a proliferation of new analyses, which allowed for the detection of lines of historical continuity behind Peronism's unconventional image. Propaganda about overcoming the past was one of the legitimizing policies of greater concern to the new regime, and consequently, each measure – nationalization, economic or social intervention – was presented as new, original and derived from Perón's political virtue and genius. State initiatives were so pronounced that Germani, after finding that during the period 1940–44 the average of strikes and the number of strikers and lost days were at their lowest since the beginning of the twentieth century, claimed that: "Affiliation to a trade union, and even participation in strikes, were not actually necessary for victories by the workers. Most of the benefits were conquered through the pressure of the [labour] Ministry" (Germani 1973: 474). State intervention in industrial relations was more than 30 years old in Argentina, but until 1943, no one had dared take political advantage of that resource: "Perón made the first move. The originality of his vision is made clear by the calmness with which his enemies inside the Army took his designation, on 27 October, as head of the National Department of Labour" (Little 1979: 332). This department was created in 1907, at the request of a group of liberal reformists, that sought to contain and prevent the labour conflicts by means of a dual policy: opening negotiation channels with socialist trade unions and revolutionary unionists and, at the same time, using repression, especially against anarchist activists. Despite not having a strong executive capacity, especially when compared to its position during the Peronist period, this department vastly increased its regulatory activities. Starting in 1937, almost half of the labour conflicts had been subjected to some sort of state mediation (Korzeniewicz 1993: 340). When the first industrial unions were being organized in the mid-1930s, even the communists leading the process sought the department's intervention to negotiate salaries, working conditions, and create hybrid (labour and state) commissions to avoid company retaliation and police intervention during strikes. Perón channelled, and subsumed an ascending unionist movement into a state logic before it became an uncontrollable storm. Thus, Argentina slowly moved from a military government that repressed labour action, to a regime with a Department of Labour that promoted the organization of trade unions.

To grasp the significance of this change, the case of the glassworkers' union will serve as an example. As a result of the efforts of a group of communists, socialists and some anarchist militants, along with workers interested in intra-plant negotiations, unions were organized in three of the biggest industrial factories in the country. In the South of Greater Buenos Aires, the Union of Glassworkers and Allied Workers was founded in March 1942 (Angélico & Forni 1995: 589). However, with the implementation of the Peronist strategy, what would have been a long-term, painful process in previous years was now changing. Several of the militants established a relationship with Perón when he was minister of war and had summoned them to ask for their opinion about the big slaughterhouse strike in September 1943. This engagement was a landmark, which historiography recognizes as the first meeting between the then colonel and the workers' movement. The activist group operated as an engine to build a process of confluence between other unions' experiences in smaller factories (more closely related to the performance of qualified workers), always with the support of the STyP (Secretaría de Trabajo y Previsión, Department of Labour and Prevision). Later in June 1944, an assembly decided on the foundation, at a national level, of the Union of the Glass Industry Workers (SOIV) which united factories in Cordoba, Rosario, Greater Buenos Aires and the capital itself. Within two weeks, the department gave it legal recognition. The union immediately started to act in collective negotiations, despite being an association with a fragmented past and smaller in comparison to other industrial groups. In a three-month period, the new union was able to update labour agreements in three of the most important companies of the sector. Later, their general secretary, José María Freire, a socialist glassworker, replaced Perón in his position at the Department of Labour in June 1946.

PERONISM AS PASSIVE REVOLUTION

In the mid-1940s, the analytical skills of Argentinian left-wing political and trade union forces were not sufficient to fully understand the changes that had been maturing over many years in the depths of society. In that context, as Daniel James (2006) suggests, the renowned official slogan "Perón cumple!" ("Perón delivers!") demonstrated a disruptive political style that attracted workers based on concrete progress, and therefore made it believable. By these means, Perón opened a path between the total discrediting of the dominant class, and the political stalemate of the left-wing organizations, persecuted by the government and ideologically compromised during the Second World War:

> The first rule I obeyed was: telling the truth and acting in an honest and loyal way because I knew that the masses were discouraged by the lack of honesty and loyalty, and the constant lying with which those who came before me proceeded. They promised everything but gave nothing. So, I put a different system into practice. Promise nothing and give everything. Instead of lying, speaking the truth. Instead of deception, loyal and honest engagement with everyone. (Perón 1952: 33)

What may allow us to better understand the significance of Peronism, especially in terms of class conflict, is the historical role played by Perón, not as a personal attribute, but rather as the power to articulate contradictory social and political interests. Undoubtedly, what made the difference was that Perón did things that others saw as necessary, but did not want to do:

> When I went to the Department of Labour and Provision, in 1944, I first took over the National Department of Labour, and there I gauged the masses. I started to talk to the men, to see what they thought, how they felt, what they wanted, what they didn't want, what were their impressions about the government, how they interpreted that moment in Argentina, what their aspirations were and what their complaints about the past were [...] What had to be done was partly what they wanted and partly what I wanted [...] Some, when I gave the first speeches in the Department of Labour and Prevision, said: "This man is a communist". And I spoke a bit about communism to them. Why? Because if I had spoken a different language to them in the first speech, they would have thrown me the first tomatoes. Because they had been into Marxism for forty years and had communist leaders. What I wanted was for them to like me a little, but I cared more about the others, the ones behind them, the ones I wanted to take away from them. The communist leaders brought me people so I would see the masses behind them. I received them and made them believe that was what I thought. But what I wanted was to take the mass away and leave them without it [...] They started to say: "There is a madman in the Department who says a few true things, things we like." So, if ten came, I would talk to those ten. If it was ten thousand, I talked to ten thousand. If it was only one, I talked to one. It was my job. My job was to persuade. During almost two years I kept persuading [...] That gradual persuasion gave me the political prestige I hadn't had before. I hadn't had any of that with the masses, but I started to obtain it. (Perón 1952: 215–16)

In fact, his power of persuasion was successful because of the combination of rhetorical devices and material rewards. At the same time, it was accompanied with coercive measures against recalcitrant unions: refusing to acknowledge their rights to negotiate; encouraging the creation of competing unions; persecuting and imprisoning both left-wing workers and loyal ones who had fallen out of favour. As Walter Little (1979) has noted, the "Peronization" of the labour movement was not achieved during the mythical initial period (1943–45). Rather, it was a long, multistage process, during which the union leaders who did not fully accept the new labour policies of the state and wanted to retain certain organizational autonomy, were progressively eliminated from office. This became possible as Perón gained the trust of the rank and file. However, the importance of the above-mentioned quote is that it shows how Perón himself recognizes the process of power building, not as a simple product of a rhetoric that was able to persuade the masses of anomic "new" workers, susceptible to domination by a charismatic leader. On the contrary, he faced the challenge of a working-class activism with a strong left-wing culture, one he had to necessarily answer by partly granting demands, albeit never all that they sought. Perón was able to resolve many accumulated labour demands, and this disconcerted labour leaderships and left-wing organizations.

Arguably we could say this analysis makes it possible to label Peronism as a *passive revolution*. This concept might take us closer to a better understanding of the logic behind the historical phenomenon and, at the same time, allows us to examine such a notion with a historical analysis, observing its subjective actions and its real consequences. According to Antonio Gramsci, the historical objective of a passive revolution is to establish a state power apparatus capable of conveying:

> [T]he necessity for the "thesis" to achieve its full development, up to the point where it would even succeed in incorporating a part of the antithesis itself – in order, that is, not to allow itself to be "transcended" in the dialectical opposition. The thesis alone in fact develops to the full its potential for struggle, up to the point where it absorbs even the so-called representatives of the antithesis. (Gramsci 1971: 109–10)

This last aspect is a characteristic that defines passive revolutions: the political initiative comes from above because what is missing is actual popular initiative from below. It is not an autonomous decision taken by subordinate classes: it is a determination born from powerful factions of the elite who seek to organize an outcome that avoids the possibility of a civil war, while acting as a collective capitalist faced by a potential crisis. What triggers these movements from above are situations considered to be in a catastrophic equilibrium, in which none of the colliding forces are able to prevail over the other, thus keeping alive the risk of a reciprocal destruction. Gramsci claims that each solution must be explained by a concrete historical analysis, and not simply by following a model. This analysis requires paying special attention to the rise of a great historical character, which he terms "Caesarism". This new character provides an arbitrary solution to the crisis. That manifestation of the phenomenon will not be pursued here, as it would lead us back to the interpretation which empowers Perón's role as a demiurge,[1] but we will prioritize another Gramscian idea: in passive revolutions the protagonists are the facts and not individual people. That is why it is important not to forget that, even if the initiative comes from above, processes are unleashed "which are certainly not revolutions, but which are not entirely reactionary either" (Gramsci 1971: 223), that is, they mobilize forces simultaneously in both directions. In the case of Argentina, the process of import substitution industrialization – strengthened by the effects of the 1929 crisis and then by the Second World War – led to a growth of the working class and stimulated union organizing with new left-wing forces such as communism, although it must be admitted that unionism at that time was still largely a social force (Torre 1990). However, within the Gramscian logic, presenting the relationship of forces between classes, not in absolute terms but in relative ones, the Argentinian situation in the 1940s created a type of passive revolution that had to adopt several popular demands:

> These movements too can have a relatively "progressive" content, in so far as they indicate that there were effective forces latent in the old society which the old leaders did not know how to exploit [...] They are rendered historically effective by their adversary's inability to construct, not by an inherent force of their own. Hence they are linked to a particular situation of equilibrium between the conflicting forces – both incapable in their respective camps of giving autonomous expression to a will for reconstruction.
>
> (Gramsci 1971: 223)

We will analyse below some of the effects caused by these processes in the light of the Peronist experience. This topic has two sides, one being the *initiative from above*, a political will applied to overcome a crisis of class domination; the second being the unleashing of ulterior processes which have the possibility of developing in an autonomous way: "molecular changes which progressively modify the pre-existing composition of forces, and hence become the matrix of new changes" (Gramsci 1971: 223). This criterion is fundamental if we seek to understand a historical dynamic, as the aforementioned "new modifications" do not necessarily follow the guidelines of the will that set the process into motion: necessity initiates, then contingency starts to play a role.

1. A demiurge in philosophy is a subordinate god who fashions and arranges the physical world to make it conform to a rational and eternal ideal.

EVERYTHING FLOWS

If Peronism is reduced to an experience of mass authoritarian manipulation, it is difficult to explain its persistence as a political identity for most of the labour movement, given that it was not always in power, and even when it was, it sometimes implemented severe anti-working-class measures, as occurred under the Peronist governments of Carlos Menem in the 1990s. This neo-populism did not rely solely on domination, on the contrary, it knows how to lead hegemonically. This is a fundamental aspect, as it allows modifications to power relationships, and is manifested in what Gramsci calls "transformism"; that is, the process of incorporating representatives of the subordinated classes into the new state:

> [W]ith gradual but continuous absorption, and obtained with methods of varying effectiveness, out of the active elements that emerged from the allied groups and even from the opponents and those who seemed irreconcilable enemies. In this sense, political leadership has become an aspect of the function of domination, since the absorption of the elites of the enemy groups leads to the beheading of these and their annihilation for an often very long period. (Gramsci 1971: 109)

Conventionally, there has been a tendency to highlight the wide variety of political support achieved by Perón: conservative politicians from the Argentina's more traditional provinces, religious sectors, different kinds of nationalists and even fascists. Less attention has been paid to the hegemonic absorption of the vanguards of subordinate classes, that is, the nucleus of Perón's long-term popular support. Here, what comes into play is avoiding the rigidities caused by the debate about the origins of Peronism that was outlined in the previous section: the "old unionism" – even when many of the militants were young – was not a rigid block, and, as it becomes readily apparent, not even those with the same ideology could ensure union politics followed similar positions. That factor helped the development of some sort of *transformist* "hoovering" up of support by Perón. In fact, Perón mainly influenced union activists with a long labour trajectory. Both revolutionary syndicalists and anarcho-syndicalists, had long ago dropped their ideological rigidities in exchange for directly negotiating with state representatives when possibilities allowed it, as happened during the Radical Civic Union (UCR) governments (1916–30). But this time the phenomenon reached much further, paradoxically managing to include entire sectors of opposing forces that were persecuted by the military regime, initiating a series of unusual crossovers. The case of Freire was mentioned above, but probably the

"Peronized" socialists with most presence in the media were the ones the historian, Raanan Rein (2008), called Perón's "second line": Ángel Borlenghi, who went from being the general secretary of the commercial workers' union to becoming a minister of internal affairs in the first two government periods; and rail workers' lawyer Juan Atilio Bramuglia, who managed to become minister of foreign affairs. When looking at all the labour unions, we can see that the list of Socialist Party members who joined Peronism was extensive. For instance: José Domenech, general secretary of the powerful railroad workers union and leader of La Confederación General del Trabajo (General Labour Confederation, CGT), who is said to have called Perón "the first worker"; David Diskin, from the commercial employees union, who founded the Labour Party together with several other union leaders, and helped build the political structure for Perón's election victory in 1946; and José Espejo, from the food workers' union who managed to become the CGT's general secretary from 1947. Besides these significant labour leaders, there were also scarcely registered transformist moves among rank-and-file activists, sometimes born out of internal rivalries, as seen in the occurrences inside the Municipal Workers Union:

> At the beginning of 1944, a group of socialist leaders of lesser rank expressed their dissatisfaction with this type of authoritarian leadership, very probably because it thwarted their desires for power. When Pérez Leirós refused to come into contact with Perón, his opponents mobilized so the government would intervene with the union. That is how the government proceeded, undoubtedly driven by its own reasons, and Pérez Leirós' opponents became intervention advisors, which allowed them to have a sort of power they wouldn't have gotten otherwise. (Horowitz 2004: 310)

To this, we should add the creation of alternative unions, which was a frequent initiative of the Labour Department itself: legal recognition was quickly granted and, therefore, the exclusive rights to negotiation that went with national recognition. This was, of course, a method to weaken opposition unions.

Trade union sectors to the left of the Socialist Party also had to face the new reality. The communist exodus towards Peronism was not of the same volume as the socialists, probably because it openly professed a virulent anti-communism. However, the changed situation caused severe tensions between the Communist Party leadership and its labour activists. For instance, within the textile union, socialists and communists competed for members, and at the same time had their own internal struggles. The Department of Labour used the dispute between the leftist parties to create a new textile union that would be aligned with the Peronist project. It is important to mention that some manufacturing sector militants sensed what might be coming:

> The situation of being an underground movement was not a problem for the leader of the Communist Textile Union (UOT), Jorge Michellón, to meet with Perón in 1943. In total, he had six or seven meetings. Before that, he had asked the Communist Party (PCA) for permission to attend. Nevertheless, some time afterwards, the party put an end to those meetings, because they did not share Michellón's conviction that they would benefit more through cooperation than from opposition. Michellón was then suspended from the party's central committee, but without losing his position in the union. In an interview carried out years later he claimed: "I told the party leadership that we could gain more from the militants than from Santamarina [a big landowner and famous conservative politician who became an anti-Peronist ally of the PCA]. But I wasn't heard." (Torre 1990: 77)

What is more, Peronism's power of attraction even managed to dazzle working-class militants connected to Argentine Trotskyism. The significance the new state labour policy had for activists, who tried to organize labour unions in the hard times of the 1930s, was reflected in many testimonies. For instance, Ángel Perelman, a steelworker activist and Trotskyist, and one the founders and leaders of one of the most important unions that supported Perón, the Union of Metallurgical Workers (UOM) recalled how:

> In our work at the union, as from 1944, we noticed incredible things: labour laws that had been violated before were now complied with; holiday requests were accepted without the need to seek law; other labour provision, such as recognition of factory delegates, assurance of not being fired and the like, had immediate and rigorous application. Internal relationships with the employers and the staff in the factory had completely changed their nature [...] The employers were disconcerted, the same way the workers were surprised and happy. The Department of Labour had become a factor of organization, performance, and support for the working class. It did not work as a state regulator from above the classes, and at union level, it acted as a state ally of the working class. (Schiavi 2011: 8)

To summarize, if we want to record and understand the range of effects of Peronism (as a form of populism with Argentinian features) the whole transformist process cannot be understood by perspectives derived from static models of analysis. Instead, they need to be interpreted in terms of Gramsci's notion of the dynamic coordinates set in motion by the *initiative from above*. The crisis of deference towards the elites, accelerated by the political attitude Perón and his circle had during those years, simultaneously loosened the knots, and increased tensions between ideology and politics in the working field, causing a reconfiguration and an unprecedented dynamism. As Horowitz (2004: 310) puts it, "the Argentinian situation in 1943–1945 was extraordinarily fluid".

HISTORICAL SHIFTS

As the volume of union members dramatically increased – from 900,000 members in 1946 to representing over 2,200,000 in 1954 (Doyon 2002) – the dynamic of the transformist mechanism, in combination with various coercive instruments of the state and direct repression, managed to complete the process of "Peronization" of the Argentinian labour movement. According to Little's analysis (1979): the toughest politico-ideological oppositions were mostly eliminated between 1943 and 1946; the unions which supported the government, while seeking to maintain a "neutral" stance, were displaced by 1951; and then only those "loyal" to Perón were legally recognized. From then on, unionist organizations' autonomy in relation to the state came to an end, and they became, to all intents and purposes, government institutions until Perón fell in 1955. There was a condition that was fundamental to this process of bureaucratization of the labour union apparatus: the rank and file mostly supported Perón, either out of political passivity or because they prioritized material needs over ideological definitions:

> Look, I knew that this was going to happen. In the years 1943–1944 people in the factories followed Perón, and I meant for my fellow workers to take the lead. Of course, they couldn't show themselves as communists [...] People said: "We're Perón's" and marched towards the Department of Labour with their demands.
>
> (Michellón 1979: 9)

With a satisfied rank and file and controlled union leaders, it might have seemed that "Perón delivered" to the elites as promised in his speeches, guaranteeing that the workers would not challenge the system or be "derailed".

However, what Friedrich Engels once claimed about historical events in general is certainly applicable to Peronism: "What emerges is something that no one willed" (Engels 1987: 380). In processes like the one analysed, we must not forget that the hegemonic initiative is just one put into play among many others, and even if it has the great advantage of counting on state resources, it must face the resistance of those whose force it wishes to lead, including the ones it benefits. Hegemony is more about direction than imposition, and because the "passive revolution" seeks to create a new arrangement between the classes to exit an organic crisis, it must necessarily free social forces which might later take an autonomous course or, paraphrasing Perón, "derail". In brief, while it is true that Perón restrained the working class, it is also true that he was restrained by it.

Between 1946 and 1948 there was a surprising number of labour mobilizations and protests. If we observe labour conflict figures for the city of Buenos Aires, the numbers speak for themselves. During the quarter of a century that preceded Perón's coming to office – between 1919 and 1945 – approximately 750,000 had participated in declared strikes. For the two-year period of 1946–48, figures were 50 per cent higher, with 1,150,000 strike participants. Regarding their frequency, in 1946 alone there were 146 strikes documented, which was the highest annual figure since 1920. If we analyse working days lost, in 1947 there were almost 3,500,000, the highest figure since the origins of the labour movement in Argentina (Doyon 1977). The tendency of the indicators seemed to descend towards the final stage of the Peronist regime, either because of a fulfilment of workers' claims, or because of the stricter discipline applied by the state to control the workers' strikes in the context of an economic slowdown and inflationary growth after 1949. Between 1950 and 1954 conflict returned, not actually expressed in frequency of strikes, but, rather, in the number of lost working days – about 2,000,000 and 1,400,000 respectively – given the long duration of the protests. In the interpretation of the workers' struggles during the Peronist period, the official version, which prevailed for a long time, pointed at the existence of a "communist plot" around 1947. By 1950, with political and ideological oppositions under control, in conflicts like that of the rail workers, the image of conspirator had mutated into a "false Peronist", as by that time any conflict had to be related to an internal struggle inside the pro-government sector.

There is considerable agreement around the idea of working-class protest never managing to represent an ideological rupture between the individual workers and Peronism, but rather was seen as a

> phenomenon that seemed to reflect the workers' decision to bring their political victory in the past elections to the economic sphere … the expansion of labour amendments … was the result of the struggles pursued by the organized workers, who in many cases projected themselves further than the government's initiatives, even to the point of clashing with it. (Doyon 2002: 274)

This last aspect is what explains the decision of political power to label those as a part of a sinister plan even when, paradoxically, the big unions, which triggered the protests, were the industrial trade unions. That is, they were the ones that had benefited the most from government policies, for instance in the cases of slaughterhouses, sugarcane mills, metal workers and textile workers. Even when it is not possible to dismiss the involvement of other groups of political and union activists displaced from their positions or persecuted, the strikes themselves did not manifest opposition towards the government: "During the conflicts, they strove to keep Perón on the margins of the protest and when it came to choosing adversaries they pointed at businessmen or government officials" (Doyon 2002: 299). Political consensus and industrial conflict thus became two sides of the same coin. That reality often remains hidden when Peronism is reduced to the old scheme of populism as class conciliation.

According to James (1981), Peronism's reformist ideology was generally accepted, but workers' resistance, to whatever threatened their triumph, challenged fundamental aspects of the capitalist organization of production inside factories. At the beginning of the 1950s, in the middle of an economic crisis, the government started to yield to the pressure of the business sector and launched a campaign to increase worker productivity through the CGT. But they faced an unyielding labour culture of resistance in the workplace. Workers believed they could negotiate their efficiency/effort bargain, i.e., how much work for specific pay, according to their standards.

In the quest for factors to explain the cycle of strikes, we can turn once again to Gino Germani (1973). Despite being extensively criticized, he was the first to outline some facts later taken up by other authors:

> Although the working mass lost their autonomy at the level of leadership during Perón's era, it must be recognized that they continued exerting a considerable pressure on the rank and file, and that pressure sometimes introduced limitations and conditions to CGT's leading power. In the conditions found in the governments that followed Perón, this experience intensified even more.
>
> (Germani 1973: 475)

Grasping this concept allowed a renewal of interpretations of the relationship between Peronism and the working class, because the focus now changed towards exploring the relationship between union *leaders* and the *rank and file*. Thus, it is possible to understand labour struggle beyond the frame of political opportunities, given to the workers by a regime procuring popular support. When these conditions faded after Perón's removal by a military coup in 1955, the combative attitude of the working-class remained intact, as shown by strike waves in 1957, 1959 and 1965, and the cycle of working-class revolts unleashed between the end of the 1960s and the mid-1970s. It is important to realize that the disciplining of the rank and file was more of a probability than a certainty. The subordination to the state, and the verticalization of various organizational levels of the labour movement, during the Peronist governments, were not enough to totally suffocate the rank and file's autonomy in relation to leaders, who were becoming more and more committed to government policies. This leadership alignment with the government was linked to the growing power of the CGT and the centralization of union finances in national unions and confederations. Parallel to a bureaucratization of the unions, we note a strong level of organization at plant level, that helped to preserve opportunities for rank-and-file representation and action. These organizations were known as *internal commissions*, composed of delegates chosen by the workers in their workplaces. Even if they had existed in stages prior to Peronism, it was only during that time that they reached a level of real power inside the factory. This enabled them to guarantee and defend the benefits and rights conquered with collective agreements: representation of plant workers before the bosses and the union; direct complaints to the management; encouragement of workers' participation; and even strike action. The legal status of strike action was very unclear, and it was not mentioned in agreements as businessmen refused to include it. Therefore, it was clearly imposed through workers' struggle: "Employers fiercely opposed the establishment of these union commissions as they very well knew they meant the end of their unilateral control over the company's working life" (Doyon 1984: 211).

We might ask ourselves what is the "revolutionary" aspect of Peronism when regarded as a process of passive revolution? The closest answer, in historical terms, is that it produced a considerable change in the power relationships between classes in the workplace, in favour of workers. With Perón's labour policy, a labour movement, with more than 50 years of history and a deep-rooted left-wing culture (Pozzi 2020), finally managed to obtain real power in the plants. Although this power did not come about in the way many union leaders expected it to, it emerged without the need to risk union organization, while stimulating activism to a point where it became difficult to control, even when the workers identified with Peronism. Daniel James (2006) gave it the name of Peronism's *ambivalent legacy* and claimed that accepting, rather than clouding it with value judgements, is more productive to understanding the history of Peronism. Within an interpretative framework that only finds capitalist authoritarian restoration in Peronism, it becomes difficult to understand and explain the tenor of the labour events and practices, such as the ones that took place in the sugarcane mills in the north of Argentina, for instance:

> Last night at eleven pm […] a group of people composed of strikers cut the water and power supplies for the inhabitants of "La Trinidad" sugarcane mill. They also cut phone lines, isolating the facilities. Immediately, and with the police unable to intervene, they committed all kinds of outrages, such as firing guns and throwing stones at the houses, especially at the accountant's residence, and intended to break down his door.
>
> (Gutiérrez 2014: 10)

Those actions usually had very positive results, as can be appreciated in the agreements reached in those sugarcane mills: in 1945 only 112 occupational categories were recognized, by 1946 they had reached 285, and by 1947 they were at 444. Being covered by these agreements benefited workers within a few years in terms of salary, seniority and a decrease in management's arbitrary decisions on post rotation.

Peronism came to provide a bourgeois exit to the crisis of domination that was emerging in those years, but the process unfolded in such a way that Perón "the general" could not beat Perón "the sorcerer's apprentice". He had unleashed forces which, while swearing allegiance to him, were slipping out of his control. A business leader from one of the most important metal manufacturers in Argentina, who also had a good relationship with the president, addressed this very issue during an interview:

> Unfortunately, during Perón's era, some sort of hierarchy rupture took place within the factories. This is one of the possible accusations to be made against the Perónist period, because authority management was distorted within the factories because of employers' intervention in the union themselves, and as a result of indiscriminate defence of workers' claims in conflicts that could have originated in the application of certain basic discipline, order and authority norms within the factories. (Schiavi 2013: 12)

Both rebellious workers' subjectivity and the new power relationships, depended on organization in the workplaces, a condition that was very evident for businessmen when they attempted to recover working productivity levels during Peronism, or afterwards. Even from 1955, when the post-coup political situation, and an open repression of the labour movement, seemed to clear the horizon in terms of rationalization, the government and many employers had to face a fierce working-class resistance:

> After an initial period of demoralization following the November coup, one finds by the middle of 1956 the emergence of a network of semi-clandestine internal commissions now led by a new generation of militants with little or no formal union experience prior to 1955 [...] Throughout 1956 and 1957 they led a stubborn and bitter defensive action against management's rationalization plans [...] Moreover, with the official intervention of the formal union structure, the role of organizing and expressing this resistance had, perforce, fallen to the internal commissions. (James 1981: 339)

In brief, we can thus claim that the Peronist passive revolution meant a greater power for workers in their workplace, but it was a power they had to defend every day, sometimes even despite the trade unions themselves.

CONCLUSIONS

So, finally, is Peronism left or right? First, it seems that finding an answer would depend on what method we choose to approach the question. Should we count the number of right-wing measures and left-wing ones? Should we focus on the political past of government officials: governors, mayors, legislators? Nationalizations: should we consider them right-oriented or left-oriented? And what about control over external trade? And labour legislation? Or maybe it would be better to create an index with several variables, but how should we weigh them?

The question about Peronism's political orientation is part and result of the historical process: for the Argentinian political/intellectual sector in 1945, it was utterly impossible to associate Peronism with the left wing. Peronism was demagogy, totalitarianism or the "possible fascism" of Argentina. The Peronists of course, felt that they were the protagonists of the "Justicialist Revolution", which began with Perón. Either way, the support of the working class and the postwar readjustments, gave results. For instance, the Communist Party, in mid-1946, softened its anti-Peronist stance and decided to "criticize the negative aspects and support the positive ones" (Gurbanov & Rodríguez 2016: 110). By 1949, the PCA returned to an overt oppositional stance, pointing out the various contradictions in the regime. Another rapprochement took place in 1951, owing to a failed *coup d'état* against Perón, in which the PCA supported the government and decided to propose unity of action with the Peronists. During 1952, they moved to deepen the relationship even more to "weaken imperialism", and they expressly began to vindicate the government's actions. But the romance only lasted a few months, because when internal pro Peronist PCA tendencies grew in strength, the party leadership expelled many of these activists in order "to avoid the risk of losing our identity" (Gurbanov & Rodríguez 2016: 110). All this flirting had its origins in the belief that there were "progressive" that is, anti-imperialist and anti-oligarchic, forces within Peronism. After the 1955 coup, the political narrative shifted again, and far from discussing the progressive aspects of Peronism, the left steered towards a more intense debate about its role in connection to socialism. In truth, this era opened a discussion about the revolutionary, or non-revolutionary, character of populist movements within a considerable part of the Latin American left. The debates in Argentina were, perhaps, some of the more intense, if we consider that an important part of the new left guerrillas that emerged in the 1960s, and gained prominence in the 1970s, identified itself with Peronism.

The purpose here is not to reject the negative view of Peronism as populism, merely because it implied a shift in power relationships favourable to the subordinate classes. It is true that the working class lost its autonomous role in the process, but Perón also paid a price for his type of leadership. This was very well depicted by James (2006: 57): "it was not through decrees, but rather through deals that we must negotiate". For that reason, even when Peronism succeeded in guaranteeing Argentine capitalism, in the end it never was a definitive hegemonic option for it. The concept of passive revolution allows us to capture some of the dynamic elements of Peronism and reinforces the need for concrete historical analysis to comprehend the complex power dynamics it represented. At the same time, the deployment of the Gramscian category of passive revolution to situate it, allows us to develop that category, insofar as a bourgeois initiative, like Peronism, might have an undesired effect over time and, consequently, open a historical conjuncture unleashed by class struggle at the core of the Peronist movement itself.

Is it possible to read Kirchner's governments after 2002 from that perspective? Obviously, we can recognize a similar loss of autonomy of many social and political sectors which had tenaciously opposed the neoliberal wave of the 1990s in Argentina: workers' organizations, unemployed workers' movements, human rights currents. But the evidence indicates that they are not comparable in one specific aspect: their results regarding subordinate power. Our conjecture is that this issue is closely related to the deep changes that have produced a recomposition of the Argentinian working class from the 1970s onwards, and that have been strengthened by the neoliberal policies of Carlos Menem's Peronist government of the 1990s. This was part of global processes of transformation in production structures, such as: automation and decentralization of work processes and an increase in unemployment; a framework of labour relationships encouraging stability, casualization, contractual flexibilization and an increase in individual or outside-agreement negotiation. That is how new dynamics were unleashed in workplaces, which led to loss of solidarity, sectorized struggles and a weakening of working identity. All of this had a negative impact on the stability of something Pozzi (2020) has considered a key element in the historical development of the Argentinian working class: a strong working culture in terms of class, a rebellious and oppositional common sense, a working identity experience in terms of "us against them". This phenomenon, which formed the basis for all the anti-establishment expressions that emerged in Argentinian working-class history, entered a process of resignification that is still ongoing.

Kirchnerism's trade union supporters assumed they were returning to a stable system of collective bargaining, but as Marticorena has argued, the reality was far from classic Peronism's working-class policies:

> The dynamism of collective negotiation was mainly expressed by signing agreements which covered salaries, and collective agreements were significantly lower in number, a situation which worsens when inflation accelerates after 2007. As regard to non-wage negotiations, what has been highlighted is the survival of various clauses and labour flexibilization conditions introduced in the 1990s, along with the usual incorporation of the "social peace" clause in collective agreements and conventions.
>
> (Marticorena 2020: 2007–8)

Taken as a whole, however, the statistics show increasing numbers of labour conflicts, with a constant tendency as we move upwards from 785 strikes in 2006 to 1,336 in 2017, that should lead us to clear analogies in relation to Perón's era. We highlighted above that the key factor from that period was the greater power workers had in the plants, but during Kirchner's governments, beyond an increase in union participation and workers' mobilizations in specific periods, the phenomenon was qualitatively more moderate:

> [T]his activation of the rank and file manifested in different forms and degrees of participation, which even when it indicates oppositionist union leaders, implies a certain control over union politics. The process of activating the rank and file many times emerges from opposing the bureaucratic traditional leaderships, and other times they result from actions by the leaderships or a response to renovating union currents with the purpose of occupying the workplace as a way of avoiding the advance of antibureaucratic and or combative sectors.
>
> (Marticorena 2020: 2017)

This means that the rank and file challenging the union leaders was not very problematic for the latter because, except for a few conflicts, most times labour mobilizations were initiated by union leaders. And apparently, neither did rank-and-file activation actually affect employer's control over production, if we observe that labour productivity per worker increased by approximately 40 per cent between 2004 and 2011. Placing these figures in comparison with classical Peronism, in which productivity levels dropped, what can our conclusion be? Was Kirchnerism a right-wing or a left-wing populism? Can we really answer this question?

Generally speaking, the idea of Kirchnerism corresponding to a left-wing populist movement was largely introduced by both the Argentinian and the international press, in combination with sectors of the political opposition. In particular, within the academic environment, positive assessments of its working policies were influenced by an opening to the Anglo-Saxon debate about "trade union revitalisation" started in the early 2000s (Ghigliani 2018). Consequently, the union conflict waves that began in 2004 were understood as a period of political opportunities for the labour movement, facilitated by the initiative of a government that searched to strengthen the union institutions also by restoring their credibility, as a means to recompose state hegemony and thus contain the generalized process of social protest rooted in the 2001 crisis, integrating the union leadership into a government coalition (Natalucci 2015). However, even those who adhere to these interpretations must be able to recognize how limited that "revival" is. Only in 2007 did real wage increases return to their pre-2001-crisis values, and from then on salary negotiations were supervised by the executive power and annual percentages were predetermined. Also, salaried employees progressively lost their right to family allowances (dependent child allowances), and salary improvements started to be paid in deferred percentual increases along the year, and more and more workers were reached by what is called Impuesto a las Ganancias (Income Tax), a situation that cumulatively caused tension for the alliance of the government with the union leaderships. Even with fluctuations, workers' salary increases continued during Cristina Fernández de Kirchner's government; still, the highest point was in the 2015 elections, when by very little it managed to temporarily surpass the maximum registered in 1996 during Carlos Menem's neoliberal government. Those were also years when repression against workers' protests returned, either directly through state security forces or indirectly through mobs organized by union leaders, among which the most tragic example is the assassination of the young militant called Mariano Ferreyra by one of the latter. Ferreyra's death took place in the context of a riot by railroad workers who fought against outsourcing, an aftermath of neoliberal reforms that still stand today and have been a key factor in workers' fragmentation into a class that represents between 30 per cent and 40 per cent of the Argentinian population. From her second period onwards,

Kirchner herself criticized workers' demands in several of her speeches, for instances those by underground workers, and teachers in provincial schools.

If we need to choose political categories to characterize both Kirchnerism in the early twenty-first century and Peronism in the mid-twentieth century, it is probably best to abandon the disjunction between left and right produced by the term *or* and recognize that the conjunction *and* better explains the phenomena that unfold *at the same time* in both periods. It is the specific combination of social, political and economic conflicts that can take us deeper, overcoming definitions based on political orientations, to find populism's base in *political economy* and focus on the power relationships and political compositions in which these results.

In the case of Kirchnerism, if it was a type of left-wing populism, it was in superstructural terms, given that its economic dynamic continued gravitating towards the structural terms established by Menemism in the 1990s. However, that very aspect at the same time works as a distinction between the two: the passive revolution was made by Kirchnerism. Menemism achieved relative adhesion to unionism, and its strength was anchored in keeping a high level of consumption in the middle of state reforms, privatizations and rise of unemployment, owing to an economic scheme sustained by the quasi-dollarization that led to a convertibility law for the Argentinian currency. When the amount of external debt caused a crisis in the second half of the 1990s, the passive consensus changed into a growing state of social protest lasting many years, aimed at changing the economic course. The largest part of the different opposing movements (social groups, workers, unemployed, human rights, small producers, university students) was captured by Kirchnerism after the big crisis in 2001. Starting with their leaders first – or perhaps their organic intellectuals – followed by a good part of the rank and file, unlike the Menemist experience, a political identity managed to be created which has been able, at least for the time being, to last beyond the economic and political developments experienced by its key figures.

REFERENCES

Angélico, H. & F. Forni 1995. "Nacimiento de una organización sindical en un régimen conservador: El Sindicato de Obreros del Vidrio y Anexos de Avellaneda (1942)". *Desarrollo Económico* 34(136): 579–94. https://doi.org/10.2307/3467285.

Doyon, L. 1977. "Conflictos obreros durante el régimen Perónista (1946–1955)". *Desarrollo Económico* 17(67): 437–73. https://doi.org/10.2307/3466641.

Doyon, L. 1984. "La organización del movimiento sindical Perónista 1946–1955". *Desarrollo Económico* 24(94): 2–. https://doi.org/10.2307/3466739.

Doyon, L. 2002. "La formación del sindicalismo Perónista". In J. Torre (ed.), *Nueva historia argentina*, 260–305. Buenos Aires: Editorial Sudamericana.

Engels, F. 1987. "De Engels a J. Bloch". In *Correspondencia, Marx, Carlos, and Friedrich Engels*, 379–381. Buenos Aires: Cartago Editores.

Germani, G. 1973. "El surgimiento del Peronismo: el rol de los obreros y de los migrantes internos". *Desarrollo Económico* 13(51): 435–88. https://doi.org/10.2307/3466131.

Ghigliani, P. 2018 "Sindicalismo y conflictividad laboral en el nuevo escenario". In P. Pérez & E. López (eds), *¿Un nuevo ciclo regresivo en Argentina? Mundo del trabajo, conflictos laborales y crisis de hegemonía*. La Plata: Universidad Nacional de La Plata.

Gramsci, A. 1971. *Selections from the Prison Notebooks of Antonio Gramsci*. New York: International Publishers.

Gurbanov, A. & S. Rodríguez. 2016. "Los comunistas frente al peronismo: 1943-1955". *Temas de Historia Argentina y Americana* 24. https://repositorio.uca.edu.ar/handle/123456789/7655.

Gutiérrez, F. 2014. "La irrupción del poder obrero en los ingenios azucareros: avances, límites y cuestionamientos. Tucumán, 1944–1949". *Quinto Sol* 18(2): 1–23. https://doi.org/10.19137/qs.v18i2.936.

Horowitz, J. 2004. "Una vez más los sindicatos y el ascenso al poder de Juan D. Perón". *Desarrollo Económico* 44(174): 307–11. https://doi.org/10.2307/3456040.

James, D. 1981. "Racionalización y respuesta de la clase obrera: contexto y limitaciones de la actividad gremial en la Argentina". *Desarrollo Económico* 21(83): 321–49. https://doi.org/10.2307/3466352.

James, D. 2006. *Resistencia e integración.* Buenos Aires: Siglo XXI.

Korzeniewicz, R. 1993. "Las vísperas del Peronismo: Los conflictos laborales entre 1930 y 1943". *Desarrollo Económico* 33(131): 323–54. https://doi.org/10.2307/3467085.

Little, W. 1979. "La organización obrera y el Estado Perónista, 1943–1955". *Desarrollo Económico* 19(75): 331–76. https://doi.org/10.2307/3466690.

Marticorena, C. 2020. "Negociación colectiva y conflicto laboral en Argentina (2003–2015): Entre la rutinización y la activación de las bases obreras". *Izquierdas* 49(98): 2001–21. https://dx.doi.org/10.4067/s0718-50492020000100298.

Michellón, J. 1979. "Reportaje a Jorge Michellón". *Controversia* 2–3: 8–11.

Natalucci, A. 2015. "Corporativismo y política: dilemas del movimiento obrero durante el kirchnerismo". *Población y sociedad* 22(2): 5–25.

Perón, J. 1952. *Conducción política*. Buenos Aires: Ediciones Mundo Perónista.

Pozzi, P. 2020. *¡Usted es comunista! clase, cultura y política en la Argentina contemporánea*. Buenos Aires: Prometeo Libros.

Rein, R. 2008. "Los hombres detrás del Hombre: la segunda línea de liderazgo Perónista". *Araucaria. Revista Iberoamericana de Filosofía, Política y Humanidades* 10(19): 78–92.

Schiavi, M. 2011. "Los sindicatos comunistas entre el 17 de octubre y su disolución. El caso textil y metalúrgico". In *IX Jornadas de Sociología*. Buenos Aires: Facultad de Ciencias Sociales, Universidad de Buenos Aires. www.aacademica.org/000-034/241.

Schiavi, M. 2013. "Movimiento sindical y Peronismo (1943–1955): hacia una nueva interpretación". *Trabajos y Comunicaciones* 39. www.trabajosycomunicaciones.fahce.unlp.edu.ar/article/view/TyC2013n39a06/pdf_6.

Torre, J. 1990. *La vieja guardia sindical y Perón.* Buenos Aires: Editorial Sudamericana.

CHAPTER 3

THE POPULIST LEFT IN CHILE: SOCIALISTS AND COMMUNISTS FROM 1936 TO 1973

Igor Goicovic

INTRODUCTION

There is only one great consensus about populism, and that is that it is a phenomenon that is difficult to define. Indeed, although Latin America has had different populist experiences since the beginning of the twentieth century, it is no less true that its conceptualization continues to be complex.[1] At the beginning of the 1970s, Octavio Ianni, one of the intellectuals who most deeply explored this issue, argued that, despite the dissimilar historical experiences lived by the countries of the region, populism burst into most of them as a mass movement that was installed in the *centre of the structural ruptures* that accompanied the crises of the world capitalist system and, by extension, of the Latin American oligarchies (Ianni 1973: 85). From these crises and with the masses constituted as political actors, the state was restructured under bourgeois leadership. The new ruling elites, supported by different social sectors, especially workers and the middle classes, carried out a profound reorganization of the economy, emphasizing state dirigisme, and based on it, redistributed part of the income expressed as social policy. This, in turn, operated as a strategy of clientelism which, on the one hand, consolidated the adhesion of the masses to charismatic leaderships and, on the other, reconfigured power relations (Ianni 1973: 106–49).[2] The regime of passions and emotions played a fundamental role in this, which in the perspective of Rosanvallon, activated the populist mobilization and rooted the bond of relationship with the leader (Rosanvallon 2020: 53–5).

1. Marco Palacios even describes it as an "ambiguous" concept (Palacios 2011: 14–15).
2. For an analysis of the main interpretative currents on the populist phenomenon see Viguera (1993) and Aldao and Damin (2013).

However, the historical rhythms of this process, as Osmar González (2007: 87–92) points out, were different. In some countries, such as Peru under Guillermo Billinghurst (1912–14) or Uruguay during the second period of José Batlle y Ordóñez (1911–15), the process began at the beginning of the twentieth century. In others, such as Brazil under Getúlio Vargas (1930–45) or Mexico under Lázaro Cárdenas (1934–40), the process began in the 1930s.[3]

But populism is not reduced only to the type of state, or to the power relations that were constituted at a given historical moment, nor is it restricted to the leader who embodied it. It also refers to the people, meaning the masses that give political force to the movement. According to this perspective, populist movements were heterogeneous. The people, summoned and mobilized by populisms, consisted of industrial workers, peasants with and without land, teachers, professionals, intellectuals, public officials and a wide range of unemployed and underemployed (Entrena 1996). In many circumstances, moreover, the appeal refers to tradition, which is built on the basis of an immanent identity (the people). This is historically constructed and, as such, is heir to the struggles of resistance to conquest, the struggles of decolonization and the struggles for independence. In these cases, the history of shared struggles acts as a programmatic resource and as an agitative factor (Adinolfi 2010).

All these actors come to constitute what Dussel (2012: 165), paraphrasing Gramsci, called the "social bloc of the oppressed". The oppressed, who are articulated not only in economic exploitation, but also in the whole broad fields of exclusion, discrimination and repression, are the ones called upon to configure the social base of support of the populist movement, whether for the purposes of its electoral mobilization or for a show of force in the public space.

In spite of the above, populism cannot be pigeonholed into a specific ideological component. On the contrary, the philosophy adopted by populist movements and governments was strongly associated with the political situation experienced at a regional or local level. This allowed them to turn to the left or to the right, depending on the correlations of forces that took shape. In the same sense, populisms tended to claim themselves as a third way, against both Marxism and liberalism (Martínez & Rubio 2017: 18–20). This was the case with the populist experiences led by Getúlio Vargas in Brazil and by Juan Domingo Perón in Argentina. In other movements, the revolutionary or transformative orientation was more clearly emphasized, as occurred with Lázaro Cárdenas and the Partido Nacional Revolucionario (PNR) in Mexico,

3. Chantal Mouffe argues that the crisis of contemporary neoliberalism has initiated a new "populist moment" (Mouffe 2019: 23–39).

with the Frente Popular in Chile or with the Movimiento Nacionalista Revolucionario (MNR) in Bolivia. For Laclau, the political logic of populism is always going to be imprecise and fluctuating, given that it operates in a social reality that is heterogeneous and changing (Laclau 2016: 150–1). Seen from this perspective, the theoretical and historiographical problems refer both to the subject, in this case the relationship between people and class, and to the project, hence to the relationship between populism and socialism (Retamozo 2017).

In Chile we can see the emergence of a left-wing national populism in the context of the crisis of the oligarchic regime of the 1920s, which matured as a political project with the Popular Front (FP), in the 1936–47 cycle, only to be exhausted in the mid-1960s.[4] This national-populist experience was anchored in both the Socialist Party of Chile (PSCh) and the Communist Party of Chile (PCCh).

For the North American historian Paul Drake, the PSCh developed *populist patterns*, at least in the cycle between its foundation in 1933, and the ideological and programmatic redefinitions adopted in 1955. In that period, the PSCh adhered to three phenomena, typical of the Latin American matrix of populism: it stimulated a mass mobilization, anchored in paternalism, personalism, nationalism and the promise of immediate gratification; it contributed to the formation of heterogeneous coalitions, mainly composed of workers, but led by sectors from the middle and wealthy classes; and it promoted economic programmes, based on the need for industrialization and functional to a wealth redistribution strategy (Drake 1992: 10). This design should have been exhausted by the mid-1950s, in the context of the criticism towards the populist front experience, to be definitively overcome in the 1960s, when the PSCh fell under the influence of the Cuban revolutionaries. However, in our opinion, its exhaustion was much slower, since an important part of the party, both in its rank and file as well as in its leadership, remained attached to populist political practices.

The case of the PCCh is much more complex. Since its foundation as Partido Obrero Socialista (POS) in 1912, it defined itself as a workers' party, whose objective was the conquest of power for the construction of socialism. However, since its incorporation into the political institutional framework in the mid-1930s, it also adopted practices and discourses typical of the populist model (Furci 2008: 53–106; Álvarez 2011: 79–104). Among them, the appeal to the construction of a national emancipation project, which demands a broad class alliance, became a fundamental component of the political identity of Chilean communists.

4. The concept of left-wing national populism is gleaned from Werz (2012: 184).

In this chapter we argue that, from the formation of the FP in 1936 until the fall of Salvador Allende's government in 1973, the Chilean left, formed by the PCCh and the PSCh, adopted the anti-oligarchic and anti-imperialist discourse of populism, while resorting to the social and electoral mobilization of the people in order to achieve power. In this regard, we propose to analyse the discursive elaborations and political practices of the populist left in Chile.

THE INSTITUTIONALIZATION OF THE POPULAR MOVEMENT AND THE RISE OF POPULISM

Towards the end of the nineteenth century and the beginning of the twentieth century, the irruption of capitalist modernity, especially in the industrial and mining sectors, and the subsequent workers' mobilizations and protests, gave rise to what intellectuals called *the social question*.[5] The extension and radicalization reached by the popular movement, and the rigidity with which the oligarchic regime confronted the process, led to successive bloody confrontations, most of which ended with massive workers' massacres.

It was in the spaces of sociability, segmented by class, that workers articulated their first cries of rebellion. In the taverns, the camaraderie, the bonds of fellowship and the profuse alcohol intake detonated the first uprisings against public authority. Later, the most skilled workers at handling tools, the strongest or most resistant at work, and those who could read and write, began to acquire a growing influence among their peers. Thus, spontaneous demonstrations began to take place, even in the face of organized and violent suppression.

Like many other workers' movements in the region, Chilean workers were influenced by the revolutionary ideas circulating in Europe, especially anarchist and socialist ideas and the so-called plebeian or Jacobin liberalism (Grez 2007: 25–65; Pinto 1999). The first workers' organizations that arose were the anarchist-oriented societies which were largely to be found around the urban manufacturing centres, and the workers' organizations, which were organized especially in the north of Chile, around the saltpetre and port activities, and in which democrats and socialists exercised most influence.

In this formative stage, the working class regularly resorted to strikes as the main form of struggle. The paralysation of productive activities and the public denunciation (rally) of the labour and material precariousness of the workers, operated as the fundamental referents of their struggles (Pizarro 1986).

5. Capitalist modernization has been analysed by Ortega (2005), while the debates surrounding the social question have been studied by Grez (1995: 9–44).

The workers, and the sectors that supported them, congregated in very large numbers in public spaces, subverting the oligarchic order. It is probably not surprising that most of their demonstrations were accompanied by looting of commercial establishments, confrontations with the forces of order, and destruction of urban equipment.

Meanwhile, the oligarchic elite showed itself incapable of recognizing the material and labour problems affecting the popular classes. On the contrary, workers' demands and protests were seen as a threat to private property and public order. For this reason, repression was systematically resorted to in order to contain the protests and the popular outburst. Both the police and the armed forces, called upon to re-establish the oligarchic order, fired regularly and purposefully against unarmed or poorly armed workers. Massacres followed: Valparaíso (May 1903), Santiago (October 1905), Antofagasta (February 1906), Iquique (December 1907), Forrahue (October 1912), Punta Arenas (July 1920), San Gregorio (February 1921) and La Coruña (June 1925).[6]

It was precisely in this context of crisis of the oligarchy and the rise of popular struggles, that the POS was formed in 1912, which would give rise, in January 1922, to the PCCh (Barnard 2017: 13–77; Urtubia 2017: 7–38). Similarly, the former organizations and societies in resistance attended the Third National Convention of the Great Workers' Federation of Chile (III Convención Nacional de la Gran Federación Obrera de Chile) in 1919, in order to transform it into the social and class referent of the organized workers. The organization, founded in 1909 in the old tradition of the mutual aid societies, was renamed Federación Obrera de Chile (FOCH) and, under the leadership of Luis Emilio Recabarren, adopted a revolutionary programme that proposed the abolition of capitalism and the conquest of power by the workers (Grez 2011: 23–170).

The above shows that the Chilean popular movement was constituted on the basis of a double matrix, social and political – a working-class base that was articulated around the union-federation as an expression of social unity, and a political base formed by the class party. This, in turn, was reflected in the formulation of a political project of a revolutionary nature that placed the conquest of power by the workers at the centre of the proposal. Likewise, the process of strengthening the workers' identity was carried out, based on symbolic devices such as the sacrificial memory, the spheres of sociability, and the rupturist mobilization, which converged and established the organizational centrality of both party and union. Consequently, during this period, the union and the workers' party became a homogeneous whole that allowed

6. Most of these episodes are recorded in monographic works. For an overview of oligarchic repression see the work of Felipe Portales (2011: 323–54; 2015: 24–34).

it to represent, socially and politically, the revolutionary demands of the subaltern classes.

With the election of the populist leader Arturo Alessandri Palma to government in 1920, the oligarchy was displaced from the administration of the state apparatus and replaced by a new fraction of the ruling class formed by the financial, commercial, and industrial bourgeoisie, supported by the United States. This administration, committed to contain the class confrontation, proposed to implement measures of a popular democratic nature, such as the eight-hour working day, the right to unionization and the improvement of workers' living conditions (Pinto & Valdivia 2001). At the same time, an anti-oligarchic discourse was begun, which favoured the cooperation of the organized popular masses. The coalition (Alianza Liberal), that brought Alessandri to government, was composed of the Partido Radical (PR) and liberal sectors, with a popular support base made up of the middle classes, artisans, and mining and urban workers.

Alessandri's government developed in the context of an acute unemployment situation, unleashed at the beginning of the 1920s, with the first saltpetre crisis. The severe damage to the saltpetre trade due to the loss of the German market and the consolidation of synthetic nitrate, led to severe unemployment, and an extended diffusion of the socialist ideology. Indeed, the displacement of unemployed saltpetre workers to the central zone influenced the creation of the first forms of peasant organization, as well as the multiplication of trade union organizations at an urban level (Pinto 2007: 183–232). Nevertheless, the bulk of the population continued to be linked to traditional trades, and proletarianization only represented a small segment of Chilean workers. In the rural sector, for example, precarious employment (seasonal labour) and the provision of personal services continued to predominate, while social legislation was practically non-existent in this sector (Yáñez 2008: 115–287).

The institutional changes that took place between 1924 and 1931 modified the situation of the workers' movement. Indeed, the social legislation, that was spearheaded by Arturo Alessandri's presidential campaign in 1920, was enacted in 1924, in the context of an acute political crisis, precipitated by the so-called *ruido de sables* (rattling of sabres). This was an action by young army officers, strongly influenced by the fascist corporativism of the time, and led by Carlos Ibáñez del Campo. It involved the officers making noisy protests in the tribunes of the National Congress by rattling their sabres against the floor as a sign of their support for the enactment of the so-called social laws. These regulations, duly grouped together, gave rise, in 1931, under the mandate of Ibáñez, to the country's first Labour Code.

The new legislation brought about the gradual move towards institutionalization of the class conflict. Several factors contributed to this. On the one hand, the bulk of the trade unionism that emerged during the period came under the regulations governing the internal structure and purposes of workers' organizations, with the result that existing class-based and independent trade unionism (socialist and anarcho-syndicalist) was increasingly weakened. On the other hand, the government of Carlos Ibáñez del Campo (1927–31) encouraged the formation of government approved (legal) unions (Confederación Republicana de Acción Cívica, CRAC), in order to form a social base of support for his government. This allowed the rapid multiplication of legal unions, while the Ibáñez administration harshly persecuted anarchist and communist unions and leaders. Finally, the administration asserted the role of the state as arbiter in the conflict between capital and labour. This idea, despite its scarce practical realization, profoundly modified the workers' perception of the state. As we have previously pointed out, the state, until 1920, had operated openly as a protector of the interests of the landowners and the bourgeoisie but, from the mid-1920s this function was partially abandoned, in order to build a State that ostensibly protected the interests of the workers (Rojas 1993: 47–142).

This process of institutionalization of the class conflict was also favoured by the incorporation of the political organizations of the left into the institutionality created by the newly agreed Constitution of the State of 1925. Indeed, after the phase of reflux that accompanied the popular camp during the Ibáñez administration, the popular parties (the PCCh and the PSCh, created in 1933), opted for a strategy of using the spaces of political representation (parliament, municipalities, legal unions, etc.), to increase their power over time (Furci 2008: 53–78; Drake 1992: 143–64). It was done through forming a class alliance with the sectors representing the national bourgeoisie, to advance towards the development of capitalism. Alongside this was the establishment of a bourgeois democratic regime in order to take power at some point in the future, with the support of a majority and mature proletariat. This was the founding phase of the Chilean left's adherence to the populist project.

By the mid-1930s, the incorporation of the left into the political institutional framework was completed with the formation of the FP. It came to power in 1938, endorsing the candidacy of the PR leader Pedro Aguirre Cerda. The FP (1938–47) was formed from a political alliance, which in turn was the expression of a class alliance (industrial bourgeoisie, middle classes and proletariat), which brought together the PR, the PCCh and the PSCh, and was supported by the Confederación de Trabajadores de Chile (CTCH), heir and successor of the FOCH (Milos 2008). Although the FP, as a political expression, ended in 1941 with the end of the presidency of Pedro Aguirre Cerda, the strategic alliance that created it, and its political programme, can be seen in the administrations of Juan Antonio Ríos (1942–46) and in the first years of the government of Gabriel González Videla (1946–47).

The FP's policy programme consisted of three fundamental tenets: the promotion of the country's economic activities, especially in the manufacturing sector; the expansion of educational coverage, with emphasis on technical-professional and industrial training; and the deployment of a policy of worker protection and the extension of unionization. By the end of 1947, the Corporación de Fomento (CORFO), which was established in 1939 to promote economic growth, had widely favoured the industrialization process, through the so-called industrial promotion and electric energy production plans. Similarly, the granting of soft credits to the industrial bourgeoisie favoured the expansion of the sector, especially the consumer goods industry (Llorca & Barría 2017: 9–29).

In the educational field, the FP created new educational establishments, especially in the area of preparatory education. It also favoured the installation of industrial high schools in the main departmental capitals of the country. The teachers' union, which benefited from the opening of new positions, became one of the mainstays of support for both the FP and the PR. Labour unions, particularly those affiliated to the CTCH, became active interlocutors of the government and achieved an exponential growth of affiliated militancy (Garcés 2018: 110–45; Henríquez 2014: 71–131). Notwithstanding the foregoing, the unions that saw the greatest improvements in their working conditions and an increase in their social and political rights, were the industrial unions, the professional associations at an urban level and the miners, especially those working in the copper sector. However, peasant unionization, a longstanding and major workers' issue, was postponed after a spurious agreement between the government, the CTCH and the Sociedad Nacional de Agricultura (SNA) (Acevedo 2017: 99–158; Illanes 2019: 247–81).

The cycle closed around 1948 with a profound defeat for the popular movement. The tensions between socialists and communists for the leadership of the workers' movement, which dated back to the beginning of the 1930s, worsened considerably during the 1940s. At the beginning of 1946, and after the workers' strike that gave rise to the Bulnes Square massacre (Santiago de Chile, 28 January 1946), the CTCH split into two factions, one led by the socialist Bernardo Ibáñez and the other headed by the communist Bernardo Araya. Later, in 1947, in the midst of the Cold War, the government of Gabriel González Videla aligned itself with Western democracies and proceeded to expel the communists from the government. In 1948 the administration introduced the Law of Permanent Defence of Democracy (3 September 1948), which outlawed the PC and systematically persecuted trade unions and labour leaders (Casals 2016: 137–90).

CONTINUITIES AND RUPTURES ON THE CHILEAN LEFT

By the beginning of the 1950s, the changes, derived from the economic modernization process initiated at the end of the nineteenth century, were evident. As previously mentioned, CORFO generated the conditions of infrastructure, equipment, technical advice and financial support necessary to deepen the industrialization of the country (Meller 1998: 47–60). As a result of this process, and of the increasing taxation that the state applied to the North American companies that exploited copper in Chile, public policy in relation to social matters was expanded. There was also a sustained growth in educational coverage, especially at the primary and secondary (industrial) levels, and a diversification of university offerings. It is not surprising, then, that the country's large cities, such as Santiago, Valparaíso and Concepción, where manufacturing and education were concentrated, began to attract increasing numbers of migrants of rural origin. The same can be observed with respect to the intermediate cities of less than 50,000 inhabitants, which were frequently the first stop for many in the subsequent process of movement towards the large cities.

The country's cities were not prepared for this growing and massive migratory process. The deficits in infrastructure and urban equipment, as well as the inadequacies of public policy on housing, made it very difficult for migrants to make their homes in the cities, and made their livelihood strategies more complex. Poverty took root in the urban peripheries and, along with it, a new social actor was formed: the urban poor. In time, this grouping came together in collective action and began to lead a series of illegal land occupations (*tomas*), which expanded the field of political action of the popular parties (Garcés 2002: 337–416; Hidalgo 2004: 267–345).

The defeats of the popular movement in the 1947–49 cycle was a lesson that revalidated the need for the classist and revolutionary project. This process was inaugurated at the beginning of the 1950s and had, as its main protagonists: the employees of the public sector (Asociacion Nacional de Empleados Fiscales, ANEF); and the private sector (Confederación de Empleados Particulares de Chile, CEPCH); the teachers (Federación de Educadores de Chile, FEDECH); the students grouped around the Federación de Estudiantes de la Universidad de Chile (FECH); and the workers of the split off CTCH. Indeed, after a series of partial mobilizations around wage demands, and rejection of the anti-inflationary policy of the government of the time, progress was made towards the formation of a Comisión Nacional de Unidad Sindical, which prepared the political and organizational conditions that allowed the foundation of the Central Única de Trabajadores (CUT), in

February 1953. The CUT clearly defined the need to abolish the capitalist regime in order to advance towards a classless society, vindicated the class struggle as a method of political action, and assumed itself as a classist and independent organization (Samaniego 2016: 27–41).

The CUT, under the direction of ANEF leader Clotario Blest Riffo, played, from this moment on, a key role in the process of revival of the mass movement and in the development of the social struggle. An expression of this was a growing trend towards the unionization of the working class which, by the end of the 1960s, had reached nearly one million workers. In addition, there was a sustained development of politicization of workers, a process that linked them to leftist organizations. Finally, there was the systematic use of the general strike and the suspension of labour activities, both to demand an improvement in working conditions, and to denounce abuse or repression, by both employers and the state.

This process of ideological and political reorganization of the working class had a profound impact on the PSCh. The internal crisis of the late 1940s had resulted in the fracture of the organization into two referents, the Socialist Party of Chile (PSCh) and the Popular Socialist Party. This led to intense critical, and self-critical, debates on the experience of class collaboration in the popular front and began a sustained process of internal deliberation that matured into the "Workers' Front" proposal which was adopted in 1955. Its central tenet was that the PSCh was to become "a strong popular organization of revolutionary character, which would serve as an instrument of struggle for the seizure of power first, and the revolutionary state later" (Jobet 1971: 20). According to this definition, it was up to the PSCh to unite all forces, political and social, willing to put an end to the capitalist regime. This new approach favoured the creation of the Frente de Acción Popular (FRAP) in 1956, a coalition of left-wing parties, and closed the door to any further engagement with class collaboration.

In later periods (1957, 1959, 1961 and 1964), the PSCh reinforced this political strategy and the FRAP presented a programme of revolutionary transformations: nationalization of basic wealth, banking and large industrial complexes; agrarian reform; and independent international policy. It put forward its own candidate, Salvador Allende, for the presidential elections of 1958 and 1964. After a crushing electoral defeat in the 1964 presidential elections, and under pressure from its left wing, the PSCh discarded the electoral route (Ordinary General Congress of 1965), as a means of gaining power. However, electoral mechanisms continued to be seen as useful tools for the mobilization of the masses. This position was later ratified at the XXII Ordinary General Congress of the PSCh, held in the city of Chillán, in November 1967. On that occasion the Chilean socialists approved a motion which in its central aspects established the PSCh as a revolutionary party:

> The Socialist Party, as a Marxist-Leninist organization, proposes the seizure of power as a strategic objective that this generation must fulfil in order to establish a Revolutionary State that frees Chile from dependence and economic and cultural backwardness and initiates the construction of socialism. Revolutionary violence is inevitable and legitimate. It results necessarily from the repressive and armed character of the class state. It is the only way that leads to the seizure of political and economic power and its subsequent defence and strengthening. Only by destroying the bureaucratic and military apparatus of the bourgeois state can the socialist revolution be consolidated. The peaceful or legal forms of struggle [...] do not in themselves lead to power. The Socialist Party considers them as limited instruments of action, incorporated into the political process that leads to armed struggle. Consequently, the alliances that the party establishes are only justified to the extent that they contribute to the realization of the strategic objectives already specified. (PSCh 1967: 6)

Meanwhile, the Communist Party (PCCh) experienced this new phase of the development of the popular struggle in clandestine conditions. The Law of Permanent Defence of Democracy, which had placed it outside the law between 1948 and 1958, had generated a strong internal debate between Luis Reinoso, secretary of organization of the party, who advocated the armed struggle against the regime of González Videla, and the bulk of the party leadership, who favoured an orderly withdrawal, and the encouragement of mass struggle. This latter position was adopted, and consolidated at the national conference of August 1952. The PCCh defined its policy of "national liberation front", as one which aimed to build broad social alliances to pursue an anti-oligarchic and anti-imperialist programme, that in turn, would be under the leadership of the working class (Furci 2008: 91–6). While the paths of the PSCh and the PCCh converged organically through the FRAP, they were split politically. The PSCh deepened its class and revolutionary position (with more than a few internal dissidences), while the PCCh continued its policies of broad alliances with the national bourgeoisie in order to advance towards the democratic revolution, which it perceived as still being possible.

One noteworthy call of the PCCh in this period was for the "peaceful road to socialism". Indeed, neither the Chilean communists nor the workers' movement in a broader sense, had ever gone down the road of armed struggle. On the contrary, their actions since the 1930s, and especially those deployed during the FP period, had prioritized the spaces provided by the institutionality, which they saw as being a known and effective path to power. This serves to explain the PCCh support for the presidential candidacy of

Salvador Allende Gossens (both in 1952 and 1958) despite the clandestine situation in which they had to operate.

By 1965, the process of radicalization of the popular movement manifested itself in a variety of ways. It could be seen through the rise of workers' struggles, the emergence of new social actors (the urban poor) and the accelerated organization of the peasantry. It also had to do with the definition of its own path by the Chilean left, with the PSCh defining itself as the most revolutionary party within the movement. The theoretical, political, and moral influence of the Cuban Revolution was also becoming increasingly evident. There now existed a series of organizations and groups that aspired to transform the political scenario through the formation of a revolutionary organization, that would place itself at the head of the mass movement in the struggle for the construction of socialism (Palieraki 2014: 8–55).

THE RISE AND RADICALIZATION OF POPULAR STRUGGLES

As we have previously pointed out, as far back as the early 1950s there was a process of regrouping and radicalization of the social and political left. Despite this, the electoral political arena continued to be the space prioritized by all of these groupings. But the discussions around the issue of attainment of power had provoked a series of splits and expulsions of militants in both the PCCh and the PSCh. These militants and some of Chile's smaller revolutionary movements found a theoretical reference and a point of support and confluence for their political struggle in the Cuban Revolution (Álvarez 2015: 55–68; Salinas 2013: 215–78).

In 1964, the electoral defeat of the left at the hands of Christian Democracy (PDC) and its candidate for the presidency, Eduardo Frei Montalva, generated a new and more profound debate within the popular sector. In the opinion of the most radicalized groups on the left, the electoral strategies had demonstrated, once again, their inadequacies and weaknesses. From this moment on, there was a much deeper split was between so-called "reformist organizations" (the traditional left) and the new left or "revolutionary left". The gap that opened up allowed those who considered themselves "revolutionary left" to take the necessary steps to form what they called the vanguard of the Chilean revolution. It was formed in August 1965 with the founding of the Revolutionary Left Movement (MIR) (Palieraki 2014: 83–138).

In its declaration of principles, elaborated upon in September 1965, the MIR set out the theoretical and political foundations that guided its actions. It presented itself as the Marxist-Leninist vanguard of the working class and the oppressed strata of Chile, and, at the same time, as the historical heir of the Chilean revolutionary traditions. Its aim was to overthrow the capitalist system and replace it with a government of workers and peasants, led by the organs of proletarian power. It set as a task the construction of socialism and the gradual extinction of the state, until reaching a society without classes. For the MIR, the Chilean bourgeoisie had demonstrated its incapacity to address the bourgeois democratic tasks: national liberation, agrarian reform and liquidation of the semi-feudal vestiges existing in the country. This incapacity exposed the absence of a progressive bourgeoisie and, consequently, the theory of revolution by stages, and the policy of class collaboration assumed by the traditional Chilean left since the end of the 1930s, were rejected. Later, the MIR denounced the political tactics used by the old left, in particular: the struggle to reform the capitalist system; electoralism; the abandonment of direct action; and the peaceful and parliamentary road to socialism. For the MIR these tactics confused, defrauded and disarmed the proletariat. The MIR proposed armed popular insurrection, as the only way to overthrow the capitalist regime (MIR: 1965).

In the Third Congress of the MIR, held in the city of Santiago in December 1967, the Castro-Guevarist sector, led by Miguel Enríquez, Bautista van Schowen, Luciano Cruz, and Andrés Pascal Allende, won a majority of the seats on the central committee (10 out of a total of 15), the five positions of the national secretariat, and the general secretariat of the party, which went to Miguel Enríquez (Amoros 2014: 91–5). The political scenario in which this event took place was marked by highly relevant international and national events. In October 1967, Commander Ernesto "Che" Guevara had been assassinated in Bolivia, something that brought into question the *foquista* strategy that had predominated within the revolutionary left up to that moment. Meanwhile, in Chile, the proposal of "Revolution in Freedom" of the Christian Democracy government (led by Eduardo Frei Montalva, 1964–70), began to be questioned, both by the political organizations of the left and by the popular movement. From that year onwards, a cycle of rising development of popular struggles began to take shape. This cycle had its starting point in the general strike of November 1967.

It was not only the MIR that underwent a process of radicalization during this time. The process of ideological and political radicalization of the PSCh had begun in the mid-1950s. At this stage, the evaluation of the failed experience of the FP led Chilean socialists to renounce poly-classist alliances and to reject political programmes of a reformist nature (Jobet 1967: 13–47). In 1955, within the framework of the XVI Ordinary General Congress of the FP collective (Valparaíso, October 1955), there was harsh criticism of the "policy of concessions" that had been developed during the popular front phase. The critical approach that the socialists adopted to bourgeois institutionality was accentuated with the electoral defeats experienced by the FRAP, in the presidential elections of 1958 and 1964. Meanwhile, the triumph of the Cuban

Revolution in 1959, with its armed assault on power, offered the socialists a new model of political action, different from the populist strategy they had followed since 1933 (Drake 1992: 276–81). It is unsurprising, therefore, that in 1965 the PSCh considered converting the Workers' Front into a Class Front that would advance towards the conquest of power (Jobet 1971: 111).

Later, in August 1966, the National Conference for Organization of the PS, sanctioned the modification of the party statutes. This established the PSCh as a Leninist organization which claimed its condition as a party of cadres to carry out a mass policy (Jobet 1971: 116). In line with this radical turn, the foreign policy of the PS, founded on the principle of proletarian internationalism, intensified its links with the Soviet bloc, especially with the German Democratic Republic (GDR), with Cuba, and with the national liberation movements of Asia and Africa.[7]

The highest point in the process of ideological radicalization of the PSCh took place at the XXII Ordinary General Congress in 1967 (Gómez 1993: 75–112). On that occasion the PSCh established that revolutionary violence was inevitable in any strategy of seizure of power (Jobet 1971: 30). However, the struggle of tendencies within the PSCh remained at very high levels during this period. The conservative tendency, which advocated the conquest of spaces of representation within the democratic institutionality, was led by the general secretary of the organization, Aniceto Rodriguez. It was represented at a mass level in the figure of Salvador Allende, and aligned a wide range of militants and social organizations around it. This tendency, while accepting the decisions of congresses, continued to support a policy of openness towards the progressive sectors of the bourgeoisie, and to maintain a commitment to democratic institutionality. The originating populist tradition of the 1930s reached its most mature expression in this wing of the PSCh. For Allende and the minority sector it was essential to reach agreements with the political centre in order to imbed change, while mobilizing the masses to maintain systematic pressure on parliament. The belief in this approach rested on the widely shared perception on the Chilean left in the 1960s, that Salvador Allende's leadership extended beyond the historical organizations of the working class.

In this cycle, the PCCh also underwent its own process of radicalization. Although it did not drag it to the point of vindication of the armed struggle, it did lead it to a redefinition of its power strategy. The notion of the "peaceful way", which had been adopted in the 1950s, was replaced by a new design,

7. At the regional level, the PSCh participated in the founding of the Latin American Solidarity Organization (LASO) in 1966, and the articulation of the Solidarity Organization for Asia, Africa and Latin America (OSPAAAL) in 1966. Both organizations had arisen as an initiative of Cuba and were part of its general strategy of stimulating global revolutionary processes.

called the "unarmed way", which tolerated, and even supported, the most radical manifestations of the mass movement (Álvarez 2011: 79). These included radical popular mobilizations such as land occupations, strikes and factory occupations, and street mobilizations involving confrontations with police forces. These mobilizations were complemented by active participation in all electoral contests called in the country, from the elections of neighbourhood, union and student organizations, to the elections of mayors, parliamentarians and the president of the republic.

The installation of the Popular Unity (UP) government in November 1970, and the implementation of the first measures of its programmatic proposal, unleashed an active and violent reaction from the political and business opposition (Pinto 2005: 9–33). In the agricultural regions, affected by the agrarian reform policy, farmers' resistance to the expropriation processes intensified while, in the manufacturing centres, the bosses declared a lockout to avoid expropriation and workers' self-management (Avendaño 2017: 247–339; Oszlak 2016: 59–141). At the same time, the US government was trying to economically suffocate Allende's administration (Harmer 2013: 39–73; Riquelme 2014: 11–43). In April 1971, the extreme right-wing organization, Frente Nacionalista Patria y Libertad (FNLP), was founded, which began to employ a systematic campaign of urban subversion, later moving on to the use of terrorist actions.

Undoubtedly, the "Chilean road to socialism" accentuated and sharpened the social and political confrontations that had already been simmering since the mid-1950s. After the failure of the developmental and populist experiences of the presidencies of the 1950s and 1960s (Carlos Ibáñez del Campo [1952–58] and Eduardo Frei Montalva [1964–70]), the UP sought to resolve the structural crisis affecting the capitalist system in Chile by accelerating the process of transition to socialism (Nazer 2021: 181–212). This was within the framework of a strict adherence to the country's existing political institutionality. However, the policy of expropriation of the means of production, sponsored by the UP, which affected the Chilean bourgeoisie and transnational capital, was a step too far for many. The violent opposition of the bourgeoisie, and an important sector of the middle class, to the UP project placed the issue of violence at the centre of discussion. Indeed, in a document presented to the congress of La Serena, Carlos Altamirano, secretary general of the PSCh, confronted the issue with the statement that the revolutionary vanguard had to overcome the vices and defects derived from the more than peaceful coexistence with bourgeois democracy (Altamirano 1971: 12).

And so the political strategy for the conquest of power was defined (the development of the revolutionary mass struggle, and the acceptance of the possibility of the use of political violence) and the type of political organization required to lead this process was established (party of revolutionary cadres). The PSCh then, like other revolutionary organizations of the period (such as the MIR, the Movimiento de Acción Popular Unitaria, MAPU, and the Izquierda Cristiana, IC), turned to the organization and broadening of the mass movement (Gaudichaud 2004; Cancino 1988). The aim was to strengthen popular power at the base of the workers' and popular movement and, to this end, the formation of "industrial cordons" was encouraged. These operated as territorial structures of power that represented factory workers and the urban poor. Similarly, in rural areas the "peasant councils" were to become the basis of social and political power in the revolutionary countryside. The communists, for their part, opted to defend the itinerary of revolutionary changes outlined by the UP government, but, at the base, their militancy also became part of the local power structures that were being constituted (Álvarez 2011: 95–104).

It was evident that a revolutionary process was taking shape in Chile associated with: the higher levels of class consciousness of the proletariat and the people; the growth of their forms of social and political organization; the development of a subjective consciousness of the possibility of triumph; the social and political economic erosion of the bourgeoisie; and the liquidation of the economic presence of imperialism. The highest point of the class confrontations of this period took place around the so-called Paro Patronal de Octubre of 1972 (Employers' Strike) which saw the mass mobilization of truck drivers, supported by a wide range of business and middle-class organizations: professional associations (doctors, engineers and lawyers); medium and small merchants; high school and university students. Through this mobilization, the opposition to the UP government sought to create conditions of ungovernability that would precipitate a *coup d'état* in Chile. However, workers, grouped around their base organizations, the communal commands and the revolutionary parties, managed to reverse the effects of the counter-revolutionary mobilization. Firstly, they denounced the seditious and conspiratorial manoeuvres. They kept the productive process going, distributed agricultural and industrial goods, dislodged the reactionary gangs from the public space and exercised political and territorial control over the productive centres and the working-class neighbourhoods. The seditious offensive of the bourgeoisie was defeated and the option of a revolutionary solution to the political crisis existing at that time was configured as a clear alternative.

It is not altogether surprising that, despite this, the opposition was not cowed but, instead, redoubled its destabilizing efforts. From March 1973 a scenario began to take shape in which conditions of ungovernability were again created that would lead to the resignation of President Allende. The plan was to carry out a bloodless coup. Thus, between March and June

1973, a series of anti-government mobilizations were precipitated which accentuated the climate of confrontation that had begun in October 1972. Among these mobilizations were the student movements against the Escuela Nacional Unificada (ENU) project, the strike of the El Teniente copper ore workers and the stoppage of public transportation in several cities. This escalation ended on 29 June, when the Army's Armoured Regiment No. 2, located in the city of Santiago, unsuccessfully revolted against the government in an attempt to precipitate the resignation of President Allende. In July, the government summoned the PDC to open dialogue in order to avoid civil war. These efforts were unsuccessful and in the Chamber of Deputies, on 22 August 1973, the PDC (together with the reactionary right) voted to declare the unconstitutionality of President Allende's government (Winn 2013: 93–121).

Simultaneously, the Armed Forces and the Carabineros Corps, invoking Law No. 17,798 on the control of arms and explosives (issued on the initiative of the Popular Unity government in 1972), proceeded to raid union headquarters and those of revolutionary organizations, as well as the territories controlled by the industrial cordons, in order to dissuade the workers from any attempt to go against the move. For their part, the employers' unions (business associations, professional associations, transporters and merchants), began a new anti-government mobilization at the beginning of August. Reactionary pressure reached its peak on 23 August 1973 when, after a mobilization of Army officers' wives, Carlos Prats González resigned as commander in chief of the Army and was replaced by General Augusto Pinochet. On the morning of 11 September 1973, a new chapter began in the history of Chile. The Armed Forces as a whole, plus the Chilean Carabineros Corps, deposed the Popular Unity government. The president of the republic, Salvador Allende, one of the main populist leaders of the twentieth century, heroically resisted the coup and died in the presidential palace. Thousands of workers and students took control of their work and places of study in an attempt to resist the coup but, lacking effective military support, they were violently evicted, most of them detained and many were tortured and killed (Rettig 1991). The overthrow of Salvador Allende put an end to the Chilean revolutionary experience and, moreover, crushed the populist tradition inaugurated in the 1930s. Indeed, both the revolutionary sectors (that had bet on the accumulation of social and political force at the level of the rank and file in order to provoke revolutionary rupture) and the more conservative sectors (which favoured alliance between the popular sectors and the bourgeoisie in order to introduce reforms) were violently evicted from the public sphere. The long populist experience of the Chilean left thus came to an end.

REFERENCES

Acevedo, N. 2017. *Un fantasma recorre al campo: Comunismo y politización campesina en Chile (1935–1948).* Valparaíso: América en Movimiento.

Adinolfi, G. 2010. "Las estructuras de los populismos: Diferenciación funcional en el populismo latinoamericano". *Nómadas. Revista Crítica de Ciencias Sociales y Jurídicas* 25: 1–17.

Aldao, J. & N. Damin 2013. "Populismos latinoamericanos en el siglo XX Apuntes para la actualización de un debate". *Historia Caribe* 8(23): 149–69.

Altamirano, C. 1971. "El partido Socialista y la revolución chilena". *Punto Final (Documents)* 121: 9–12.

Álvarez, M. 2015. *La constituyente revolucionaria. Historia de la fundación del MIR chileno.* Santiago de Chile: LOM Ediciones.

Álvarez, R. 2011. *Arriba los pobres del mundo. Cultura e identidad política del Partido Comunista de Chile entre democracia y dictadura. 1965–1990.* Santiago de Chile: LOM Ediciones.

Amoros, M. 2014. *Miguel Enríquez: Un nombre en las estrellas. Biografía de un revolucionario.* Santiago de Chile: Ediciones B.

Avendaño, O. 2017. *Los partidos frente a la cuestión agraria en Chile, 1946–1973: Representaciones de intereses, gradualismo y transformación estructural.* Santiago de Chile: LOM Ediciones.

Barnard, A. 2017. *El Partido Comunista de Chile 1922–1947.* Santiago de Chile: Ariadna Ediciones.

Cancino, H. 1988. *Chile: La problemática del poder popular en el proceso de la vía chilena al socialismo, 1970–1973.* Copenhague: Aarhus University Press.

Casals, M. 2016. *La creación de la amenaza roja: Del surgimiento del anticomunismo en Chile a la campaña del terror de 1964.* Santiago de Chile: LOM Ediciones.

Drake, P. 1992. *Socialismo y populismo: Chile, 1936–1973.* Valparaíso: Universidad Católica de Valparaíso.

Dussel, E. 2012. "Cinco tesis sobre populismo". In M. Márquez, E. Pastrana & G. Hoyos (eds), *El eterno retorno del populismo en América Latina y el Caribe*, 159–79. Bogotá: Editorial Pontificia Universidad Javeriana.

Entrena, F. 1996. "Los populismos y la formación del Estado-nación en América Latina". *Anuario de Estudios Americanos* 53(1): 101–21. DOI: 10.3989/aea.1996.v53.i1.434.

Furci, C. 2008. *El Partido Comunista de Chile y la vía al socialismo.* Santiago de Chile: Ariadna Ediciones.

Garcés, M. 2002. *Tomando su sitio. El movimiento de pobladores de Santiago, 1957–1970.* Santiago de Chile: LOM Ediciones.

Garcés, M. 2018. *El movimiento obrero y el Frente Popular (1936–1939).* Santiago de Chile: LOM Ediciones.

Gaudichaud, F. 2004. *Poder popular y cordones industriales: Testimonios sobre el movimiento popular urbano, 1970–1973.* Santiago de Chile: LOM Ediciones.

Gómez, J. 1993. *La rebeldía socialista. El Partido Socialista en la década de los sesenta. 1959–1970.* Santiago de Chile: FLACSO.

González, O. 2007. "Los orígenes del populismo latinoamericano. Una mirada diferente". *Cuadernos del CENDES* 24(66): 75–104.

Grez, S. 1995. *La cuestión social en Chile. Ideas y debates precursores (1804–1902)*. Santiago de Chile: DIBAM.

Grez, S. 2007. *Los anarquistas y el movimiento obrero. La alborada de la idea en Chile (1893–1915)*. Santiago de Chile: LOM Ediciones.

Grez, S. 2011. *Historia del comunismo en Chile. La era de Recabarren (1912–1924)*. Santiago de Chile: LOM Ediciones.

Harmer, T. 2013. *El gobierno de Allende y la Guerra Fría interamericana*. Santiago de Chile: Ediciones Universidad Diego Portales.

Henríquez, R. 2014. *En estado sólido. Políticas y politización en la construcción estatal: Chile, 1920–1950*. Santiago de Chile: Ediciones UC.

Hidalgo, R. 2004. *La vivienda social en Chile y la construcción de espacio urbano en el Santiago del siglo XX*. Santiago de Chile: DIBAM.

Ianni, O. 1973. "Populismo y relaciones de clase". In G. Germani, T. Di Tella & O. Ianni (eds), *Populismo y contradicciones de clase en Latinoamérica*, 83–150. Mexico: Ediciones Era.

Illanes, M. 2019. *Movimiento en la tierra. Luchas campesinas, resistencia patronal y política social agraria. Chile, 1927–1947*. Santiago de Chile: LOM ediciones.

Jobet, J. 1967. "El Partido Socialista y el Frente Popular en Chile". *Arauco* 85: 13–47.

Jobet, J. 1971. *El Partido Socialista de Chile*. Santiago de Chile: Prensa Latinoamericana.

Laclau, E. 2016. *La razón populista*. Mexico: Fondo de Cultura Económica.

Llorca, M. & D. Barría. 2017. "Introducción. Historia empresarial de Chile en el siglo XXI". In M. Llorca & D. Barría (eds), *Empresas y empresarios en la historia de Chile: 1930–2015*, 9–29. Santiago de Chile: Editorial Universitaria.

Martínez, P. & P. Rubio 2017. *América Latina actual. Del populismo al giro de izquierdas*. Madrid: Los Libros de la Catarata.

Meller, P. 1998. *Un siglo de economía política chilena (1890–1990)*. Santiago de Chile: Editorial Andrés Bello.

Milos, P. 2008. *Frente Popular en Chile: Su configuración, 1935–1938*. Santiago de Chile: LOM Ediciones.

MIR 1965. *Declaración de principios*. Santiago de Chile, septiembre de 1965.

Mouffe, C. 2019. *Por un populismo de izquierda*. Mexico: Siglo XXI Editores.

Nazer, R. 2021. "La crisis del modelo de desarrollo y las reformas estructurales, 1952–1970". In M. Llorca & R. Miller (eds), *Historia económica de Chile desde la independencia*, 181–212. Santiago de Chile: RIL Editores – Universidad de Valparaíso.

Ortega, L. 2005. *Chile en ruta del capitalismo: Cambio, euforia y depresión (1850–1880)*. Santiago de Chile: LOM Ediciones.

Oszlak, O. 2016. *La trama oculta del poder: Reforma agraria y comportamiento político de los terratenientes chilenos, 1958–1973*. Santiago de Chile: LOM Ediciones.

Palacios, M. 2011. *Populistas: El poder de las palabras. Estudios de política*. Bogotá: Universidad Nacional de Colombia.

Palieraki, E. 2014. *¡La revolución ya viene! El MIR chileno en los años sesenta*. Santiago de Chile: LOM Ediciones.

Partido Socialista de Chile. 1967. *Voto sobre la posición política nacional adoptado en el XXII Congreso Nacional Ordinario*. Chillán, 24 al 26 de noviembre de 1967. *Punto Final* (*Documents*) 46: 16 de enero de 1968: 6–7.

Pinto, J. 1999. "Socialismo y salitre: Recabarren, Tarapacá y la formación del Partido Obrero Socialista". *Historia* 32: 315–66.

Pinto, J. 2007. "Donde se alberga la revolución. La crisis salitrera y la propagación del socialismo obrero (1920–1923)". In J. Pinto (ed.), *Desgarros y utopías en la pampa salitrera. La consolidación de la identidad obrera en tiempos de la cuestión social (1890–1923)*, 183–232. Santiago de Chile: LOM Ediciones, Santiago de Chile, 2007.

Pinto, J. 2015. "Hacer la revolución en Chile". In J. Pinto (ed.), *Cuando hicimos historia. La experiencia de la Unidad Popular*, 9–33. Santiago de Chile: LOM Ediciones.

Pinto, J. & V. Valdivia 2001. *¿Revolución proletaria o querida chusma? Socialismo y alessandrismo en la pugna por la politización pampina (1911–1932)*. Santiago de Chile: LOM Ediciones.

Pizarro, C. 1986. *La huelga obrera en Chile: 1890–1970*. Santiago de Chile: Ediciones SUR.

Portales, F. 2011. *Los mitos de la democracia chilena. Desde la conquista hasta 1925*. Vol. 1. Santiago de Chile: Editorial Catalonia.

Portales, F. 2015. *Los mitos de la democracia chilena. Desde 1925 a 1938*. Vol. 2. Santiago de Chile: Editorial Catalonia.

Retamozo, M. 2017. "La teoría política del populismo. Usos y controversias en América Latina en la perspectiva posfundacional". *Latinoamérica. Revista de Estudios Latinoamericanos* 64: 125–51. https://doi.org/10.22201/cialc.24486914e.2017.64.56836.

Rettig, R. (ed.) 1991. *Informe de la Comisión Nacional de Verdad y Reconciliación*. Santiago de Chile: Ministerio del Interior.

Riquelme, A. 2014. "La Guerra Fría en Chile: Los intrincados nexos entre lo nacional y lo global". In T. Harmer & A. Riquelme (eds), *Chile y la Guerra Fría global*: 11–43. Santiago de Chile: RIL Editores-PUCCh.

Rojas, J. 1993. *La dictadura de Ibáñez y los sindicatos (1927–1931)*. Santiago de Chile: DIBAM.

Rosanvallon, P. 2020. *El siglo del populismo. Historia, teoría y crítica*. Barcelona: Galaxia Gutenberg.

Salinas, S. 2013. *El tres letras. Historia y contexto del Movimiento de Izquierda Revolucionaria*. Santiago de Chile: RIL Editores.

Samaniego, A. 2016. *Unidad sindical desde la base. La Central Única de Trabajadores de Chile, 1953–1973*. Santiago de Chile: Ariadna Ediciones.

Urtubia, X. 2017. *Hegemonía y cultura política en el Partido Comunista de Chile. La transformación del militante tradicional (1924–1933)*. Santiago de Chile: Ariadna Ediciones.

Viguera, A. 1993. "Populismo y neopopulismo en América Latina". *Revista Mexicana de Sociología* 55(3): 49–66.

Werz, N. 2012. "Populismos y democracia en América Latina". In M. Márquez, E. Pastrana & G. Hoyos (eds), *El eterno retorno del populismo en América Latina y el Caribe*, 181–97. Bogotá: Editorial Pontifica Universidad Javeriana.

Winn, P. 2013. *La revolución chilena*. Santiago de Chile: LOM Ediciones.

Yáñez, J. 2008. *La intervención social en Chile, 1907–1932*. Santiago de Chile: PEDCH-RIL.

CHAPTER 4

THE LEFT AND THE WORKERS' PARTY IN BRAZIL: A PARTY BETWEEN POPULISM, SOCIAL POLICIES AND THE POPULAR VOTE

Reinaldo Lindolfo Lohn and Silvia Maria Fávero Arend

On the first day of 2007, Luiz Inácio Lula da Silva took office for his second term as president of the republic of Brazil. The event marked an important political moment for left-wing Brazilian and Latin American political forces. As if it was not enough to have won the presidential elections for the first time in 2002, the Workers' Party – Partido dos Trabalhadores (PT) – now demonstrated that it could lead a government in an environment of relative institutional stability and achieve its continuity by democratic means. Unlike what happened at the first inauguration, when around 150,000 people took over Brasília with many red flags to welcome the new government, the second presidential inauguration was more discrete and less effusive. Once the novelty of four years earlier had passed, the inauguration of a president with Lula's personal and political trajectory no longer generated so much impact.

But it cannot be said that presidential inaugurations of democratically elected presidents in Brazil had become so frequent that they no longer attracted attention. Since the founding of the city of Brasília in 1960, a landmark of Brazilian modernist architecture and an expression of the developmental nationalism that had inspired government policies in the period immediately following World War II, it was only the sixth time that a president, elected by universal suffrage, had begun their mandate. The military dictatorship, imposed after the 1964 *coup d'état*, interrupted a relatively open and competitive political process that had begun in 1945. However, even in the brief democratic experience that the country had lived until the military took power, the left and popular forces had few opportunities to directly contest the popular vote and present a programme of social change. The Brazilian Communist Party was legalized in 1945, ran for presidential elections and managed to elect a small but symbolic and combative group of congressmen. However, in the context of insertion of the country into the geopolitics of the Cold War, the communists were forced to return to their usual clandestine activity, being outlawed from national political life in 1947.

Thus, in a country in which, for most of the twentieth century, the main leftist forces had been persecuted and banned from the formal political process, the continuity of a government derived from significant popular struggles was not unremarkable. Lula and the PT constituted themselves at the centre of a new left, organized during the process of political transition of the 1980s. This involved the last years of the dictatorship and the formation of the so-called "New Republic". The party has had continuous electoral successes since those initial years of democratization, culminating in its arrival into Brazilian central government at the beginning of this century.

The mainstream press, in addition to stressing the "maturity" of Brazilian democracy, highlighted that, in his first term, Lula and the PT had reproduced the traditional relations of Brazilian politics and been a government, in different aspects, below expectations. It was of little use for supporters to try to highlight the so-called "social advances" of the period. The economic growth rates showed a modest performance and urban violence gained dramatic contours in journalistic narratives. Furthermore, an expression had become common in the analysis of the columnists and political commentators: "Lulismo" – henceforth referred to as Lulism. Its use related Lula's government to personalist political practices and the memory of strong and centralizing leaders in different Latin American countries. Directed at the PT, the term sounded like a provocation, which was aggravated by right-wing critics who began to use the expression "lulopetismo", as if the party were nothing more than an accessory to its charismatic leader. In its trajectory until then, the party had rejected identifying itself with personalities and movements that, although popular, evoked a past of authoritarianism and manipulation of the masses. The expression Lulism also referred to forms of relationship between politicians and the popular electorate that had been called "populist" in the not-so-distant past. Militants and activists identified for years as "Petistas" – a term that sought to emphasize the importance of collective and non-personalist party organization – began to have to deal with a designation that generated discomfort.

In his inaugural speech at the start of his second term in 2007, Lula promised to make a government aimed at "accelerating, growing and including", and dedicated a brief passage to critics from both the right and the left when he said: "our government has never been, nor is it populist". This government was, is, and will be popular (Folha OnLine, 2007).

Days after the inauguration, an important Brazilian newspaper carried an article by a renowned sociologist dedicated to the study of labour relations in Brazil and its political implications. Based on a reading inspired by Gramsci, Ricardo Antunes placed Lula on a list of charismatic leaders which included Perón, Getúlio Vargas, Jânio Quadros, Adhemar de Barros, João Goulart,

Leonel Brizola and even Fernando Collor de Mello. He argued that Lulism continued a political trajectory that, in this case, mixed progressive and conservative elements, the latter increasingly taking the place of the former. Lula was losing his working-class origins and Lulism was expressing nothing more than a pragmatism, moulded to the routine circumstances of Brazilian politics. Although Antunes never used the expression "populism", it seems to be one of the possible conclusions of his reflection, in which Lula appears as a conciliatory politician, addressing the poor directly and no longer to the left, in addition to being involved in alliances and coalitions without any progressive dimension (Antunes 2007).

That reference in Lula's inaugural speech inspires the problematic from which this chapter was built. Here, the intention is not to present definitive answers, but to suggest questions about the alleged "populist" characteristics of the PT after its arrival in power, and to propose a reflection that takes account of the historical trajectory of the process of democratic construction in Brazil since the end of the last military dictatorship. The dynamics of the political transition process that took place at that time are considered here, as well as the trajectory of the political use of the notion of populism in Brazil, while avoiding conceptual generalizations. In this text, we explore possible relationships between the political action of the PT and Lula when they came to power in 2003; the social policies implemented at that time, focusing on the analysis of the "Bolsa Família" programme; and the electoral behaviour observed among the popular classes in Brazil, which are generally the target of what is called populism. A class marker can be seen in the use of this term in Brazil: it is usually used in reference to the electoral behaviour of the country's poorest populations. Therefore, the meaning of populism used here differs from its recent use in some countries and contexts, which is to designate leaders of right-wing extremist movements.

There are certainly important distinctions between a "popular" and a "populist" government, which Lula and his party were always keen to emphasize. Leftist forces in Brazil have a long history of criticism and rejection of so-called populist practices. In a way, the PT forged itself as a critic of its opponents that it accused of adopting populist postures. Hence, it was legitimate for its leaders and militants to question the use and scope of terms such as "Lulism" and "populism" to characterize the party in the twenty-first century.

THE ORIGINS OF BRAZILIAN POPULISM

The debate around populism (or even neo-populism) suggests a historical discussion about political relations in Brazil prior to the military dictatorship. In the late 1960s, Octavio Ianni claimed that the dictatorship had been the result of the collapse of the Brazilian populist experience. Populism had been the dominant political form in that society, situated in the transition from agro-export to industrialization in the mid-twentieth century, accommodating traditional political power and keeping intact the social control over workers. The masses were manipulated by techniques of political power that were necessary to maintain the compromises and accommodations of the period. This excluded a large part of the left, which adopted a nationalist and reformist programme that brought together the popular classes but did not lead to breaks with the dominant structures. The exhaustion of import substitution industrialization would have imposed on the capitalist sectors the need to reconsider alliances and commitments to populist democracy. The dictatorship was necessary to deepen the internationalization of the Brazilian economy, imposed by the ruling classes that got rid of the charismatic leaders of the past (Ianni 1968).

Another author who dedicated himself to the theme throughout the 1960s and 1970s was Francisco Weffort, who sought to understand the dynamics of social classes and the political presence of the popular masses in Brazil from 1945 onwards. In the postwar period, the extension of universal suffrage had given the popular classes the possibility of exerting pressure on the political system. Populism represented the emergence of popular classes and their importance in the context of industrial development in Brazil, incorporating them into the intricacies of politics (Weffort 1980: 61). However, the absence of effective autonomous party and union organizations committed to social change, led to a direct relationship between the electorate and politicians, thus reproducing and expanding the scope of populism. Weffort places the discussion within the scope of social conflicts in Brazil, taking populism as a particular historical situation. The popular masses were able to participate with some autonomy in the world of politics, arousing the aversion of conservative and elitist sectors. However, populism prevented such masses from acting as a class, instead maintaining their political dependence on charismatic leaders. To break with populism, union autonomy, pluralism and political education would be essential. These were the basic pillars assumed by the groups that founded the PT in the late 1970s. In the context of military dictatorship versus uncertain democracy, the party presented itself as different to the Brazilian left which had existed in the period prior to the 1964 *coup d'état*.

Nowadays, it is clear that the popular struggles pre-1964 had complex characteristics and were not simply subordinated to self-interested populist leaders. Different leftist groupings acted on the basis of a labour movement formed by workers, largely drawn from the massive rural exodus that took place in those years. In the early 1960s, some of the social struggles anticipated demands for union autonomy that would later mature in the more urbanized areas of the country (Negro 2004). In the rural areas, social struggles were also happening, with socialist and communist movements and leaders galvanized into action, and calling for agrarian reform. This was one of the main fronts of struggle in the country.

In addition, an important movement took place at the base of the Brazilian Labour Party – Partido Trabalhista Brasileiro (PTB) – an organization created in the 1940s around Getúlio Vargas, one of the paradigmatic figures commonly cited as a "Brazilian populist". Sectors of the Varguistas' social base in the big cities, particularly among the union organizations, moved closer to the left. In the absence of a large, designated, left-wing party capable of garnering votes from progressive voters, it fell to the Vargas party to be the channel of the demands for social change in the country. On the other hand, PTB leaders did not abandon their links with conservative sectors, thus maintaining a level of ambiguity. This ambiguous position was accentuated during the government of João Goulart (1961–64), a direct political heir of Vargas. This was seen by many observers as leading to paralysis of his power, and ultimately to an inability to resist the coup.

Despite appealing to the masses, populist politicians like Goulart were unable to persuade them to overcome their historical conditions. The defeat of the left, and the rapid imposition of the dictatorship, fuelled images of the poor as passive victims of deceivers, making the likelihood of their resisting the coup unlikely. The term populism came to designate the inconsistency of the political participation of popular groups, it being restricted to electoral suffrage. As important as taking academic discussions into account, it is therefore necessary to understand the political use of the term "populism" in Brazil.

The use of the term "populism" dates back to studies that have gained importance since the 1950s. It was often associated with elitist methods of disqualifying the political participation of popular groups, with the terminology applied to it used to discredit the political behaviour of the poorest sectors of the population in Brazil. Popular groups were presented as being passive and silent victims of deceptive forms of electoral campaigns, subject to messianism and political conformity.

It was argued that Brazilian society would be incapable of managing its contradictions, as there was not a full formation of social classes, endowed with awareness of their "historical role". Thus, the state was presented as a force, endowed with powers over an inconsistent society, capable of leading the process of modernization and industrialization. For Jorge Ferreira, this placed Brazilian workers as part of a "gelatinous" or "weak" civil society, dependent on an all-powerful state dedicated to manipulation, co-option and corruption. Thus, populism in Brazil involved the blaming of the state and the victimization of society (Ferreira 2001: 62–3).

One of the early applications of the populist tag in Brazil was applied to Getúlio Vargas in 1945. It was coined by the liberal-conservative opposition of the time as a way of undermining the popular support for the then dictator. Around the expression, an image of the "people" as a mixture of the ignorant and the alienated was created by the left, and also by many academics. Arising from this came the historical trope of Brazilian politics in the twentieth century as a succession of authoritarianisms followed by moments of imperfect democracy, led by devious politicians. The people could only observe the exercise of power, without the agency to alter their destiny.

When Lula came to power through the popular vote at the beginning of the twenty-first century, it is not surprising that both his trajectory and that of his party were built on a social base and a political programme that rejected the populist past. The PT had emerged from the popular bases that had broken away from the heirs of Varguism, from nationalism, as well as from communism of the 1960s and 1970s. According to Eder Sader (1988), a new popular left was forged in Brazil during the military dictatorship. Grassroots movements came together with popular sectors and developed their own political culture, connecting with the progressive church, popular education movements and demands for housing and decent living conditions. Political organizations, who had been involved in armed struggle against the authoritarian regime, also sought to build bridges with popular groups. At the same time, other groups were emerging into the public space, groups seeking women's rights, the defence of minorities, anti-racist policies and social protection policies for children and adolescents (Sader 1988). The demand for individual freedoms and, in particular, human rights also grew, after a period in which the dictatorship had set up a repressive apparatus that had turned persecution, violation, torture and death of both opponents and vulnerable social groups into state policy.

To the forefront of this movement of diverse social struggles, was a renewed labour movement with young leaders coming from a working-class base in the most industrialized region of Brazil, São Paulo. Among its members were just some of those hundreds of thousands of workers who had been displaced from the poorest rural areas of the country after World War II to work in the industrialized cities. These displaced persons formed the working base of the large national and multinational industries that produced modern consumer goods (especially cars), for the market which consisted of the middle classes and elites. However, they also participated in new forms of organization in the restricted spaces of struggle and critical expression opened up amidst the authoritarianism of the dictatorship and the control systems of factories.

This combination of diversity in mobilization and identified social needs provided for a constant dialogue between socialists, communists, Christians and humanists and, ultimately, led to, what came to be called "new unionism", which gained expression in the great strikes of 1978–81.

It was during those strikes that the country learned of the existence of a worker and unionist who, decades later, arrived in Brasília to assume the presidency of the republic for two terms, from 2003 to 2010. Born in Pernambuco, in the northeast region, and having migrated with his family as a child to São Paulo, Luiz Inácio da Silva, better known as Lula, gradually came to be seen as not just another union leader. Around the new unionism, of which Lula was the most frequent exponent, conditions were created and positions articulated that would lead to the formation of the PT in 1980. As pointed out earlier, The PT's historical trajectory was linked to grassroots social movements, new unionism, the progressive church, and the new left of the 1960s and 1970s. It rejected both the model of the Sovietized parties and social democracy (Secco 2011: 35–43).

The end of Brazil's military dictatorship and the subsequent democratization process took place in the context of a neoliberal turn (Villareal 1983), beginning under the presidency of João Figueiredo. The transition was marked by the slow negotiation of a political opening that would not threaten the rulers of the authoritarian regime, or undermine the predominance of liberal-conservative forces. This meant the construction of democratization from above, which provided for only small changes in institutional structures. The liberal-conservative coalition came to see, in the formalization of democracy, the possibility of opening up the economy and dismantling a state seen as spendthrift and essentially corrupt. It provided for neoliberal reforms to be imposed under a government with more political legitimacy than the dictatorship. Meanwhile, popular movements and the most combative opposition to the regime fought for a democracy that would mean the real expansion of civil, political and social rights. These were antagonistic perspectives. The expansion of rights meant more public policies, therefore, more state. The neoliberal position involved a significantly lesser role for the state (Viscardi & Perlatto 2018). The drafting of the 1988 Constitution and the presidential elections since then revolved around this fundamental tension.

SOCIAL POLICIES

During the process of transition, the PT transformed itself into a significant electoral force, particularly from the end of the 1980s and throughout the following decade. This occurred over a period after the fall of the Soviet Union, when internationally, the left was experiencing crises that proved, in many cases, insurmountable. In its rise, the PT was able to align itself with the urgent public agenda in the country of those years. This placed the fight against extreme poverty, through direct measures of income distribution, centre stage. Television images of people suffering extreme poverty, both in the countryside and in large cities, increased social awareness around the need for urgent policies to address this issue. Popular campaigns, mainly the one conducted under the leadership of sociologist Herbert "Betinho" de Souza, mobilized millions of people around the alleviation of poverty and hunger. Right-wingers and conservatives of different stripes found it difficult to control the public debate around it, at exactly the most favourable historical moment for their advancement in the international sphere. Certainly, the disappointment of the people with the brief government of Fernando Collor de Mello, and the difficulties of the second term of Fernando Henrique Cardoso, contributed to this.

The PT assured the left a dominance that it had never experienced before in the country, becoming the party with the most consistent popular social base in Brazil. Lula's "Caravans of Citizenship" travelled the country in the 1990s. While they did not generate direct electoral benefit, they brought to the heart of the action of the Brazilian left the need to produce specific public policies and government action programmes for the country's most vulnerable sectors. This meant a shift from comprehensive platforms for the transformation of society (so dear to the left) and the so-called structural reforms, including agrarian reform. Internationally tested mechanisms, or those developed in municipalities under the party's administration, such as microcredit and the transfer of basic income to poor families, gained traction and became central tenets of party policy. When the party rose to federal government in 2003, the political effect of income transfer measures to the poorest workers in the country was significant. At the beginning of the first Lula government, the "Fome Zero" (Zero Hunger) programme was launched, later replaced by the merging of several income transfer programmes into a single system, capable of ensuring universal coverage of social protection, known as "Bolsa Família" (Family Allowance), a conditional cash transfer family welfare programme.

Among the social programmes implemented during the Lula government, Bolsa Família was the greatest success. It was the largest conditional cash transfer programme in the world and stood out as one seeking to change the poverty conditions of a significant portion of families. It guaranteed basic social rights such as access to education and to health care. In order to be eligible, families had to ensure that children attended school and got vaccinated. Child labour was an issue among poor Brazilian families, both urban and rural, for most of the twentieth century. This was something which greatly contributed to the social reproduction of poverty, with well-paid employment increasingly demanding a higher level of education towards the end of the twentieth century into the twenty-first. It is worth noting that since the first government of Getúlio Vargas (1930–45) child school attendance was theoretically mandatory in Brazil. However, there was a wide gap between federal and state policy and what actually happened in people's daily lives.

From an early age, boys and girls in rural areas worked long hours in agriculture and/or taking care of animals, on the small and medium-sized properties of their families. In the urban world, the picture was more complex. Young boys, and teenage boys and girls, worked in industry and in commerce and services and were poorly paid. This made it more difficult for men to get work that paid enough to provide for their families. This, in turn put further pressure on individual families to send children out to work. With the aim of defraying family expenses, poor girls, generally from the age of 12 onwards, entered the labour market, mainly acting as domestic servants in the homes of the middle classes. The issue of minors not attending school was not seen as a social problem for much of the Brazilian middle class. Increasingly, on the streets of large Brazilian urban centres, there were significant numbers of children and adolescents working informally or begging (Frontana 1999). Over the years, some of them, especially males, have engaged in the emerging and illegal narcotics trade.

Those responsible for formulating social policies for children during the military dictatorship advocated their transfer to public or private shelters. Public resources were provided to institutions to provide shelter, food and clothing for the children and to give them an education. Reality, however, presented a picture of lack and neglect. Even so, this and other actions in the fields of social assistance, such as the distribution of basic foodstuffs, were of great importance for the maintenance of a network of political support for the dictatorial regime. Social issues, such as these, were dealt with as part of a vast system of social control and political power, in which the authoritarian state's role was to ensure that the poor did not get out of control (Zaluar 2012).

When media censorship was eased at the end of the dictatorship, serious allegations of human rights violations in the children's institutions began to surface. Throughout the process of political transition and democratic construction, this issue featured increasingly on the public agenda (Arend 2016). Its uncovering was instrumental in the introduction of federal legislation, the Statute of Children and Adolescents, in 1990. This statute guaranteed the rights of children and adolescents in the country, as well as providing for social policies targeted at the poor. Its introduction was certainly influenced by the presence of the new Brazilian left and its programmes. Their direct engagement with the popular classes was raising awareness among the people and pointing to the need for more compensatory social policies. There was a move away from dependence on charitable and philanthropic organizations and actions and also from the policies of sheltering children in large institutions. The period of Fernando Henrique Cardoso's government (1995–2002), saw some movement in this regard at national level. However, it was during the two Lula administrations that the really significant move was made towards universality of social protection (Rego & Pinzani 2013).

The Bolsa Família social programme was instituted in 2003 during Lula's first government, building on policies and actions that had already been instituted. The social programme targeted families in both urban and rural areas, located on the spectrum between poverty and extreme poverty. Each family received a differentiated payment, based on the number of children aged under 17 years and the presence of pregnant or nursing women. Beneficiaries received a monthly payment directly from the federal government through a state bank. The conditionalities of the social programme were: children and teenagers should attend school; pregnant women should undergo prenatal examinations; and children between zero and six years old should have their weight, height and vaccination control verified by the health system. These conditionalities were designed to break with the generational cycle of poverty, thus creating possibilities for people to enter the labour market, after completing the school cycle (Pires & Jardim 2014).

POLITICAL INTERMEDIATION

The social programmes, as constituted, were seen as capable of reorienting the social assistance and support mechanisms built throughout the twentieth century in Brazil. They moved away from a situation where politicians routinely adopted the role of intermediary in the delivery of services in exchange for votes. The use of family registration systems, that involved objective criteria, reduced the level of personalization of social policy. Ensuring the institutionality built throughout the New Republic and governing within the limits of the political frameworks created, the PT presented itself as capable of distributing income, without increasing social conflicts. The political effect on the trajectory of the PT and part of the Brazilian left would be considerable. However, there is still much debate about the extent to which the policy of minimum wage, social security mechanisms and social programmes succeeded in deconcentrating income and reducing social inequalities. Critics from both the right and the left were highly critical of what they saw as the institutionality of paternalism by the government.

The 1990s and the years immediately prior to the electoral victories of the beginning of the twenty-first century, saw significant changes in the performance of the PT, consolidated on its arrival into government in 2003. There were some important factors that influenced party actions in the political sphere over those years. First, after the military dictatorship, Brazilian democracy was institutionally guided by the centrality of mechanisms of political representation as the main means for its construction; this applied with strict limits (Pitkin 2004). Thus, political forces had little choice but to organize themselves around the functions of electoral campaigning. In the case of the PT, subordinating the party to the electoral politics of governing municipalities and states meant, for most of its leaders, creating alliances and coalitions, organizing themselves for costly electoral campaigns, as well as making party programmes more flexible.

Second, the PT had come to identify strongly with combating extreme poverty through social programmes applied at local level. However, it was hugely challenging to build a comprehensive left-wing programme, while acting within the limits of an economic management, subordinated to the limits of conservative fiscal and monetary measures. Expanding social rights amid neoliberalism became a difficult problem to resolve. The so-called "macroeconomic tripod", inherited from the 1990s, was preserved with an economic policy, based on the generation of a primary surplus, inflation targets, and a floating exchange rate (Braga & Santos 2020).

Finally, in what would later prove to be a bitter and contradictory condition, the PT emerged as an ethical bulwark amid a political system marked by deviations and scandals in different areas of state management. What has come to be called "coalition presidentialism" (Abranches 1988), was a common practice in post-dictatorship Brazil. This is where presidents are only strong and stable when they form vast parliamentary majorities in exchange for advantages in accessing power, resources, state companies and ministerial positions. The consolidation of institutional schemes, guided by parliamentary protagonism, led the various governments of the New Republic to adopt forms of interaction with the National Congress that involved intense negotiation in the division of the public budget and in the structuring of the state itself. The PT, despite controlling the executive functions of the state, was far from having a majority in the parliament. Being part of this type of unwieldy coalition of varied interests with the primary focus on being in government, meant the party was in office when huge campaign funds were sought, and provided, by large companies to further electoral success. This meant the party was cited in press coverage of accusations of practices considered corrupt and was also investigated by parliament and the judiciary in relation to these matters. Such accusations featured in the middle of Lula's first term in office, when PT leaders and important members of the government were accused of ethical deviations and corruption.[1]

1. Years later, after leaving the government, Lula himself would be convicted of, and imprisoned for, corruption and money laundering, involving the oil company Petrobras and contractors. The finding was contentious, with serious doubts raised about the intentions, and possible collusion, of the prosecutors and the judge. Subsequently, the judge was declared partial by the Supreme Court, the conviction was quashed, and Lula was freed.

Towards the end of his first term, Lula's government was no longer clearly on the left. He and the PT had found it impossible to conduct a programme of real social reform within a government with a substantial neoliberal element. This was compounded by the right-wing opposition, which exploited the political ambiguities and corruption scandals that beset the government and made the front pages of newspapers. It seemed, if the forecasters were to be believed, that Lula's first term was heading towards a melancholy and demoralizing end and that the possibility of a second term in office was an impossibility. But it was exactly at this point that the concept of "Lulism" appeared (Singer 2009). In a discussion first published in 2009, Singer appropriated the term that had circulated among critics of the PT from different ideological spectrums. He described "Lulism" as a term that goes far beyond a variety of populism. He pointed to the contradiction in the criticism and asked the question, how could the PT government be neoliberal (as it was accused of by the left) and populist, in the Brazilian style of the 1950s (as claimed by conservatives, and some leftists)?

Lula's trajectory, in the years immediately prior to his becoming president, made him the most popular candidate, but it was the measures his government took to increase the minimum wage, extend social programmes and transfer income, that would be fundamental to the phenomenon of Lulismo. More than a specific exercise of power, or a direct attempt to gain voter approval at election time, it was a movement that brought about consistent change in the electoral behaviour of significant sectors of popular groups in Brazil, both in relation to the PT, but mainly in relation to Lula. Electoral data, systematized by Singer, demonstrates that, prior to 2006, Lula performed best with voters in middle-income groups, those with monthly incomes of up to two minimum wages. Latterly, post-2006, the Lula voters were made up of individuals with difficulty finding formal jobs or as self-employed service providers. These voters were disconnected from union organizations and in a frequent condition of instability and seasonality. A large proportion of them lived in the poorest areas of the country, especially in the north and northeast regions, in places that for decades were departure points for emigrants to the large Brazilian cities. This "sub-proletariat", marked by informality and difficult conditions in the world of labour, forms a contingent of the working-class that the Brazilian left has historically failed to reach. The successive elections that took place after the country's redemocratization showed a marked conservatism among these voters (Singer 2012).

"Lulism" brought to the PT a contingent of voters that the party was not used to. Vulnerable and precarious, they were inclined to reject uncertain and insecure radical proposals for fear of a rupture in the social order. Their life experience tended to show that periods of crisis and instability only aggravated their poverty. A significant portion of the middle classes, the better paid and organized sectors of the working class, and civil servants tended to vote for the PT in the 1980s and 1990s. They were inspired by a post-materialist ethic (Inglehart 1990) and in search of an alternative to the political and cultural practices in the country. Meanwhile, the poorest gave their support to right-wing politicians. They were very much subject to a worldview, influenced by consolidated hierarchies and a popular religiosity, that prompted distrust of political protest and deviation from the status quo.

As can be seen, Brazilian society is more complex than a very structured social class scheme allows for. The inability of the leftist discourse to attract the poorest is indicative of that. The historical political violence, perpetrated in the interior of the country against the poor when they engaged in popular protest, contributed to creating a common sense of fear and prudence. Further to that, voting is seen as almost a community activity where consensus, within both family and community, is valued and conflict is feared, and avoided. Thus, voting becomes less of an individual choice, and more of an adherence to the norms of the society in which the poor are located (Palmeira 1992). Thus, politics operates as a mode of interaction between the rich and the poor, that keeps the poor away from power. Researching the lives of poor workers in an area on the outskirts of São Paulo between the 1970s and 1980s, Teresa Caldeira analysed and described experiences that indicated a vague belief in the concept of social mobility and the possibility of improving life through individual effort, with the support and encouragement of family. This belief in the possibility of upward mobility through individual effort impacts the political perceptions and electoral choices of very poor populations in Brazil (Caldeira 1984). Any analysis of Brazilian politics in recent decades must consider the electoral decision-making of such workers and must avoid subordinating it to the mere reproduction of politicians' ideas and speeches.

CONCLUSION

In terms of macroeconomic policy, the Lula government maintained continuity with its predecessors, but through its expansion of a universal basis for the protection of rights of the popular classes, it reduced the power of practices of social control by local elites over the poor. In parallel, measures such as the expansion of public credit and state investments resulted in the maintenance of low inflation rates and the stability of fundamental food prices, all supported by consistent adjustments in the minimum wage. The macroeconomic conservatism was accompanied by public and private investment that contributed to the generation of jobs and increased employment.

Meanwhile, an economy of popular goods, cheap food, affordable civil construction materials for self-construction of homes, among other factors, boosted an underground economy.

Public mechanisms ensured a more or less stable base of income, food security and the protection of children and the elderly. The government saw its programme of measures as one that respected the dignity of the poor. This constituted a significant change in the historical trajectory, where the poor were accustomed to a routine of disrespect, oppression and discrimination. Lula sought to maintain relations with the unionized working class, now a decreasing number, as a result of productive restructuring and deindustrialization. He also reached out to a broader electorate of workers, who were not necessarily unionized, but who saw the opportunities presented by Lula's government, such as education for their children and, for the first time, access to consumer goods (refrigerators, washing machines, etc.).

Singer characterizes Lulism as being based on "weak reformism" and having a political practice that brings it closer to conservative power relations (Singer 2012). Its success came through its appeal to the most precarious sectors of society, and the resultant fundamental shift in its longstanding voting allegiance to the right wing. Through this, Lula and the PT promoted a realignment of political forces in Brazil that was maintained throughout the first decades of the twenty-first century. The limitations of the movement are marked by its inability to bring about structural changes. That is to say the trajectory of the PT government, and of the labour movement that supported it, was conditioned by the change in labour relations, including a marked increase in precarization. It is also necessary to consider the importance of social protection policies in a country with so many inequalities and contradictions like Brazil.

The political process in Brazil following the military dictatorship, the negotiated transition and the perspectives that guided the construction of a limited democracy must be considered when evaluating the trajectory and behaviour of left-wing party organizations in Brazil. The development of the PT was also influenced by these processes, despite its unique path to power. The party became increasingly identified with Lula as an individual, thus reconfiguring the way it was perceived by the popular classes. And even if he had wanted to, and the PT had tried to, it was impossible to return to the pre-1964 populist political order, given the political and economic changes that had taken place since, under the military regimes and their successors.

The concept of populism alone is insufficient to account for the issues of present-day Brazil, or even to fully characterize a party like the PT, without considering the trajectory of its political use. At various historical moments, the accusation of populism was used, by both right and left respectively, to undermine the popular vote. The democratization of power through popular participation cannot, by itself, be deemed "populist". Neither can social struggles, and the system of rights they sought to build, be reduced to populism. The limits of the political system, that allowed for the election of Dilma Rousseff twice through the popular vote, could not stop the steady rise of the far right after 2014, despite the conciliatory position of the PT. In short, politics cannot be reduced to populism and its opposite.

REFERENCES

Abranches, S. 1988. "Presidencialismo de coalizão: O dilema institucional brasileiro". *Dados* 31(1): 5–38.

Antunes, R. 2007. "Fenomenologia do lulismo." *Folha de S. Paulo*, 3 January, A-1.

Arend, S. 2016. "Ditadura, imprensa e o 'problema do menor': assistência à infância no Brasil (1980–1985)". *Delaware Review of Latin American Studies* 17(2): 1–9.

Braga, R. & F. Santos 2020. "The political economy of Lulism and its aftermath". *Latin American Perspectives* 47(1): 169–86. DOI: 10.1177/0094582X19887806.

Caldeira, T. 1984. *A política dos outros: o cotidiano dos moradores da periferia e o que pensam do poder e dos poderosos*. São Paulo: Brasiliense.

Ferreira, J. 2001. "O nome e a coisa: o populismo na política brasileira". In *O populismo e sua história: debate e crítica*, 59–124. Rio de Janeiro: Civilização Brasileira.

Folha OnLine 2007. "Veja a íntegra do discurso de posse do presidente Lula." *Folha de S. Paulo*, 1 January. www1.folha.uol.com.br/folha/brasil/ult96u88185.shtml.

Frontana, I. 1999. *Crianças e adolescentes nas ruas de São Paulo*. São Paulo: Loyola.

Ianni, O. 1968. *O colapso do populismo no Brasil*. Rio de Janeiro: Civilização Brasileira.

Inglehart, R. 1990. *Culture Shift in Advanced Industrial Society*. Princeton, NJ: Princeton University Press.

Negro, A. 2004. *Linhas de montagem: o industrialismo nacional-desenvolvimentista e a sindicalização dos trabalhadores (1945–1978)*. São Paulo: Boitempo.

Palmeira, M. 1992. "Voto: racionalidade ou significado?". *Revista Brasileira de Ciências Sociais* 20(7): 26–30.

Pires, F. & G. Jardim. 2014. "Geração bolsa família: escolarização, trabalho infantil e consumo na casa sertaneja (Catingueira/PB)". *Revista Brasileira de Ciências Sociais* 29(85): 99–112. DOI: 10.1590/S0102-69092014000200007.

Pitkin, H. 2004. "Representation and democracy: uneasy alliance". *Scandinavian Political Studies* 27(3): 335–42. DOI: 10.1111/j.1467-9477.2004.00109.x.

Rego, W. & A. Pinzani. 2013. *Vozes do Bolsa Família: autonomia, dinheiro e cidadania*. São Paulo: Unesp.

Sader, E. 1988. *Quando novos personagens entraram em cena: experiências, falas e lutas dos trabalhadores da Grande São Paulo (1970–80)*. Rio de Janeiro: Paz e Terra.

Secco, L. 2011. *História do PT, 1978–2010*. Cotia: Ateliê Editorial.

Singer, A. 2009. "Raízes sociais e ideológicas do lulismo". *Novos Estudos CEBRAP* 85: 83–102. DOI: 10.1590/S0101-33002009000300004.

Singer, A. 2012. *Os sentidos do lulismo: reforma gradual e pacto conservador*. São Paulo: Cia das Letras.

Villarreal, R. 1983. "La contrarrevolución monetarista en el centro y la periferia". *El Trimestre Económico* 197(50): 429–71.

Viscardi, C. & F. Perlatto. 2018. "Cidadania no tempo presente". In J. Ferreira & L. Delgado (eds), *O Brasil republicano, 5. O tempo da Nova República (1985–2016)*, 447–77. Rio de Janeiro: Civilização Brasileira.

Weffort, F. 1980. *O populismo na política brasileira*. Rio de Janeiro: Paz e Terra.

Zaluar, A. 2012. "Juventude Violenta: Processos, Retrocessos e Novos Percursos". *Dados* 55(2): 327–65. DOI: 10.1590/S0011-52582012000200003.

CHAPTER 5

BRAZIL, BOLSONARO AND POPULISM OF THE RIGHT

Victor de Oliveira Pinto Coelho

In the political analysis of Latin America and Brazil, when we mention "populism", we immediately think about the long tradition of figures such as Getúlio Vargas (Brazil), Juan Domingo Perón (Argentina), Lázaro Cárdenas del Rio (Mexico) or José María Velasco Ibarra (Ecuador). It relates to a time when Latin America was going through a period of intense and complex processes of modernization and inclusion of the working class, within the framework of labour laws and political democracy. More recently, we have witnessed a "return" of populism in Latin America as elsewhere, but now in a conservative version and in a particular context in macroeconomic terms. Unlike the "classical" era of populism, the current neoliberal hegemony has led to a reduction of the role of the state, in favour of greater freedom for capital flows and a shrinking of the labour market, of social policies, of labour rights, and so on. Latin American presidents, characterized by their populist appeal, were very much part of this conjuncture, such as Alberto Fujimori (Peru) and Fernando Collor de Mello (Brazil). What does this new populism of the right signify? How does it relate to the classic populism and the original incorporation of the masses into the democratic order?

These debates are not just a concern from a historiographical or sociological point of view. They are part of the current political process itself, in the sense of building a political programme and claiming political traditions. In this sense, as a way of trying to counteract the neoliberal agenda put into practice in Brazil throughout the 1990s, and also of forming a political opposition to the governments of Fernando Collor de Mello and Fernando Henrique Cardoso, the Workers' Party – Partido dos Trabalhadores (PT) – claimed the tradition of national developmentalism (Perlatto 2016). This tradition, which came from Getúlio Vargas (and the subsequent governments of Juscelino Kubitschek and João Goulart) implied a commitment to industrialization and modernization of the country and included the incorporation of the working population into citizenship via the

Labour Court. However, it was achieved without shaking the foundations of the primary sector of the economy, based on the large exporting rural areas, and thus was some kind of compromise state.

The anti-PT movement,[1] which gained strength during the years when the PT was represented in the federal government (2003–16), was encouraged by the liberal opposition, whether by political parties, especially the PSDB,[2] or by the media in general. One of its foundations was the criticism of the "populism" of the PT's social and macroeconomic policies. This criticism, of course, also took into account the Latin American context, in which the centre-left governments of Lula and Dilma ruled at the same time as the regimes of Hugo Chávez and Maduro (Venezuela), Kirchner (Argentina), Evo Morales (Bolivia), Rafael Correa (Ecuador) and José Mujica (Uruguay). In analytical terms, we can see why the "populist" label was deployed against governments that proposed a break from the neoliberal logic (Cortés 2016). Attacks on populist rhetoric, on the charismatic and "manipulative" character of its leaders were common. The spectre of the "Chavista dictatorship" became a symbolic theme extended to any left-wing government, serving as a political weapon, bringing to bear the menace of populism to haunt decent free-spirited and entrepreneurial souls.

With regard to Brazil, there are controversies around the effective national-developmental character of the PT governments. In practice, they implemented forms of labour flexibility, openness to private management of public services (such as health services) and created a central role for agribusiness as the country's adaptation to the flow of commodities, with a tendency towards deindustrialization (see Gonçalves 2013). In the public sphere, especially after the global financial crisis of 2008, the mainstream media carried sustained criticism of "public spending" and defended austerity policies. However, the result of President Dilma Rousseff's removal through impeachment in 2016 did not represent a smooth return to the neoliberal agenda, as set out in the "Bridge to the Future" platform, defended by Vice President Michel Temer's party (the PMDB), which would then take over the government. The neoliberal, or ultraliberal, agenda would assert itself within the ambit of an extreme right-wing populism which became known as Bolsonarismo, an ideological formation forged around the figure of Jair Messias Bolsonaro.

Bolsonaro was an obscure figure in Brazilian political life. In 1986, he was arrested by the Army due to an interview given to a magazine, in which he complained about the low wages paid by the institution. The following year,

1. Political opposition to the PT party, "antipetismo" in Portuguese.
2. Party of the Social Brazilian Democracy, originated in 1988 (year of the promulgation of the current Federative Constitution of Brazil) and which, despite its name, implemented neoliberal policies during the presidency of Fernando Henrique Cardoso (1995–2002).

the same magazine published an article that pointed to Bolsonaro as one of the suspects of having planned a bomb attack against the Agulhas Negras Military Academy (Academia Militar Agulhas Negras, AMAN), to force a salary increase, being acquitted by the Supreme Military Court. Retired from the army in 1988, aged 33, Bolsonaro has begun a long and not particularly illustrious political career, first as a councillor in Rio de Janeiro, later as a federal deputy. He has always defended conservative agendas, especially those related to public safety. In general, he did not defend neoliberal projects and was faithful to the authoritarian developmentalism from the time of the military dictatorship (1964–85), for which he was always an apologist and continued to be, even as president-elect in 2018. On taking up office Bolsonaro appointed the staunch defender of neoliberalism Paulo Guedes as minister of the economy. Guedes had acted as economic advisor to his campaign. Finally, there was a well-known connection between Bolsonaro and his sons with militia[3] members in Rio de Janeiro.

The guiding thread of our reflections is: how could a figure from the lowest level (in the practical and symbolic sense) of Brazilian politics be elected president of the country? How can the concept of populism help us to understand the phenomenon? In order to try to answer these questions, we will divide this chapter into two parts.

First, we will highlight the crisis in the legitimacy of the political system at the global level, which is linked to the rise of right-wing populism. We seek to portray the relationship with neoliberal policies and the underlying social demands, emphasizing the eruption of popular demonstrations in Brazil from 2013 onwards. For this, we intend to show the similarity with, and even the influence of, the Spanish 15-M Movement. Second, we will discuss how, in the midst of a complex scenario, the Bolsonarist discourse managed to establish a hegemony, in which such complexity is translated as "us *versus* them" bipolarity. Ernesto Laclau's discourse theory (which influenced the leaders of Podemos, in Spain) will be an important reference for our explanation.

Finally, we will seek to demonstrate how the neoliberal agenda was updated through the populist agenda of Bolsonarism. Here we suggest that, in its maximum degree of polarization, approaching a neofascist phenomenon, Bolsonarism allowed social demands to be subsumed by the neoliberal agenda. This final section refers back to the first section, where we put forward elements of neoliberal subjectivity that emerge simultaneously with the process of deregulation of the labour market.

3. Criminal organizations formed, especially by former police officers, operating in low-income urban communities such as housing developments and slums. They claim to act to combat the crime of drug trafficking, but start to live off the extortion of the population and clandestine exploitation of gas, cable television, slot machines, loan sharking, premiums on real estate sales, and so on. On Bolsonaro's link with the militias, see Manso (2020).

REPRESENTATION CRISIS: THE GLOBAL WAVE THAT ARRIVED IN BRAZIL IN 2013

In the analysis of the populist phenomenon, there are some common topics one has to consider: the nature of the "populist" political leader, the discourse that seeks to antagonize the fields of the "people" versus the "corrupt elite", and the broader relationship between populism and democracy. Is populism a type of politics antagonistic to democracy or does it represent a permanent internal tension, present in moments of crisis of representation? Cas Mudde and Cristóbal Rovira Kaltwasser (2017) in analysing the relationship between, on the one hand, a society that presents demands and, on the other, an institutionalized political system, present two hypotheses. Such a system may manage to fulfil those demands; or, on the contrary, it fails to fulfil those demands, thus generating frustration. In this last hypothesis, we have the example of the crisis surrounding social democratic governments such as Zapatero in Spain (2004–11) or Papandreou in Greece (2009–11), which decided to follow "responsible" economic austerity policies. The populist phenomenon relates to moments such as dramatic economic crises and, above all, political crises related to revelations of cases of systematic corruption. This was the case, as the authors point out, with the rise of Berlusconi in Italy, of Chávez in Venezuela, of Podemos in Spain, of Syriza in Greece. Furthermore, the very perception that the political system does not respond to the demands of the population is, in itself, a potential factor leading to the emergence of populism. As we will see further on, such factors were present in the context of the Bolsonarist rise in Brazil.

If we think specifically about the rise of right-wing populism in Europe and the US, it is no coincidence that, as several analyses demonstrate, there is a correlation between phenomena such as the reduction of the middle class[4] (resulting from the events of the postindustrial era, and neoliberal and globalization expansion) and that of anti-immigration ideology (response to migratory flows that are linked to demand for precarious jobs). In the political field, the structures of political institutions and parties, representatives of this "system", exploded after the 2008 crisis. As we know, one of the dramatic and direct effects was the subprime mortgage crisis due to the bursting of the mortgage bubble, with Spain being a country in which this had a major impact.

When citizens begin to feel that the differences between traditional political forces are less significant than what unites them, they then begin to look outside the traditional order for solutions to issues that concern

4. See, for example, Guilluy (2020).

them (Tormey 2019). This was the context in which Spain experienced the irruption of the Indignados Movement – or 15-M, as it would come to be known – and, a few years later, the creation of the Podemos party. On 15 May 2011, there was the first massive protest in which Spanish protesters had, as their main target, what they defined as anti-social measures. These measures were defined by bankers and led to official policies of economic adjustment: on the one hand, cuts in the social spending, and on the other hand, the financial rescue of banks, rightly seen as responsible for the economic crisis (Alcaide 2011).

This injustice ended up causing, in turn, a crisis of legitimacy of the political and economic system that had emerged with the redemocratization of Spain (after the Franco dictatorship) in particular with the "Pact of Moncloa" and the promulgation of the Constitution of 1978. One of the guidelines of the movement, driven by the web page ¡Democracia Real YA!, was the end of bipartisanship – constituted by the two main parties, the Popular Party (PP) and the Spanish Socialist Workers' Party (PSOE) – also eroded by accusations of corruption. It is worth emphasizing the strategic role of social networks, not only for organizing and calling protests, but also for their repercussions – the term "Spanish Revolution" came to life on internet social networks. All these elements formed a repertoire, still remembered by authors and activists, as a form of inspiration for "another policy".

Between 2013 and 2014, the demand for "another politics" also exploded on the streets of Brazil. It is impossible to think about the streets taken over by young people in 2013 without considering a double tension: (1) the loss of traditional political references, resulting from the transformation in the world of work, and (2) the crisis of representation of traditional parties, due to their continued adherence to the same public management model, clearly shown to be inefficient in reducing the structural problems of a society as unequal as the Brazilian one. This complex crisis was reinforced by a series of corruption scandals.

Although some Brazilian analysts tend to see a direct correlation between the popular irruption of 2013 and the hegemonic rise of the far right, in fact these social demands and organizational forms relate, in form and principle, to the Arab Spring, 15-M and Occupy Wall Street. In 2014, protesters chose 15 May and the acronym "15-M" to protest, in several cities in Brazil, against the hosting of the World Cup, contrasting the financial cost of the sporting event with unmet social demands, such as teachers' salaries and removals of families due to road works (Época 2014). It should be noted that the motto "We want FIFA standard public hospitals" was launched in June 2013. In 2015, there were the pro-impeachment protests, which – although targeting the PT government and with a strong anti-communist focus – had a similar repertoire and made similar social demands, including around health and education. In 2016, student occupations in public schools and universities in several states of the country took place. On 28 April 2017, there was a general strike with broad participation, including from non-union sectors and, finally, 2018 saw a truck drivers' strike (with the presence of Bolsonarist leaders) in a context of presidential elections and great political polarization.

As Ricci (2018) has pointed out, the movements that first emerged in June 2013 had characteristics such as: temporary and discontinuous; communitarianism and self-organization; horizontality, as self-organization and rejection of formal and institutionalized instances of the political and social world, such as occurred in Spain; anti-institutionalism and an anti-systemic culture, founded "on distrust of the great organizational structures and universal rules of behaviour that supposedly inhibit individual freedom". Anti-institutionalism recalls the author, "was already expressed in the 1980s through the New Social Movements (NSMs) that emerged in Latin Europe and Brazil, a field of European and Brazilian sociology in the 1980s and part of the 1990s" (Ricci 2018: 96). In addition to these four characteristics that, as we emphasize, represent a relationship between form and content, the author highlights a fifth characteristic, perhaps more controversial in character, namely individualism:

> The mark of hyper-individualism that starts to determine choices fragments society into multiple needs and interests, to the detriment of universal values and even the notion of rights. It is the instant demand that becomes valued and motivates group actions or small-scale associations. Such a situation engenders, in many cases, the advent of "magical thought", the personal demand that one's will must be instantly respected or fulfilled as a legitimate determination. (Ricci 2018: 95–6)

Our emphasis is on how this dimension of individualism, as described by Ricci, leads to political ambiguity, if we analyse some aspects of a more sociological nature, related to the world of work in Brazil in recent years, especially with regard to young people. This may serve as a reflection on why the irruption of agendas, linked to the demands for more participation and more social justice, ended up being followed by the political rise of the far right.

During most of the Lula and Dilma Rousseff administrations, the contradiction between the transformations in the world of work – a tendency towards precariousness – was mitigated by the access to the "consumerist citizenship", accompanied by the generation of jobs, including formal jobs, while the economy went through an upturn. That is, in the case of Brazil, the mass of workers, especially those in the informal sector who, in 2018, would end up casting their vote for Bolsonaro, "did not miss the dismantling of a welfare state and did not necessarily lose their job because of crisis, as they probably never had one", as highlighted by Rosana Pinheiro-Machado (2021: n.p.). On the contrary, during the PT governments, these people saw improvement in their lives within a horizon of economic growth. But, *a posteriori*, it is now possible to analyse more clearly the gap between, on the one hand, those low-income youths, with access to university and acquisition of goods, and on the other, the depoliticization around the Workers' Party.

This gap was fuelled by the new situation in the world of work, as the flexibilization of work and neoliberalism grew, the idea of a society of wage and rights and, with them, the notion of public and universal education imploded (Costa 2019: 291–2). Empirical research carried out with a group of student-workers from a dynamic sector of post-Fordist capitalism is significant for the analysis of the political situation. The last phase of the research interviews with these young people, who worked in technology companies, call centres, commerce, electronic marketing and information security, coincided with the period of the 2014 presidential campaign (see Costa 2019). In general, they showed superficial political-ideological assessments of the political context in which they were living; they saw their well-being as dependent above all on their individual initiative; their educational qualification itself was seen in an instrumental way as a somewhat bureaucratic employer requirement.

It is therefore necessary to highlight the aspect of individual aspirations of groups such as platform workers, their focus on their individual life projects, their goal of "working hard and dreaming of changing their lives and getting along", with the emphasis on possessions and property as a crowning point of individual effort. Thus, instead of analysing informal work and unemployment under a negative category, such as "lack or resentment", we need to realize that what Bolsonaro does – like the Philippine President Duterte[5] – "is to manipulate this logic and speaking for the positive aspect: 'you are the guy, the problem is everything else, stop mimimi [whining]'" (Pinheiro-Machado 2021).

When the political and economic crisis worsened in 2015 – with the first clear economic data on the decrease of the gross domestic product and of economic activities in industry and in the services sector – the government reference against which to protest was, of course, the PT government. Hence, the new allegations of corruption, which weighed heavily on the party since the Lula government and the *mensalão* (big monthly allowance) scandal, would gain political prominence due to legal and media actions such as those of Vaza Jato (Operation Car Wash). This operation was a set of

5. We cite the research done by Rosana Pinheiro-Machado together with the anthropologist Cristina Martins, a comparative analysis with other countries in the global South that have known a period of economic growth followed by the rise of the far right – namely, India and the Philippines.

investigations carried out by the federal police, commanded by the Federal Public Ministry (MPF) based in the city of Curitiba. Its aim was to investigate a money laundering and bribery scheme and its main target was PT leaders and large companies, such as the state-owned Petrobras and Odebrecht construction company.

Both dissatisfaction with the political system and demands for participation were reinforced by a new element in mass politics: the internet. Individualism, the logic of affective group formation, the demand for political participation without the intermediation of the traditional "castes" of "old politics" and the internet, came together to form the basis of the Italian 5 Star Movement and the rise of right-wing populism in the world, including in Brazil (see Empoli 2020).

As president of Brazil, Jair Bolsonaro consistently attacked the press, with the exception of two television networks. These received public funds and presented "news" favourable to Bolsonaro, and provided a regular platform for him to "speak directly to the people". In particular, they continued to reinforce the spectre of "PT communism".

THE ANTI-PT MOVEMENT AND THE RISE OF BOLSONARISM

The anti-PT movement (antipestismo) was a critical element in galvanizing votes for Bolsonaro in the 2018 election. With regard to the profile of his voters, Jairo Nicolau (2020) showed that, for the most part, they had middle and higher levels of education, The PT presidential candidate, Fernando Haddad, maintained the pattern of the elections of Lula (second term) and Dilma (two terms), showing a good performance in the northeast, a region historically marked by poverty, but which had seen significant improvements during the PT administrations. This was largely due to income transfer social programmes, infrastructure works and flexible credit policies. The anti-PT movement, according to the opinion polls analysed for this research, was supported by about 30 per cent of voters, while the percentage of people outside the "PT versus anti-PT" conflict was close to 50 per cent.

It is not the point here to analyse the radical opposition to the PT in quantitative terms only. In order to measure the potential of a political leadership, it is not so much the percentage of votes that matters but, as Mudde and Kaltwasser put it, "the ability to put topics on the public agenda (agenda-setting) and the capacity to shape public policies (policy impact)" is a particularly relevant distinction "when we think about the success and failure of populist actors. After all, in many places in the world populists attract a fairly limited number of votes, but nevertheless, they play a notable role in terms of agenda-setting and policy impact" (Mudde & Kaltwasser 2017: 98). The same reasoning holds for the strategic role of the neo-Pentecostal churches, the social sector where Bolsonaro had the highest percentage of votes, and which provided an ideological and political underpinning for Bolsonarism.[6] Although neo-Pentecostalists represent just under 30 per cent of the electorate, they played a strategic role in political mobilization (see Alves 2018).

At this point, our objective is to highlight the co-optation of the demand for new politics by the far right. First, that appropriation led to the massive election of parliamentarians from the Social Liberal Party (PSL), a party founded in 1994 and insignificant, until Bolsonaro ran for office under its banner. Second, it also brought into play parties and groups that had previously emerged in the post-2013 wave, independently of Bolsonaro. These groups, such as the New Party[7] and the Free Brazil Movement (Movimento Brasil Livre, MBL) positioned themselves as "liberals on the economy and conservatives on customs". A demonstration of MBL's conservatism can be seen in an action in 2017 against an artistic performance that, inevitably, conjures up images of the Nazi condemnation of "degenerate art".[8] Finally, there emerged in Brazil a conjunction with the global extreme right-wing discourse that protested against "dictatorship of the politically correct", "gender ideology", and so on, creating a link between "corruption" (as in the stealing of public money) and "corruption of values".

A study of the anti-PT movement and conservatism on Facebook analysed discussions within right-wing groups – such as the MBL itself – and concluded that the moral judgements around sexual themes or those related to the spectre of "banditry" ascribe wrongdoing to "left-wingers", who are perceived as "the enemies" that keep "the population ignorant and hostage to social programmes that perpetuate corrupt politicians in power". Former President Lula was portrayed as "the head of this gang that has control of the

6. On the Bolsonarist "political theology", see Mata (2020).
7. Founded in 2011, but only officially registered in 2015. João Amoêdo's candidacy for the presidency sank in the face of the Bolsonaro versus PT dispute, but the party managed to elect a small but significant bench for Congress and the governor of one of the main electoral colleges of the country, the state of Minas Gerais.
8. In September 2017, there was a performance at the Museum of Modern Art (Museu de Arte Moderna, MAM), in São Paulo, in which a nude artist was inspired by the work Bichos, by artist Lygia Clark, in which aluminum sculptures can be manipulated by the public. On the occasion, a video was circulated of a child quickly touching the artist's hand, shin, and feet. This was enough for the MBL to accuse MAM of promoting "eroticization of children". Later, the MBL would also be accused of censorship for having campaigned against the exhibition Queermuseu (Queer Museum), which exhibited works addressing diversity of gender expression. The exhibition, held on the premises of a private bank in the city of Porto Alegre, was eventually cancelled due to the controversy.

Judiciary, as he appointed the ministers of the STF, and of social movements and unions" (Ribeiro 2018: 89–90). The anti-PT movement had become such a strong political force that it is correct to say that, between 2014 and 2018, Brazil experienced its third great anti-communist wave – the other two being 1935–37, and 1961–64 (Motta 2002) both of which were followed by dictatorships.[9]

A very important element of Bolsonaro's success was the strong military support for his campaign, which would translate into the effective military control of the government between 2019 and 2021. After he became president, seven out of the 22 ministers appointed were from the armed forces This group came to be known as the "Military Party", a cohesive, albeit informal organization, made up of soldiers from the "1970s generation", that is, they began their military careers in the middle of the dictatorship. Having become generals in the 2000s, they achieved prominence with the participation of the Brazilian armed forces in the United Nations stabilization mission in Haiti and in the guarantee-of-law-and-order operations in Brazilian territory. Their dissatisfaction with the PT government came to a head with the National Truth Commission (Souza 2021), which had as its main objective the investigation of crimes committed by the dictatorship. In 2018, the commanding general of the Brazilian armed forces, General Eduardo Villas Bôas, gave an interview in which he reverted to the typical anti-communism of the National Security Doctrine (in force during the Cold War) to criticize the "ideology" – "gender ideology", "environmentalist ideology", and so on – that, in his view, divided society and justified the Bolsonaro candidacy (Victor 2018).

POPULISM, LEFT AND RIGHT

As in the past, we believe that anti-communism, now in opposition to the PT, and to the left in general, functions to shift social contradictions to an imaginary (but mobilizing) of the conflict between the "nation" and "communism". In the sense given to it by Ernesto Laclau (1978), this would be a type of popular interpellation – that is, directed at the "people" in general – in a synthetic-antagonistic set that organizes the elements around a common axis, while projecting undesirable elements as "outside".

Laclau, in further reflections on populism and in partnership with Chantal Mouffe (Laclau 2018; Laclau & Mouffe 2015), continued to develop theorization about these discursive forms that have popular demands, both as a basis and as a result. These diffuse demands acquire strength when they establish

9. We refer respectively to the Estado Novo (New State), which begin in 1937 under the command of Getúlio Vargas, and the military dictatorship, which started in 1964.

a chain of equivalence – which does not necessarily eliminate their relative differences – insofar as, through discourse, they establish an antagonism – us ("the people") against them ("the elite"). In other words, the political field is formed and intensified when a chain of demands is articulated directly (or through discourse) and is strengthened, to the extent that a logic of antagonism is established, through discourse. For Laclau (2018), this political-discursive logic would be the populist reason itself. We take this discourse analysis model here as a heuristic model,[10] which allows us to analyse how diffuse agendas for social justice ended up being galvanized by the far right. It should be noted that the central element of Laclau's theory of populism – the opposition "people" versus "elite" – is a common element in the analysis of populism, but he also considers the dynamics of discursive constitution of this opposition.

When Laclau wrote *The Populist Reason*, Latin America was going through a phase of left optimism around popular governments, such as the PT in Brazil. In this historical context, two of the main leaders of the Spanish Podemos party were politically inspired by Latin American politics and Laclau's theory. In 2006, Íñigo Errejón, one of the founders of the left-wing student association Contrapoder, invited Bolivian president Evo Morales to give a lecture at the Facultad de Ciencias Políticas and in 2012, he defended his thesis, *The Struggle for Hegemony During the First MAS Government in Bolivia (2006–2009): A Discursive Analysis*. Juan Carlos Monedero, for his part, worked as an advisor to the Venezuelan government of Hugo Chávez between 2005 and 2010. These personal, political and intellectual experiences around the emergence of popular programmes in Latin America, where indigenous people's agendas played an important role, stimulated a conjunction of the political-discursive and electoral strategies of Podemos to build its own political platform for Spain (Schavelzon 2015; Bringel 2015). In 2014, the same year that the PT government began to face a political crisis and the beginning of a loss of hegemony, Podemos was created as an opposition party, claiming the legacy of the 15-M, defending greater public participation in decision-making, policies of social redistribution and the end of corruption and clientelism, and achieving significant victories.[11]

10. It is not the aim of this chapter to expose or analyse important and controversial debates around Laclau and Mouffe's theory of discourse and politics, such as criticisms of its ontological character, its own antagonism towards inclusive perspectives, or the difficulty of differentiating what would be a right-wing and a left-wing populism.
11. Podemos, created in 2014, made an immediate advance in the 2014 European elections, winning 9 per cent of the vote and five seats in the European Parliament. In the Spanish general elections of 2016 and 2017, it received about 20 per cent of the popular vote, breaking the bipartisan system in force since the end of the Franco dictatorship. In 2015, Ada Colau and Manuela Carmena, political activists allied with Podemos and 15-M, were elected mayors of Barcelona and Madrid, respectively.

The 2013 mass demonstrations in Brazil erupted at a time when, as pointed out earlier, there was not yet an economic crisis – on the contrary, there was still favourable indicators regarding the employment rate and material improvement of life conditions. Hence, both Rousseff (see Mendes 2013) and Lula (Silva 2013) posed an interpretation of it as demands around employment policies, income distribution and access to universities which, in turn, would have fuelled the desire for more rights, more health, more education.

It is worth recalling here some points already highlighted. Throughout the PT governments, a growing tension was set up between, on the one hand, a group of workers already engaged in the new labour market, in large part constituted of young people in precarious and temporary jobs and, on the other, the "new middle class". In this scenario, it is simplistic to categorize the PT governments as "purely" left (since there was a good measure of adaptation to parameters of neoliberal "management") or as a government of the "Traitor's Party", since there was still an alignment with popular agendas, such as programmes of income transfer, creation of university access, implementation of a quota system, attention to family farming, and so on. Likewise, it is simplistic to categorize the June 2013 protesters, and even a large part of those present at the 2015 demonstrations, as left or right, particularly in terms of the traditional party-political horizon.

However, from 2014 onwards, there was a growing antagonism towards the PT and the idea of the left in general. In addition to the rising anti-communism in the form of an anti-PT discourse, the anti-corruption Car Wash Operation played a fundamental role in generating anti-PT sentiment. The prosecutors from the Public Prosecutor's Office (Ministério Público Federal [MPF]) involved in the operation, alongside the trial judge Sergio Moro, came to be perceived as national heroes in the "fight against corruption". Selective leaks to the media and special reports, in addition to the use of social networks, were important for the political effect of the operation. The partnership between the Brazilian prosecutor's office and the media was inspired by the Italian Mani Pulite Operation, of which Moro (2004) had spoken in an article some years before. Many critics, including those from the legal world, warned of abuses in the conduct of operations – abuses that would be exposed later after the Vaza Jato scandal[12] – especially the partnership between the prosecutor and the judge (Moro). Despite this, the Car Wash Operation, and Moro's decisions, had a very significant impact, on the country's political destiny and contributed to the political crisis that would

12. Term by which the leaked conversations, carried out through the instant messaging software Telegram, between Moro and the prosecutor Deltan Dallagnol and other members of the Car Wash Operation task force, became known in the Brazilian press. The case was highlighted after the disclosure made by Intercept Brazil.

lead to the impeachment of Dilma and the controversial arrest and jailing of Lula in 2018,[13] when the former president was leading in the electoral polls.

Here we highlight a significant episode, in relation to the above, that occurred in 2016. In March of that year, Judge Moro leaked to the press a wiretapped telephone conversation between then-president Dilma Rousseff and ex-president Lula. Lula was being asked to occupy the Civil House, something that would have the double advantage of Lula becoming the political articulator of a government in crisis and, at the same time, the position could save Lula from criminal prosecution. The leaking of the call by Moro was a criminal act under the Constitution. Therefore, a lawsuit was filed against him, to be judged by the Federal Regional Court of the 4th Region (TRF-4), in Porto Alegre. By 13 votes to 1, they delivered an opinion that cited German conservative jurist, Carl Schmitt's, theory of exception:

> At first, it is important to note that these legal rules (secrecy of telephone communications, Constitution, act. 5, XII) can only be correctly interpreted in light of the facts to which they relate and in any way verified that they fell within the scope of normality covered by them. The legal norm focuses on normality, not applying to exceptional situations.
>
> (Tribunal Regional Federal da 4ª Região 2016: 4)

Following the spirit of Schmitt's theory (see Schmitt 1988), the opinion of the TRF-4, by recognizing and not punishing a crime, transferred the sovereign power to the one who "acted in an exceptional situation".

It is undeniable that the Car Wash Operation, "carwashism" (*lavajatismo*),[14] contributed to the creation of the conditions for Bolsonarism. Its motto of "fighting corruption" and its actions, such as the issuing of a bench warrant for Lula's arrest (a frequent and irregular activity), emerged in an election year, and raised what we might call "legal populism" to its political paroxysm. If one of the pillars of the far right is the figure of the public enemy, the promoters of the Car Wash Operation, and its partnership with the big media, established a major pillar for the emergence of "Bolsonarism". Judge Moro played a direct role in Bolsonaro's election and was subsequently appointed his Minister of Justice. The "friend versus enemy" polarity gave the "us versus them" populist polarity an extreme degree of intensity.

---

13. Sanctioned by the Supreme Court, in a climate of legal populism, unconstitutional imprisonment was allowed after a trial in second instance – even though, in the process, there was no direct evidence of Lula's involvement with passive corruption or money laundering.
14. Neologism to designate pejoratively the Car Wash Operation *modus operandi*.

FINAL CONSIDERATIONS: BETWEEN NEOFASCISM AND NEOLIBERALISM

> Principled, moralised, anti-pluralism and the reliance on a non-institutionalized notion of the "people" helps explain why populists so frequently oppose the "morally correct" outcome of a vote to the actual empirical result of an election, when the latter was not in their favour. (Müller 2017: 31–2)

After the 2018 elections and again amid the drop in Bolsonaro's government's popularity in 2021, and his poor electoral projections for 2022, he once again reverted to claims that the 2018 election had been "fraudulent" because, according to him, his real victory should have been in the first round. For Simon Tormey, populism in itself is not undemocratic, but it can become so, especially when authoritarian populist leaders attack the very existence of liberal institutions and democratic processes: "Populism becomes nativist or nationalist in character when this antagonism is combined with an idea about the ethnicity, religion or nationality of the people in question" (Tormey 2019: 198).

As we have already highlighted, Bolsonarism is an extreme right-wing populist phenomenon, similar to the global wave of political populism that arose from a situation of crisis of democracy across Europe and the Americas. It is directly linked to transformations in economies (growth of neoliberalism) that have been causing profound change in labour markets, increasing inequality and forced change in expectations. When dealing with new forms of subjectivation, expectations are eventually frustrated and right-wing populism has been actively exploiting such frustration, relating society's ills to evils from abroad – the "globalist" agenda[15] – and internal agents. In Brazil, "Bolsonarism" made explicit the return to an authoritarian agenda and the re-energizing of the anti-communist tradition, updated through the anti-PT movement, and supported by the neo-Pentecostal churches. Bolsonaro also tapped into the xenophobia of voters from the south and southeast regions of the country in relation to the people of the northeast, personalized in the electoral dynamics between him and Haddad in the 2018 election.

Recent studies on the populist phenomenon have discussed issues such as whether it would be possible to clearly differentiate a left-wing populism from a right-wing one (or more precisely, an extreme right-wing one), and

15. According to Olavo de Carvalho (2009: n.p.), the Brazilian version of Steve Bannon, guru of the international extreme right, globalism is "a revolutionary process", the "vast and most ambitious of all", encompassing "the radical mutation, not only of the structures of power, but from society, from education, from morals, and even from the most intimate reactions of the human soul".

whether such right-wing populism could imply a form of fascism or neo-fascism. Regarding the left-wing version, Carla Brandalise says: "certain left-wing populisms may well have legitimacy as non-demagogic progressive manifestations, in the name of an appreciation of sectors effectively excluded from society and condemned to marginality" (2021: 41).

The question of links between right-wing populism and fascism is a much debated one, although fascism is a word frequently used to describe the Bolsonarism phenomenon. The literature examines the many similarities – such as the attack on institutions, the appeal of leadership and its direct relationship with the people and the division of society between "them" and "us", which has nationalist and even xenophobic connotations. However, the general view is that, despite the similarities, they differ fundamentally, in that fascism is considered to be a defined movement, ideologically, doctrinally and historically, while populism is seen as an unpredictable phenomenon, linked to crises, most particularly of democracy itself. It is, nonetheless, significant that the commonalities between far-right populism and fascism turn out to be the visible features of the Bolsonarism phenomenon.

In the first instance, Bolsonaro, has long been a habitual apologist for the dictatorship. As president, he dedicated himself to the hollowing out of federal agencies and constantly made direct attacks on state institutions. At a discursive level, let us consider the elements that Jason Stanley (2018) listed to categorize "how fascism works": the mythical past (for Bolsonaro and the Bolsonarists, the post-1964 civil-military government that hunted communists and aggrandized the nation); propaganda (the massive use of digital media and fake news by the Bolsonaro family and their supporters); anti-intellectualism (attack on public universities and "communist indoctrination in schools"); unreality (distortion of facts, turned to tragedy during the Covid-19 pandemic); hierarchy (symbolized in the electoral slogan "Brazil above everything, God above everyone"); victimization (at the hands of the "dictatorship of the politically correct"); law and order (core to the authoritarian conception of the world); sexual anxiety (creating suspicion, and fear, of "gay dictatorship", "gender ideology", etc.); Sodom and Gomorrah; or "*Arbeit macht frei*"[16] (hard work, meritocracy and freedom from the laziness of those who live on state benefits).

The June 2013 demonstrations, despite the attempts of co-option by the dominant political forces and aside from the biased media coverage,[17] represented pressure from outside the "system" of the governing coalition

16. "Work sets you free", a phrase at the gates of the Nazi concentration camps of Auschwitz and Buchenwald.
17. First, the attempt to criminalize the demonstrations and legitimize police repression, and then the construction of the anti-government narrative.

around the PT, but also from the official opposition and by the media and corporations.

Several surveys, mainly focused on São Paulo, indicated that between 70 per cent and 80 per cent of protesters were young people, from the middle and working classes. "The struggle for social rights (public transport, health, and education) was the main motivation for the vast majority of protesters, even though the 'fight against corruption' was also mentioned by a significant portion" (Calil 2013: 389).

In the electoral contest for the country's presidency in 2018, a candidate was elected with no public administration experience beyond three decades served as a deputy and an earlier obscure career in the army. How was this possible? Our hypothesis, as presented, is that the "war on corruption" became a high-level "empty signifier", open to different meanings in different contexts, as theorized by Laclau. Around that "war", two sets of "empty signifiers" were formed by the Bolsonaro camp. On the one hand was Haddad and the PT, presented in terms of: constructed state apparatus; populism; inefficiency, vote-buying of the poor; politically correct dictatorship; corruption of values. On the other was Bolsonaro, associated with language such as: freedom; entrepreneurship; reduction of the state; honesty through work without favours; meritocracy; and, of course, war on corruption. The use of this polarizing imagery presented the election as a struggle of the "people" against a "corrupt political elite".

The neoliberal – or ultraliberal – agenda is articulated, in the language of "fighting ideology and partisan interests". In his inaugural speech at the National Congress in January 2019, Bolsonaro told the people: "Brazilians can and should dream. Dreaming of a better life, with better conditions to enjoy the fruit of their work by meritocracy." Later that same day, in a brief speech to the chamber of deputies, he said: "We are going to unite the people, value the family, respect religions and our Judeo-Christian tradition, fight gender ideology, preserving our values. Brazil will once again be a country free from ideological shackles and education with a communist bias" (Veja 2019: n.p.). Four months later, in a speech on Labour Day, he again referenced meritocracy and proclaimed his "commitment to full economic freedom, the only way to provide, on his own merit and without state interference, the aggrandizement of each citizen" (G1 2019: n.p.).

It was not our intention in this chapter to homogenize right-wing groups that had different trajectories and social roots. On the contrary, we emphasize the constitutive role of discourse, in the sense of symbolic articulation and production of antagonism. We also show how Bolsonarism, as a movement, shows up the fragility of the line between right-wing populism and (neo) fascism in the current context. More than ever, it is necessary to analyse the populist phenomenon in the light of democratic agendas and from a transformational perspective.

REFERENCES

Alcaide, S. 2011. "Movimiento 15-M: los ciudadanos exigen reconstruir la política". *El País*, 11 May. https://elpais.com/politica/2011/05/16/actualidad/1305578500_751064.html.

Alves, J. 2018. "O voto evangélico garantiu a eleição de Jair Bolsonaro". *Ecodebate*, 31 October. www.ecodebate.com.br/2018/10/31/o-voto-evangelico-garantiu-a-eleicao-de-jair-bolsonaro-artigo-de-jose-eustaquio-diniz-alves/.

Brandalise, C. 2021. "Populismos de extrema-direita: heurística possível na temporalidade presente?" In A. Priori, E. Batista & G. Bomba (eds), *Política, autoritarismo e violência no Brasil (século XX)*, 13–45. Maringá and São Paulo: Edições Diálogos and ANPUH-GTNHP.

Bringel, B. 2015. "15-M, Podemos e os movimentos sociais na Espanha. Trajetórias, conjuntura e transições". *Novos Estudos Cebrap*, November: 59–77.

Calil, G. 2013. "Embates e disputas em torno das jornadas de junho". *Projeto História* 47: 377–403.

Carvalho, O. 2009. "A revolução globalista". https://olavodecarvalho.org/a-revolucao-globalista/.

Cortés, A. 2016. "Chile: aquém ou além do populismo?" In F. Perlatto & D. Chaves (eds), *Repensar os populismos na América do Sul: debates, tradições e releituras*, 47–69. Macapá: UNIFAP.

Costa, H. 2019. "Estudantes do Prouni na crise do lulismo". *Plural, Revista do Programa de Pós-Graduação em Sociologia da USP* 26(1): 289–311.

Empoli, G. 2020. *Os engenheiros do caos*. Translated by Arnaldo Bloch. Reprint 1st Edition. São Paulo: Vestígio.

Época 2014. "Protestos de grevistas e contra gastos com a Copa marcam 15M". https://epoca.oglobo.globo.com/tempo/noticia/2014/05/protestos-de-grevistas-e-contra-gastos-com-copa-marcam-15m.html.

G1 2019. "Bolsonaro diz no Dia do Trabalho que o governo tem compromisso com a 'plena liberdade econômica'". https://g1.globo.com/politica/noticia/2019/05/01/bolsonaro-diz-no-dia-do-trabalho-que-governo-tem-compromisso-com-a-plena-liberdade-economica.ghtml.

Gonçalves, R. 2013. *Desenvolvimento às avessas: verdade, ma-fé e ilusão no atual modelo brasileiro de desenvolvimento*. Rio de Janeiro: LTC.

Guilluy, C. 2020. *O fim da classe média: a fragmentação das elites e o esgotamento de um modelo que já não constrói sociedades*. Translated by A. Bonrruquer. Rio de Janeiro: Record.

Laclau, E. 1978. *Política e ideologia na teoria marxista: Capitalismo, fascismo e populismo*. Rio de Janeiro: Paz e Terra.

Laclau, E. 2018. *A razão populista*. Translated by M. de Moura. São Paulo: Três Estrelas.

Laclau, E. and C. Mouffe 2015. *Hegemonia e estratégia socialista. Por uma política democrática radical*. Translated by J. Burity, J. de Paula Jr. & A. Amaral. São Paulo and Brasília: Intermeios and CNPq.

Manso, B. 2020. *A república das milícias: dos esquadrões da morte à era Bolsonaro*. São Paulo: Todavia.

Mata, S. 2020. "A Teologia Política do Governo Bolsonaro". In B. Klem, M. Pareira, and V. Araujo (eds), *Do Fake ao Fato: Des(atualizando) Bolsonaro*. Kindle: Editora Milfontes.

Mendes, P. 2013. "Dilma defende protestos e diz que governo ouve 'vozes pela mudança'". *G1*, 18 June. http://g1.globo.com/politica/noticia/2013/06/dilma-defende-protestos-e-diz-que-governo-ouve-vozes-pela-mudanca.html.

Moro, S. 2004. Considerações sobre a operação mani pulite. *Revista do Centro de Estudos Jurídicos* 26: 56–62.

Motta, R. 2002. *Em guarda contra o "Perigo Vermelho": o anticomunismo no Brasil (1917–1964)*. São Paulo: Perspectiva FAPESP.

Mudde, C. and C. Kaltwasser 2017. *Populism: A Very Short Introduction*. New York: Oxford University Press.

Müller, J.-W. 2017. *What is Populism?* London: Penguin.

Nicolau, J. 2020. *O Brasil dobro à direita. Uma radiografia da eleição de Bolsonaro em 2018*. Rio de Janeiro: Zahar.

Perlatto, F. 2016. "Adeus ao populismo? Reviravoltas de um conceito e de uma política no Brasil do tempo presente". In F. Perlato & D. Chaves (eds), *Repensar os populismos na América do Sul: debates, tradições e releituras*, 70–94. Macapá: UNIFAP.

Pinheiro-Machado, R. 2021. "O que Lula deu e Bolsonaro abocanhou". *El País Brasil*, 22 June. https://brasil.elpais.com/opiniao/2021-06-21/o-que-lula-deu-e-bolsonaro-abocanhou.html?mid=DM67937&bid=612833664.

Ribeiro, M. 2018. "Antipetismo e conservadorismo no Facebook". In E. Gallego (ed.), *O ódio como política: a reinvenção da direita no Brasil*, 85–90. São Paulo: Boitempo.

Ricci, R. 2018. "Movimentos e mobilizações sociais no Brasil: de 2013 aos dias atuais". *Saúde Debate* 42(3): 90–107.

Schavelzon, S. 2015. "A formação do Podemos. América do Sul, populismo pós-colonial e hegemonia flexível". Translated by M. Passos. *Novos Estudos Cebrap*, November: 33–57. www.scielo.br/j/nec/a/8WjDYDZKWgS8gytW6SVdRvR/?lang=pt.

Schmitt, C. 1988. *Théologie Politique. 1922, 1969*. Translated by J.-L. Schlegel. Paris: Gallimard.

Silva, L. 2013. "The message of Brazil's youth". *The New York Times*, 16 July. www.nytimes.com/2013/07/17/opinion/global/lula-da-silva-the-message-of-brazils-youth.html?searchResultPosition=1.

Souza, M. 2021. "Generais arrastam Forças Armadas para a política e governam o país com 'partido militar'". *Folha de São Paulo*, 17 July. www1.folha.uol.com.br/ilustrissima/2021/07/generais-arrastam-forcas-armadas-para-a-politica-e-governam-o-pais-com-partido-militar.shtml.

Stanley, J. 2018. *Como funciona o fascismo. A política do "nós" e "eles"*. Porto Alegre: L&PM.

Tribunal Regional Federal da 4ª Região 2016. *P.A. Corte Especial nº 0003021-32.2016.4.04.8000/RS*. Relator: Des. Federal Rômulo Pizzolatti.

Tormey, S. 2019. *Populismo: uma breve introdução*. São Paulo: Cultrix.

Veja 2019. "Leia a íntegra dos dois primeiros discursos do presidente Jair Bolsonaro". https://veja.abril.com.br/politica/leia-a-integra-dos-dois-primeiros-discursos-do-presidente-jair-bolsonaro/.

Victor, F. 2018. "Mal-estar na caserna". *Piauí* 138. https://piaui.folha.uol.com.br/materia/mal-estar-na-caserna/.

CHAPTER 6

POLITICAL DILEMMAS OF THE GOVERNMENT OF LÓPEZ OBRADOR: BETWEEN POPULISM, DEMOCRACY AND THE LEFT IN MEXICO

Patricia Pensado Leglise

INTRODUCTION

> The notion of populism has had an uneven academic life. The variety of political movements to which the term is applied and the complex nature of the phenomenon itself, ranging from the left to the right of the ideological spectrum, has raised doubts about its plausibility [...] Populism is not the first controversial issue in social science, nor is it surprising that the discussion about its semantic field is tinged with political connotations [...] We scholars have not agreed yet about the forms in which the phenomenon manifests itself [...] Since the seminal studies of the 1960s, it was not clear whether its ideological dimension (the populist ideas) or its organizational forms should be emphasized. (Maldonado 2017: 153–4)

Talking about populism is fashionable nowadays. The term is enunciated in political debates, social networks and scholarly circles, and it is used interchangeably to praise or denigrate political figures of any ideological sign. Without going deeply into the intricacies of the term, its historical contexts and characteristics, maybe it is worth remembering that it first referred to late nineteenth-century social movements as different and distant as those of Russia and of the United States, whose only common traits were their closeness to "the people" and opposition to the established order.

The "populist wind" arrived in Latin America several years later. The names of Brazil's Getúlio Vargas and Argentina's Juan Domingo Perón remain in the collective memory and history. To them, we must add the most recent and abounding wave: Carlos Menem, Hugo Chávez, Néstor and Cristina

Kirchner, Evo Morales and Rafael Correa, each in their own context. More recently, Andrés Manuel López Obrador has joined this list. If there is one thing these leaders have in common, it is their "personal style of governing", as Daniel Cosío Villegas used to say.

The populist "rebirth" has been propelled by economic transformations: widening social and educational inequalities, those related to gender, race and access to public services; increasing poverty; various forms of violence; social exclusion and dysfunction; and biases of the democratic systems. According to the French historian and sociologist Pierre Rosanvallón:

> The specificity of the current populist moment is its globalization. One could say that until about fifteen years ago, populism had two definitions, a historical one referred [to] Latin America history [and] it corresponded to what we could call situations of transition in the countries of the region, situations of transition from caudillismo to democracy, from authoritarian regimes to democracy [...] The second definition [referred to] a sort of revival of European extreme rights parties [...] Nowadays, the specificity of populism is its universality. (Annunziata 2020: n.p.)

It seems to me that reflecting on populism, as it is done in this collective volume, should allow us to explore, as objectively as possible, the conditions that have transformed it into a universal phenomenon in the twenty-first century, rather than seeking exhaustive or schematic definitions.

AMLO AND THE "NATION PROJECT"

Andrés Manuel López Obrador (AMLO) has served as president of Mexico since 2018. I suggest that in 2022, halfway through his term, the concept that would best define him would be as a wilful politician characterized by a *chiaroscuro* politics in his actions. He "received" a country with serious and longstanding problems such as increasing violence, low economic growth for more than 30 years, widening social inequalities, predominance of precarious jobs and a low tax revenues treasury, all of which describe a country affected by accumulated social malaise.

Regarding his administration, I would stress his support for the poor. However, this commitment lacks a discernible strategy and public policies to overcome the vicious circle of poverty, as has been pointed out by several experts on the issue. Besides money transfers, educational and economic programmes are required and, above all, the acceptance that there can be no social development without sustained economic growth and good, formal, and well-paid jobs. AMLO's slogan, "For the good of all, the poor first", forces the state to address a serious social issue, poisoned by decades of mediocre economic growth and the unpunished scourge of organized crime. Whether AMLO's government is populist (or popular) is an open question. Is it one that moves towards the demolition of unfair structures, or is it incapable of laying the foundations of a mixed economy articulated by a national investment programme and a social state of law and universal rights, sustained by sound, flexible and transparent public finance? As Ricardo Raphael puts it:

> López Obrador's popularity can be understood in part because he embraces important causes for a large part of the electorate, who also shares his diagnosis. No less important is the extended weariness with corruption, as well as the indolence of the affluent class. However, he is limited by a messianic view of politics, his frequent irritation in the face of criticism [and] the occasional virulence of his language. (Raphael 2018: n.p.)

What we need is a sharp and detailed analysis of our daily life – a present that seems to be frozen – to understand how we have arrived at such a conflictive and confused situation that contaminates our political discussions, which, it seems to me, did not begin with López Obrador's government.

As president-elect, in 2018, Andrés Manuel López Obrador presented his *Proyecto de Nación*, the guiding document for his then imminent administration, in which he proposed to reverse 35 years of crisis and inequality in Mexico along the following lines: (1) politics and government; (2) social development; (3) economy and development; (4) education, science, moral values and culture. In his view, it was possible to introduce policies to right longstanding and deep-rooted problems, so a team was established to design proposals to bring about a change of course in order to achieve national reconstruction. "We want to live in a fair, democratic, sovereign, peaceful and transparent Mexico in 2024" (*Proyecto de Nación* 2018: 3).

The approval and support for AMLO's project has not been homogeneous – contrasting opinions define it as leftist, populist or reformist. However, compared to the many years of estrangement between the previous federal administrations and society, in an atmosphere of impunity, corruption and indifference to the social tensions that boiled in the veins of Mexico's social body, AMLO's proposal seemed to herald a change that could only come from a popular left-oriented coalition. But given the lack of clarity of the candidate, and his party, on how to carry out the reforms they claimed would stimulate economic growth and distribute its fruits, and given the plurality of opinions on this, it was hard to see the viability of the project. This, in turn, gave rise to further interpretations of it, as well as conjecture as to what could happen in the near future. Nevertheless, AMLO represented a leftist option "that in broad strokes we can call nationalist and populist, yet singularly austere" (Gómez Bruera 2021: 3). Without ignoring AMLO's former militancy in the Partido Revolucionario Institucional (PRI), his discourse was interpreted by many as hopeful, as he focused on social issues with slogans such as "For the good of Mexico, the poor first".

AMLO's moral discourse and his vocal disassociation from previous governments helped to legitimize him among various social groups that felt aggrieved by the many years of corruption and impunity of those governments. Above all, he sought to "put into context" a comment made by his predecessor Enrique Peña Nieto, who called corruption an endemic evil of Mexicans. AMLO was quick to counter this, saying that corruption is in the neoliberals' DNA, a vice completely alien to the people, whom he generically described, and continues to describe, as good and wise. He has resorted to this binary and reductionist discourse to debar opponents of his policies. He presents honesty as the antithesis of corruption. In his view, whoever is not honest is corrupt. From this assertion he has gone further: "honesty can be Mexico´s salvation"; corruption "is the main cause of inequality and national tragedy; honesty is a virtue that is a part of the moral patrimony of the people" (*Proyecto de Nación* 2018: 30–1). Pronouncements like these do not take account of the complexity of phenomena that transcend Mexico's reality, which must be put in a global context. It is not the case that values, such as honesty alone, can solve the economic injustices of globalization, nor can it be thought of as genetic material that is transmitted from generation to generation.

LEFT-WING POPULISMS

AMLO, like many others, is not against the Latin American leftist position that argues that social change is related to the reaffirmation of national projects, designed and implemented by the state to bring about social and economic reform, aimed to eradicate poverty. As Rolando Cordera Campos pointed out, when commenting on this position: "a policy for redefining the general interest and the common good" to repair the social fracture was needed (Cordera Campos 2021c: n.p.). Therefore, it is not surprising that AMLO promised to defend the rule of law, fight corruption, eradicate poverty and recover peace, financial viability, gender equality and sustainable development, among other commitments.

In a pioneering study of Latin American populism in the 1960s, Alistair Hennessy defined the phenomenon as an expression of a discontented but thriving middle class who is distant from the main spheres of political power (Hennessy 1969: 40). It is capable of joining together divergent social groups, showing itself to be a cross-class political project, and constituting itself as "a unifying, binding social force" (Turner 1971: 19) that achieves social consensus, and stimulates the political participation of groups that have been excluded from politics by the dominant culture. These are referred to as "the people".

Luis Villoro argues that "the people", despite being a vague term, refers to a collective entity with a clear identity and characteristics of its own, that are linked to a territory and have equal rights. For other intellectuals, "people" is a mere abstraction which, with the passage of time, has become a rhetorical device at the service of authoritarianism. In opposition to this idea is the approach of Hernán Gómez Bruera. He argues that we are experiencing a cultural change, that expresses itself as a partial recovery of

> the dimension of the collective and the community. Nowadays, in addition to speaking of "citizenship", we have recovered a notion of the "people" that had fallen into disuse and that is important because it involves thinking of ourselves as a whole with an identity closer to the interests of the majorities.
>
> (Gómez Bruera 2021: 21)

If it were possible to single out a common feature of the diverse forms of populism in the twenty-first century, it would probably be their origins since all of them have emerged from social unrest against liberalism. In Mexico the advantages of the democratic transition were not socialized because corruption swiftly corroded the institutions, violence increased, the economy did not grow at the expected pace, and inequality gaps widened, all of which contributed to stirring up deep resentments within and among social groups. Several analysts have argued that, to the extent that a process of deinstitutionalization of society comes about, the state is pushed away. In the Mexican case, despite the sizable public expenditures for social programmes and the creation of autonomous public agencies since the presidency of Vicente Fox (2000–06), the social fabric has not been reconstituted, nor have far-reaching policies been implemented to improve socioeconomic conditions, close inequality gaps and sustainably reduce poverty indexes.

Without attempting to detail the causes of this situation, we will mention some problems that have contributed to worsening it: flawed design of social programmes; insufficient evaluation of results; lack of social participation in decision-making; and unsatisfactory economic growth. It must be said that the AMLO's administration has not found answers to these problems, despite its seemingly genuine concern for serving the most disadvantaged social groups and improving their material conditions. The harshest criticism of the current administration comes from social democratic intellectuals, such as Gilberto Guevara Niebla, for whom AMLO's government is not only populist (in the derogatory sense), but also "destroys the spirit of community and undermines the shared public space that makes possible the nourishment of democracy by sincere dialogue between political actors" He goes on to say: "populist leaders are unscrupulous demagogues who indifferently speak truths and lies [...] do not educate critical thinking [nor] political intelligence, but instead promote prejudice and distrust among fellow citizens" (Guevara Niebla 2021a: n.p.).

Guevara Niebla's criticism is shared by other intellectuals who do not distinguish left-wing populism from right-wing and consider them to be the same, as both undermine democracy to the point of embracing authoritarian positions that restrict freedom already attained. In the face of this criticism, it is useful to recall that the early populist governments in Latin America emerged in contexts of economic modernization, in which they inserted nationalist development models that forced the recognition of labour rights and the dignification of the working classes, considering them active subjects of social change. These experiences occurred in political contexts without democratic traditions, where workers were oppressed. Thus, it is unsurprising that the reception of populism by the working classes is generally positive.

The point is that, in the current debate, those who rule out all populism, whatever its nature,

> have created a universe of their own [...] impervious to the others' ideas and needs, and by considering themselves as self-sufficient [their criticism] becomes a link that leads to fanaticism [...], a blinding obsession that finds it impossible to recognize the diversity that shapes the world. (Woldenberg 2021a: n.p.)

THE STATE REFORM INITIATIVE

Economist Rolando Cordera Campos has long insisted on the need to reform the Mexican state and undertake a new course of development that, in his opinion, should be the result of collaborative efforts between the various sectors and political actors "to reorient and resume production with the already installed productive forces and capacities" (Cordera Campos 2021a: n.p.). Such a course of development should be based on

> new forms of relationships that sustain a political economy with a public purpose [...] the reconstruction of the economy and the state; the reinvention of the public-private economy and the gestation of social accords capable of deliberating and agreeing on new and safe links of redistribution along the productive and distributive chain. (Cordera Campos 2021b: n.p.)

According to Cordera Campos, governments should be able to smooth the way for the leading economic forces to reach consensus. Like other economists, he has underlined the need to address the fiscal issue as a national priority. Cordera Campos is the coordinator of the New Course of Development Group, a team for reflection and analysis which has been proposing concrete economic measures since 2009. In its most recent document it states:

> The welfare state must be articulated in terms of purpose and of commitment to the general development of society, [economic] growth, expansion of the productive forces and implementation of new and fair redistributive forms and methods of the fruits of technical progress and the collective effort of social production.
> (Grupo Nuevo Curso de Desarrollo 2021: 12)

In his electoral campaign in 2018, AMLO expressed his commitment to separate the state from the interests of the market, and to convert it into a driving force of political, economic, and social development of the country (*Proyecto de Nación* 2018: 26). However, he did not propose any strategy for this reform in a social or legal sense. And what has actually happened is a trend towards a greater control and centralization of political power, a feature that bears great resemblance to the Latin American populist governments of the past. This is mainly due to the fact that, the Mexican government has not completely abandoned the corporate model created in the 1930s, to control the social sectors in order to carry out its economic modernization project. It is also the case that the democratic transition was limited to the political-electoral field, not only by successive governments, but also by the leftist sectors in general. This fact, combined with the low economic growth, left the central issues of inequality and poverty unattended.

Clearly state reform must be based on social reform as its central axis to focus on rebuilding the basic social fabric and processes of the nation. This necessarily involves the redistribution of power, a fundamental rearrangement of the relations and counterweights between the economic sphere, resource allocation and income and wealth distribution.

One of AMLO's most criticized undertakings has been the initiative to remove or curtail power (depending on how one sees it) of the autonomous public agencies created in recent years. His attempts have provoked strong debate because these agencies, despite their defects and constraints, are seen as facilitating the "public good" and as having opened up political and information spaces. AMLO's opposition to them has been interpreted as a fear of their autonomy, assuming that allowing them freedom to function independently would fracture political power and limit executive control. In this sense, AMLO's position can only be interpreted as a desire to concentrate the power of the state in his own hands, a position that José Woldenberg has called "hyper-presidentialism without counterweights" (Woldenberg 2021b: n.p.).

Pedro Salazar confirms that it is the case that these autonomous agencies perform specialized functions previously performed by the executive branch and that they were created originally "to dismantle the hyper-presidential system of post-revolutionary and authoritarian Mexico" (Salazar 2021: n.p.). They were created at different political moments. The Bank of Mexico (Banxico), Federal Electoral Institute (formerly INE), Human Rights National Commission (CNDH) and National Institute of Geography and Statistics (INEGI) came first and contributed to democratizing and liberalizing the country in political terms. The National Institute for Educational Evaluation (INEE), National Telecommunications Institute (IFT), Federal Commission of Economic Competence (COFECE), National Institute of Transparency and Access to Information (INAI), National Council for the Evaluation of Social Policy (CONEVAL) and Attorney's General Office (FGR), formed later, "share a common juridical character but their functions are very dissimilar [...] Some of them are administrative authorities with sanctioning powers for political or administrative authorities, and public or particular interests entities" (Salazar 2021: n.p.). Other agencies have a human rights protection function (CNDH); others perform regulatory functions with sanctioning power (IFT, COFECE); others are responsible for strategic economic functions (Banxico); others generate technical data (INEGI, CONEVAL); and others prosecute crime (FGR). According to jurist Leticia Bonifaz Alfonso, these autonomous agencies "are a product of the exhaustion of the hegemonic political party model that we have left behind" (Bonifaz Alfonso 2021: n.p.).

AMLO also oversaw the elimination of subsidies to civil society organizations. The allegation, which had some validity, was that programmes were being poorly implemented and that money was being diverted for personal gain. However, the action was taken without any proper investigation of those supposedly responsible, and thus provoked an outcry of indignation and criticism. Sergio Aguayo interpreted this action as proof of AMLO's aversion to citizens "who organize themselves, submit projects to the authority and support those who organize to demand respect for their own rights" (Aguayo 2021: n.p.). Another poorly informed decision by AMLO that was harshly criticized was the elimination of 109 trust funds which were designed to finance long-term projects in the arts, science, sports, human rights and other areas. While some of the government's arguments for the elimination of these funds were in line with trumpeted republican austerity, the money saved was not reallocated to areas of social need, such as the much-deteriorated health system.

SOCIAL POLICY AND ITS IMPLEMENTATION

One way for AMLO's government to obtain economic resources to finance social programmes is through so-called "republican austerity", whose stated main aim is to eliminate corruption. Another is to avoid indebtedness, a policy that has been highly criticized since there is a lack of liquidity in the country, a shortage that has halted productive investments. This situation was worsened by the closure of non-essential economic activities because of the Covid-19 health crisis, and the government refusal to provide economic support to medium and small firms. This, in turn, has increased unemployment as well as precarious or informal work. In the year 2020, 647,000 formal jobs were lost, and more than one million businesses closed their doors (González 2021). About 1,789,638 workers have been forced to withdraw a part or all of their pension savings due to the loss of their jobs (Fuentes 2021).

On the other hand, it is the case that the government has, so far, kept its promise to increase the minimum wage every year. The National Minimum Wage Commission increased it by 16 per cent in 2021. Another source of income that has cushioned the fall of purchasing power is remittances from Mexican migrant workers in the United States, which totalled $41,832 trillion in 2020. "It can be estimated that about seven million Mexican households receive remittances [...] which means that millions of families receive an average income between 7,000 and 14,000 pesos a month" (Quintana 2021b: n.p.).

From the beginning, AMLO's government committed to developing a social policy that would be the guideline for governmental activities (*Proyecto de Nación* 2018: 424). The Welfare Secretariat would be responsible for organizing the Basic Welfare Programmes, through which money would be transferred to the previously registered population. Of the total federal government spending for 2021, 51.5 per cent (112,143 million pesos) was allocated for social development. The largest part of this (51,694 million pesos) was allocated to housing and public services; 21,280 million pesos to health services; 12,147 million pesos to social protection; 12,509 million pesos to environmental protection, and 10,341 million pesos to education (Márquez Ayala 2021).

A sizeable part of the social budget was allocated to pensions for senior citizens over 65 (the base age was reduced from 68) and the amount of the individual pension increased to almost equate to the cost of the basic food basket (Zamarripa 2021). Funding is provided for the purchase or extension of houses. There are also allowances for people with disabilities, single mothers, children in day care centres and young people between 15 and 29 years old (Young People Building the Future programme) who are neither studying nor working, to support them in gaining access to the labour market. There are scholarships for students at elementary, middle and high school levels. There is also a direct transfer fund for parent-teacher committees of 51,000 schools, and undergraduate and graduate scholarships for poor students (Toledo 2021). There is a programme for promoting reading, through which Fondo de Cultura Económica, the Mexican state publishing house, has printed and distributed more than 1.5 million free books

Health care is a constitutional right in Mexico but, in reality, access is very limited. At the beginning of his mandate, AMLO pledged that his government's main healthcare goal would be to strengthen the Public Health System (PHS). According to official data, in 2017 about 20.5 million people had no access to the PHS. In 2020, this figure was reduced to 15 million, but diseases related to malnutrition, drugs and alcohol abuse, overweight and heart conditions, among others, increased. AMLO's government proposed to address this situation with the establishment of the National Institute for Health Care and Wellbeing (INSABI). Unfortunately, the coordination entanglements in transitioning from the PHS system to the new INSABI collided with the Covid-19 emergency, which caused a setback in both health care service and coverage.

Among the issues related to sustainable development and environment, the government decreed a gradual reduction in glyphosate and hybrid corn imports in December 2020, with a view to having these imports cancelled by 2024. Transgenic crops and the fracking technique for hydrocarbon extraction were banned.

There has been significant criticism of many of AMLO's government policies and actions. On cash transfers it has been said that they "replicate neoliberal logics in a perverse way, so eroding the social support institutions and making the individual entirely responsible for his own wellbeing and to keep his head afloat in the middle of a competitive market economy" (Bravo Regidor *et al.* 2021). Another criticism is that cash transfers are not enough to eradicate poverty. Gilberto Guevara Niebla commented: "poverty cannot be eradicated unless we start by producing more wealth. The engine of national productivity and the energy that drives the welfare state or the socialist democracies is education" (Guevara Niebla 2021b). According to him, the government must invest money in substantive areas of education such as better teacher wages, new teaching posts, continuing education provision and school infrastructure.

The majority of the population knows little about "social policy" and its various programmes. Far from understanding that these are constitutional rights, they are seen by many as generous government handouts, a form of patronage, the purpose of which is perceived as being to achieve electoral gain and maintain power. Further to this, just as many do not know their rights, nor do they understand their obligations as beneficiaries of the programmes. The lack of solid research data in identifying the population living in extreme poverty, and in assessing the outcomes of the various programmes have also been criticized. Assessment, when it does take place is irregular and poorly executed

In addition to the issues identified with the social programmes, the combination of the economic crisis and the Covid-19 health emergency has led to deteriorating social conditions. According to official data from CONEVAL, between 2018 and 2020 the number of poor in Mexico went from 51.9 million to 55.7 million, and the number of extreme poor went from 8.7 million to 10.8 million (Woldenberg 2021c). As several scholars have pointed out, "the best social program to reduce poverty is jobs creation" (Hernández Licona 2021: n.p.).

There is a need to rethink the programmes in order to design and implement economic and social policy strategies that generate development, which does not seem to be a priority for AMLO's government.

ENERGY, LABOUR AND AGRICULTURE

AMLO's government's reform policies were intended to be congruent with his political project but, as observed by Víctor Toledo, former secretary of the environment, this policy "has not been free of *chiaroscuros* and contradictions", despite "[AMLO] having proposed a path of honesty, support for the poor, rescue of the State and the nation, social and environmental regeneration, historical memory recovering and invoking the main universal values" (Toledo 2021: n.p.).

The reform of the energy industry was based on supporting the country's economic development, largely through the productivity of PEMEX and CFE, state-owned companies that had been privatized by previous governments. They were considered essential for economic development and seen as flagships of national sovereignty. Their strengthening was an absolute priority in the effort to reduce Mexico's energy dependence. In a further initiative to reform the laws governing the oil and electricity industries, the government was granted power to temporarily suspend licences to suppliers if it considered that they were a threat to national security, energy security or the national economy (Galván Ochoa 2021a). It was also established that "the authority may take control of the permit holder's facilities and hand them over to PEMEX or CFE for operation" (Quintana 2021a: n.p.). The Business Coordinator Council described these reforms as "indirect expropriation that will result in greater subsidies to the CFE and more expensive and polluting electricity", generating serious environmental and economic impacts (Cortés 2020: n.p.). Regarding this, the government has stated its intention is to accelerate the transition to renewable energies, but there is still no clarity on this issue.

Several labour law reforms were introduced to strengthen union freedoms and democracy, labour court independence and subcontracting or "outsourcing" regulations. With regard to the latter, "the prohibition of subcontracting personnel for specialized services other than the social purpose and the main economic activity of the contracting company" was established (Galván Ochoa 2021b). Agreement 189 of the Interamerican Labour Organization (ILO) on the rights of domestic workers was ratified (Bravo Regidor *et al.* 2021). This reform was described as transcendental because it contributes to the reduction of informality and precariousness of labour and to an increase in public revenues. According to the Organisation for Economic Co-operation and Development (OECD), "Mexico's per capita GDP is 64 per cent lower than that of most advanced economies of the organization. Inequality is greater than in most developed countries, where 20 per cent of the households with the lowest income are 5 per cent of the total" (Cortés 2021: n.p.).

One of AMLO's campaign pledges was to support the agrarian and rural sector, which had been harmed by the policies of previous governments, such as the promotion of the agro-export industry and the intensive use of technologies that deplete natural resources. According to AMLO, this sector can be "one of the main engines of economic growth, a source of well-being for people living in the countryside, the basis for achieving food security for all Mexicans, and a pillar of the sustainable and inclusive development required by the nation" (*Proyecto de Nación* 2018: 350).

AMLO's policies recognized the conditions of the indigenous cultures and focused on strengthening the country's multicultural character and combating discrimination, while committing to respect the forms of community organizations and support for economic development projects. The approach also diagnosed the diversity of the rural sector, with the classification of rural workers (*ejidatarios*, communal farmers, small landowners, day laborers) and agriculture forms (domestic, market or non-market, entrepreneurial). There was an emphasis on: the fit, sustainable and responsible use of natural resources for resilient agriculture; the strengthening of institutions for integrated environmental management in a global context; the cultivation of corn and beans through the Enlarged Corn Field with Fruit Trees Programme (MIFA); a programme of guaranteed prices for basic agricultural products (Production for Wellbeing) and the Sowing Life Programme (Soto 2021). This approach was seen as being appropriate for the Mexican countryside. On the negative side, some large infrastructure projects across the countryside, such as the trans-isthmus corridor and the Santa Lucía Airport, have been the subject of considerable criticism because they affect rural territories and rural and urban indigenous communities, especially in the southeast of the country.

MIGRATION AND INSECURITY

Migration to the United States is, and has long been, a major feature of Mexican society. A particular and increasing difficulty in this regard is the strong anti-immigration movement in the US and the activities of anti-immigration activists along the Mexico/US border. Alongside this, due to the worsening economic, social and security problems in Central America there is an increasing migratory pressure on Mexico's southern border. AMLO's government has proposed to not only protect,and defend migrants' human rights but to modernize border crossings facilities and immigration stations on its southern border. As medium and long-term measures, AMLO has promoted the signing of trilateral programmes (US-Mexico-Central America) to develop rural regions and urban centres in Central America, as well as to build an economic and commercial corridor in the Isthmus of Tehuantepec. In respect of national security and the fight against organized crime, Mexico's government has sought agreements with the United States government to fight drugs, arms and people trafficking on the US–Mexico border.

Violence and crime are major issues in Mexico. The causes are well-known, springing primarily from insecurity, as a result of structural phenomena such as inequality and poverty. AMLO's government has proposed to address these issues in the fight against crime. While it is true that tackling inequality and poverty will help to make Mexico's poor less vulnerable to recruitment by organized crime, it is also the case that there is an urgent need to address the more structural legal issues and the many forms of corruption. The government's response to these problems has not been sufficiently broad-based. It has increased the numbers in the security forces but has not improved training. The National Guard, which replaced the inherited security forces, was to be under civilian command, but it has ended up under military control. Little has been done to reform the administration of justice or to implement social crime prevention programmes.

THE OTHER LEFT

Although in the short term there is no glimpse of a greater definition of the López Obrador government towards the left, it remains to be seen what the consequences of the international crisis will be, the expressions of which will be interdependent and multidimensional. This will contribute to exacerbating the contradictions and conflicts, especially among the groups that today dispute recognition, autonomy, justice, equality and that have been involved in recent mobilizations, such as the National Indigenous Council, in which the EZLN participates, feminist groups, groups from the LGBTQIA+

community, environmentalists, relatives of the disappeared and of inhabitants of popular neighbourhoods.

However, the social fragmentation and the lack of political will of the groups seeking a common front are striking, as well as the limited political scope, even more so if one considers the indifference of the government to the expression of problems. Also notorious is the regrouping of old and new militants of leftist parties that, for a long time, had ceased to have a presence; this is the case of communists, Trotskyists and anarchists who now acquire a presence in social movements.

Regarding the intellectual left, the one that comes from the student and union movements of the 1960s, which participated in the formation of the first political party of the unified Mexican left in the second half of the twentieth century, the Unified Socialist Party of Mexico, it identifies more with social democracy and only has limited examples of political participation. Although it has a daily presence in the media, it does not manage to transcend and be able to offer options in terms of proposals of a national scope that may contribute to the solution of the many pending issues, among which the following stand out: respect for the San Andrés Agreements; do justice to the victims of violence; put an end to impunity, especially that which comes from public officials; stop megaprojects that affect the environment and peasant and/or indigenous communities and develop a programme to promote increased formal employment.

CONCLUSION

Having reviewed the government programmes and policies that have received greater disapproval or rejection from public opinion, we can now distinguish two positions: those who have expressed scepticism and rejection of AMLO since he was a candidate, considering him a return to authoritarianism; and those who have focused their criticism on the lack of technical support for economic policies, which seem to them wholly insufficient. Among these we can include sectors inclined to social democracy or the democratic left, such as the New Course of Development group.

We note that several issues that have been submitted to public debate have not been sufficiently explained, such as the popular consultations to cancel the construction of the new international airport of Mexico City or the Constellations Brands brewery in Mexicali. Therefore, it is necessary to call for dialogue in order to reach consensus and collectively solve these, and other, problems.

Regarding the government's social programmes and infrastructure works, it is not possible to spend what is required and spend it well if the state lacks a robust and transparent treasury. Certainly, the government has improved tax collection, but this is not enough. To think that social programmes and large infrastructure works can be financed by transferring money from other parts of the federal budget – which seems to be affecting the functioning of the administrative apparatus – is illusory. As AMLO himself said: "Social policy cannot be the sum of palliative programs, but a general and deep transformation of state policy" (*Proyecto de Nación* 2018: 425).

Finally, we can note that President AMLO, unlike historical cases of Latin American populism, does not seem interested in creating a strong political party and his party, Morena, is far from following the corporate or sector-based mass party model. The way out of the negative dynamics in which Mexico finds itself currently seems clear. The consequences of the Covid-19 emergency on the economic, social, and political conditions of life are significant. If social transformation is now truly sought, the emphasis must be on a clear and explicit commitment to build a constitutional rule of law and rights. This is the only way to firmly resume a path of economic growth with social justice.

REFERENCES

Aguayo, S. 2021. "La resistencia". *Reforma*, 28 April. www.reforma.com/la-resistencia-2021-04-28/op203726.

Annunziata, R. 2020. "El populismo como democracia limite. Entrevista a Pierre Rosanvallón". *Andamios* 18(46). www.scielo.org.mx/scielo.php?script=sci_arttext&pid=S1870-00632021000200259.

Bonifaz Alfonso, L. 2021. "Vistazo a los órganos autónomos". *El Universal*, 16 June. www.eluniversal.com.mx/opinion/leticia-bonifaz-alfonzo/vistazo-los-organos-autonomos.

Bravo Regidor, C., P. Iber & H. Beck 2021. "AMLO, inamovible". *Opinión*, April. https://nuso.org/articulo/amlo-inamovible/.

Cordera Campos, R. 2021a "Oración y Penumbra", *La Jornada*, 17 January. www.jornada.com.mx/2021/01/17/opinion/013a1pol.

Cordera Campos, R. 2021b. "El mundo en peligro", *El Financiero*, 18 February. www.elfinanciero.com.mx/opinion/rolando-cordera-campos/el-mundo-en-peligro/.

Cordera Campos, R. 2021c. "Preguntitas sin destinatario", *La Jornada*, 21 February. www.jornada.com.mx/2021/02/21/opinion/013a2pol.

Cortés, M. 2020. "Esperada renuncia de Alfonso Romo". *Excelsior Sección Opinión y Blogs*, 3 December. www.dineroenimagen.com/maricarmen-cortes/esperada-renuncia-de-alfonso-romo/129032?utm_source=headtopics&utm_medium=news&utm_campaign=2020-12-03.

Cortés, M. 2021. "OCDE: debilidades de México y recomendaciones". *Excelsior Sección Opinión y Blogs*, 15 April. www.dineroenimagen.com/maricarmen-cortes/ocde-debilidades-de-mexico-y-recomendaciones/132707.

Fuentes, M. 2021. Nuevas pensiones envueltas en un remolino de crisis. *Silla Rota*. https://lasillarota.com/opinion/columnas/2021/1/6/nuevas-pensiones-envueltas-en-un-remolino-de-crisis-355507.html.

Galván Ochoa, E. 2021a. "Dinero: No habrá expropiaciones: AMLO". *La Jornada Sección Economía*, 30 March. www.jornada.com.mx/notas/2021/03/30/economia/dinero-no-habra-expropiaciones-amlo-siembran-inquietud-los-cambios-a-la-ley-de-hidrocarburos-el-cannabis-es-tan-adictivo-como-los-opiaceos/.

Galván Ochoa, E. 2021b. "Dinero: Pacto obrero-patronal para un outsourcing… limitado". *La Jornada Sección Economía*, 6 April. https://jornada.com.mx/notas/2021/04/06/economia/dinero-pacto-obrero-patronal-para-un-outsourcing-limitado-don-millonesimo-quiere-ser-diputado-el-reparto-del-actor-alfredo-adame/.

Gómez Bruera, H. 2021. *Una radiografía para escépticos*. Mexico: Océano.

González, L. 2021 "Le importa a AMLO la Secretaría de Economía". *El Economista*, 6 January. www.eleconomista.com.mx/opinion/Le-importa-a-AMLO-la-Secretaria-de-Economia-20210106-0002.html.

Grupo Nuevo Curso de Desarrollo 2021. Renovar políticas: para un nuevo curso de desarrollo en Méxcio. www.nuevocursodedesarrollo.unam.mx/docs/GNCD_2021.08_Renovar_%20Politicas.pdf.

Guevara Niebla, G. 2021a. "Credo antipopulista". *Crónica Sección Opinión*, 26 January. www.cronica.com.mx/notas-credo_antipopulista-1175763-2021.

Guevara Niebla, G. 2021b. "El futuro en sombras". *Crónica Sección Opinión*, 11 April. www.cronica.com.mx/notas-el_futuro_en_sombras-1183100-2021.

Hennessy, A. 1969. *América Latina en Ghita Ionescu y Ernest Gellner (compiladores): Populismo. Sus significados y características nacionales*. Buenos Aires: Amorrortu.

Hernández Licona, G. 2021. "Covid-19 empleo y pobreza durante 2020 en México". *Animal Político*, 6 March. https://mexicocomovamos.mx/animal-politico/2021/03/covid-19-empleo-y-pobreza-durante-2020-en-mexico/.

Maldonado, M. 2017. "Las bases afectivas del populismo". *Revista Internacional de Pensamiento Político* 12: 151–67. www.upo.es/revistas/index.php/ripp/article/download/3257/2533/9694.

Márquez Ayala, D. 2021. "Reporte económico: Ciudad de México. Presupuesto 2021". *La Jornada*, 1 February. www.jornada.com.mx/notas/2021/02/01/economia/reporte-economico-ciudad-de-mexico-presupuesto-2021/.

Proyecto de Nación 2018. https://drive.google.com/file/d/1yOdkHHTeKKHCwzAjyacQ_15LbqvHUHa6/view?vsp=sharing.

Quintana, E. 2021a. "La oportunidad que se nos está yendo". *El Financiero*, 9 April. www.elfinanciero.com.mx/opinion/enrique-quintana/2021/04/19/la-oportunidad-que-se-nos-esta-yendo.

Quintana, E. 2021b. "Ya somos dependientes de las remesas". *El Financiero*, 5 May. www.elfinanciero.com.mx/opinion/enrique-quintana/2021/05/04/ya-somos-dependientes-de-las-remesas/.

Raphael, R. 2018. "AMLO: de la polarización a la reconciliación", *El Financiero*, 1 June. www.elfinanciero.com.mx/culturas/amlo-de-la-polarizacion-a-la-reconciliacion/.

Salazar, P. 2021. "Estos OCA no son gansos". *Nexos*, 1 March. www.nexos.com.mx/?p=53611.

Soto, L. 2021. "Elecciones México 2021: Encuestas de salida, noticias de candidatos y PREP por estados EN VIVO". *El Heraldo de México*, 6 June. https://heraldodemexico.com.mx/elecciones/2021/6/6/elecciones-mexico-2021-encuestas-de-salida-noticias-de-candidatos-prep-por-estados-en-vivo-303724.html.

Toledo, V. 2021. "Votar por la decencia, la vida y el planeta". *La Jornada*, 1 June. www.jornada.com.mx/notas/2021/06/01/politica/votar-por-la-decencia-la-vida-y-el-planeta/.

Turner, F. 1971. *La dinámica del nacionalismo mexicano*. Mexico: Editorial Grijalbo.

Woldenberg, J. 2021a. "Vivir encerrado". *El Universal*, 26 June. www.eluniversal.com.mx/opinion/jose-woldenberg/vivir-encerrado.

Woldenberg, J. 2021b. "¿Democracia o autoritarismo?". *El Universal*, 4 May. www.eluniversal.com.mx/opinion/jose-woldenberg/democracia-o-autoritarismo.

Woldenberg, J. 2021c. "Así no se puede". *El Universal*, 11 August. www.eluniversal.com.mx/opinion/jose-woldenberg/asi-no-se-puede.

Zamarripa, G. 2021. "Programas sociales en las campañas: aumento de pensiones". *Excélsior*, 27 March. www.dineroenimagen.com/guillermo-zamarripa/programas-sociales-en-las-campanas-aumento-las-pensiones/132201.

CHAPTER 7

THE BOLIVARIAN PROCESS IN VENEZUELA: SOCIALISM, POPULISM OR NEOLIBERALISM?

Roberto López Sánchez

INTRODUCTION

Hugo Chávez won the presidential elections in December 1998 after a decade of neoliberal policies in Venezuela. The previous period had seen: two successive governments implementing neoliberal economic programmes; the spontaneous popular uprising of February–March 1989, which shook the two-party political system in place since 1958; two nationalist and leftist military uprisings;[1] and a sitting president removed from office by parliament on charges of corruption.[2]

The so-called "Bolivarian process", that began in Venezuela with the electoral triumph of Hugo Chávez in 1998, was the popular response to the crisis of legitimacy of the political model of representative democracy that had been in place since 1958 (López Maya 1994: 32; Carvallo & López Maya 1989: 49). The failure of the productive model of import substitution, the foundation of representative democracy for 30 years, had become evident by the mid-1980s, with a profound economic crisis that worsened with the fall in oil prices in 1986.

The spontaneous popular uprising of 27–28 February 1989, known as the "Caracazo" (Barrios-Ferrer 1990: 55; España 1989: 118), revealed the great discontent of the population with a political-economic system that did not satisfy their fundamental needs. The government's brutal repressive response caused hundreds of deaths in the neighbourhoods of Caracas and nearby cities. It reinforced the view that those who governed did not deserve to enjoy the popular support that had sustained the ruling two-party political model

1. On 4 February and 27 November 1992.
2. Carlos Andrés Pérez was dismissed by parliament in May 1993.

for three decades. The two parties in question were the Acción Democrática (AD [Democratic Action]) and Partido Socialcristiano (COPEI [Social Christian party]).

However, in the absence of alternative political options, and with a left in crisis, both in its electoral versions and in the groups that maintained the armed struggle, the two-party system would remain in power for another decade. But the decomposition of the political model continued, and in 1992 two military uprisings followed one after the other. They both failed but they showed that the ship of representative democracy was still sinking.

The military rebellions of 1992 marked a profound break in the dominant power bloc that had ruled since 1958.[3] A very large sector of middle ranking officers in the armed forces, unhappy at having been used by the government as "executioners" of the people during the events of February 1989, decided to rebel, raising anti-corruption slogans, and promoting a diffuse nationalist and popular political change. The revolt was defeated but the dominant bloc was now fragmented and was unable to recompose in the following years.

In the decade before Chávez, the second government of social democrat Carlos Andrés Pérez (1989–93) had inaugurated the first fully neoliberal economic plan in Venezuela[4] (Lander 1994: 103). The package of measures implemented at the beginning of his government, such as the liberalization of prices and the elimination of subsidies (including the important subsidy on gasoline), were the triggers for the Caracazo. Pérez was finally dismissed in 1993 by the legislature, accused of corruption. In reality, however, his dismissal was a manoeuvre by the ruling elite (AD, COPEI and the business and military elite) in an attempt to contain the social and military discontent, and to prop up a system whose legitimacy was in question (Prato Barbosa 1994: 21).

The Pérez government was succeeded by the Christian Socialist, Rafael Caldera (1994–99). This was also his second period in office but, despite being the founder of COPEI, he had now broken with it, and won the elections with the support of the left-wing parties. But Caldera's government, instead of being consistent with its discourse, which was critical of the neoliberal plan implemented by his predecessor, applied the same economic recipe of the

3. A power bloc made up of the AD and COPEI parties, the military high command, the business elite grouped in Fedecámaras, the church hierarchy, the mass media and the trade union bureaucracy of the CTV (Confederación de Trabajadores de Venezuela). The formation of this power bloc is considered by historians to be based on the Punto Fijo Pact, signed in October 1958 by the AD, COPEI and URD parties. The governments between 1959 and 1999 are called "Punto Fijo" governments.
4. In 1979 the Social-Christian government of Luis Herrera Campins (1979–84) timidly applied some neoliberal measures such as price liberalization. But the strong social protest presented made him give up after a few weeks.

International Monetary Fund.[5] Citizens' rejection of this new neoliberal turn was manifested in the elections of 1998 and allowed Hugo Chávez to present himself as the nationalist and popular alternative to 20 years of economic failure and 40 years of a discredited two-party political model (Ellner 2009).

HUGO CHÁVEZ: FROM THE THIRD WAY TO SOCIALISM

Lieutenant Colonel Hugo Chávez had led the "Bolivarian" military rebellion of 4 February 1992,[6] and planned the uprising of 27 November 1992 from prison. After his release, he decided to found a legal party (Movimiento Quinta República, MVR) and entered the 1998 elections. In a dizzying electoral surge throughout 1998, Chávez prevailed over the unified candidate of the AD and COPEI parties, which had taken turns in power since 1958. With a main proposal to convene an assembly to draft a new constitution, Chávez had a political-economic programme very close to the welfare state, in a global neoliberal context. His electoral proposal announced an endorsement of the diffuse "Third Way" formulated by British leader Tony Blair and others (Martínez 2018).

Upon coming to power, Chávez was labelled a populist leader, similar to others throughout the twentieth century in Latin America.[7] Populism has been considered an ambiguous concept that can encompass extreme interpretations in the political sphere with the study of its expressions in Latin America based on different approaches (Rengifo & Medina 2019: 236). Given this, we consider that Hugo Chávez's government had similar characteristics to the populist governments of the mid-twentieth century (Stanley 2000: 351) such as: the presence of a charismatic leadership; the imposition of a democracy with authoritarian overtones (in the case of Chávez, this involved participation of the military in relevant government positions); broad popular support that was constantly mobilized; and a radical discourse that was very appealing to the large impoverished masses.

---

5. The neoliberal economic plan implemented by Caldera from 1996 onwards was called "Agenda Venezuela".
6. Calling himself the "Bolivarian military movement", Chávez always postulated the thoughts of Simón Bolívar as the ideological foundation of his programmatic proposal. Hence his anti-imperialist and nationalist stance. Bolívar had defeated and expelled the Spanish Empire from South America and was the founder of what are now six nations on the continent (Venezuela, Colombia, Ecuador, Peru, Bolivia and Panama).
7. So-called "Latin American populism" has been identified with governments and political leaders who, throughout the twentieth century, responded to the crisis of the oligarchic order that emerged after independence. They represented the response of certain fractions of the industrial bourgeoisie, of new "intermediate" fractions and of broad sectors of the popular masses to this crisis (Vilas 1988).

But his performance at the helm of government quickly transcended the frameworks of traditional populism, moving closer to models of "socialist revolution" such as Cuba. This was in the global context of the collapse of the Socialist Bloc in Eastern Europe a decade earlier, the failure in Latin America of attempts at political change through armed struggle (as in El Salvador and Guatemala) and the crushing of socialist attempts by "peaceful means" (Chile). Thus Chávez, at the end of the twentieth century and the beginning of the twenty-first, followed a rethought ideal of "socialist revolution", that linked the principles of national sovereignty and continental integration formulated in the War of Independence, with the traditions of popular revolutionary struggle expressed in the last century. Chávez defined his revolution as "socialist", during his participation in the Porto Alegre Social Forum in January 2005 (Biardeau 2015). The basic principles of this "socialism" were participatory and protagonist democracy of "popular power" (as opposed to liberal representative democracy); "equality and justice"; and "civil-military" unity.

In recent decades, governments of different tendencies that coincide in developing processes of sociopolitical change and economic programmes of a nationalist, Keynesian or even self-described "socialist" nature have been designated as "populist" in Latin America. The populist label generally comes from conservative analysts, who question governments that in some way attempt to oppose neoliberal economic schemes and move away from the traditional subordination to the US government. The general economic and political situation in Latin America, at the end of the twentieth century, included considerable citizen rejection of the neoliberal "shock" adjustments implemented in the previous two decades. There was also accumulated popular discontent at the disastrous results of these adjustments, which had led to a reversal of the labour rights won in the postwar period, and a significant drop in the income levels of the working classes (Alayón 2007: 181). This reality forced many progressive parties and leaders to speak out against neoliberalism and its main promoter, the International Monetary Fund (IMF), and to postulate alternative paths that included Keynesian, and socialist proposals.

In Venezuela, Chávez's electoral triumph in 1998 contributed to reversing this process of falling income levels for the working class, as all the neoliberal plans that had been implemented since February 1989, began to slow down and in some cases, to be reversed, due to the explicit policies of the new government (Alayón 2007: 184). In particular, the processes of privatization of public companies[8] were halted, including the

8. The Caldera government privatized the Siderurgica del Orinoco, the National Telephone Company (CANTV) and the airline Aeropostal. It sold to the private sector the banks that had gone bankrupt and had been under state control since the banking crisis of 1994.

so-called "oil opening", proposed by Pérez, and initiated by Caldera in 1995 (Toussaint 2009: 255; Mateo Tomé 2010: 44). A major transformative step taken by the government was the convening of a Constituent Assembly in 1999. The new constitution significantly expanded social rights and some new political rights such as the mid-term recall referendum for the president of the republic and other elected positions in the executive and legislative branches.

In the economic sphere, the Chávez project was defined by anti-neoliberalism and the overcoming of oil rentierism (Rodríguez Rojas 2010: 195) and its replacement by a neo-developmentalist policy, with strong state intervention, in strategic areas. The trial was carried out in a process of polarized struggle between the government, the political right, and the traditional business sector (which emerged in the period 1958–98).

The Chávez period revitalized the workers' struggle, changing labour relations and forms of ownership. In terms of labour rights, the Constitution, approved in December 1999, ratified fundamental workers' rights, already enshrined in the 1947 and 1961 Constitutions. These included: the right to unionize; the autonomy of trade unions from the employer and the state; the right to collective bargaining; the right to strike; the right to social security as a public service and the obligation of the state to guarantee it; the right to work, and the inclusion of new rights such as equality and equity between men and women in the exercise of the right to work; the recognition of household work as an economic activity that creates added value and produces wealth and provides welfare; the right of housewives to social security; the progressiveness of labour rights and their inalienable nature; and finally, the reduction of the daytime working day from 48 to 44 hours a week (López Sánchez 2017a: 34).

These constitutional rights come from the most progressive visions of the welfare state,[9] having the historical merit of being ratified after two decades of neoliberal policies at the global level, which had among their main objectives the annihilation of such rights and the "flexibilization" of labour relations. In the years that followed, Venezuelan workers embarked on a process of profound reorganization of their trade union structures, raising demands and political proposals that confronted and transcended the previous neoliberal decade and opened up prospects for the anti-capitalist direction of the Venezuelan political process (Chirino 2005: 36).

9. In the main Western capitalist countries, labour rights do not have constitutional status but appear in specific laws and regulations. Venezuela was one of the first countries, after Mexico (Constitution of Querétaro 1917), to constitutionally endorse the fundamental rights of the working class, with the Constitution that emerged from the Constituent Assembly of 1947.

CHÁVEZ'S PROGRAMME OF NATIONALIZATION

A failed *coup d'état* in April 2002 was closely followed by an employer-led general strike (known as the "oil strike" or "oil lockout") in December 2002, carried out by the Puntofijista[10] elites. The strike was a further failed attempt to overthrow the Chávez government, Resistance to that strike generated the rise of the workers' struggle throughout the country. Its failure was taken as a victory by the sectors of Bolivarian workers who were beginning to organize independently, outside of the CTV (which was one of the organizers of the strike, together with Fedecámaras).

From 2003 onwards, Venezuelan workers took back companies that had been paralysed and demanded the nationalization/renationalization of industries in the hands of the national or foreign private sector. At the same time, the workers' struggle began to try out novel forms of organizing productive activity through workers' councils and workers' control, proposals that found an echo in the Bolivarian government and ended up becoming state policies (López Sánchez 2017a: 34). Workers' control, which emerged as a slogan for action during the 2002–03 strike, launched the slogans of "Factory stopped, factory occupied" and "Workers' control of productive activity", leading to the occupation by the workers of numerous companies that had ceased activity. This occurred in Venepal (Carabobo), Venezolana de Válvulas (Los Teques), Textiles Fénix (Guárico), Cristine-Carol Perfumes (Caracas), and others (López Sánchez & Hernández 2016: 184).

From 2004, when Chávez ordered the expropriation of Venepal, "Workers' Control" began to be considered a policy of the Venezuelan state, although it was only in 2009 that it was included as a government guideline, in what became known as the Guayana Socialist Plan (López Sánchez & Hernández 2016: 184). The aim of Workers' Control as a policy was to achieve the full exercise of participatory and protagonist democracy by the workers, inside and outside the factory (Adarfio 2011: 43). It constituted an experiment in the workers' battle to replace the bourgeois state with a new state of transition to socialism, and was designed not to repeat the fatal mistakes of the Soviet experience (Carcione 2010: 56).

Another aspect of workers' organization was the Prevention Delegates and the Health and Safety at Work Committees (CSSL), whose promotion was in the hands of INPSASEL,[11] an institute attached to the Ministry of Labour. These committees were set up throughout the country, in various companies,

10. Puntofijista derives from the Pact of Punto Fijo, signed in 1958 between the participating political parties.
11. National Institute for Prevention, Health and Safety at Work.

and in both public and private institutions, which made them an organizational tool almost as widespread as the trade unions themselves. Prevention delegates played a role as defenders of workers' rights, especially in small companies, where there were no trade unions (López Sánchez 2017b: 201).

In May 2012, a new Labour Law (LOTTT)[12] was passed, restoring the rights violated in the Caldera reform of 1997[13] and also incorporating a suite of new labour and political rights (López Sánchez 2017b: 234). The approval of the new LOTTT was seen as an outstanding legal contribution to the workers' struggle against neoliberalism and against capitalist exploitation in general, according to the definition contained in its article 25, which states: "The social labour process has as its essential objective to overcome the forms of capitalist exploitation" (López Sánchez 2017a: 35).

One of the most stark expressions of the anti-neoliberal programme, implemented during the Chávez government, was the nationalization of a range of large companies throughout the country (Carcione 2009: 14):

- February 2007: Nationalization of the oil fields operated in the Orinoco Belt by transnational companies from the US, UK, France and Norway.
- May 2007: Nationalization of the company Electricidad de Caracas, creation of the National Electricity Corporation (Corpoelec), and nationalization of regional private companies.
- May 2008: nationalization of CANTV,[14] buying the shares of the US company Verizon.
- April 2008: Renationalization of Siderúrgica del Orinoco (SIDOR),[15] which was owned by the Italian-Argentine multinational Techint, a company closely linked to the Kirchner government.
- 2008: Nationalization of the country's main cement industries, which were owned by Mexico's Cemex, Switzerland's Holcin and France's Lafarge.
- May 2009: Nationalization of briquette companies such as MATESSI, and the pipe factory TAVSA.
- 2009: Nationalization of 76 medium-sized companies that provided services to the oil industry.
- 2009: Nationalization of the sardine processing company La Gaviota and Café Fama de América.

12. Organic Law of Labour and Workers.
13. The main point, which had been a central element of Chávez's programmatic discourse during the 1998 election campaign, was the reinstatement of the retroactive calculation for the payment of seniority (payment of social benefits on the basis of the last salary). In addition, double compensation in the case of unjustified dismissal was reinstated.
14. Compañía Anónima Nacional Teléfonos de Venezuela (National Telephone Company of Venezuela).
15. It had been privatized during the second government of Rafael Caldera in the 1990s.

- 2009: Nationalization of the Banco de Venezuela, which was owned by the Spanish Santander group.
- 2007–09: Occupation of idle land and nationalization of numerous large estates in various states of the country.

The highlight of this process was the renationalization of SIDOR, as a result of a long struggle by its workers. In 1997, SIDOR had been handed over to a private Argentine consortium[16] (Giacalone 2003: 53–87). After 15 months of struggle by its workers, President Chávez's decision to nationalize the company was the trigger for the strengthening of "Workers' Control" and the approval in 2009 of the Guayana Socialist Plan (Pérez Borges et al. 2009: 24). The Plan Guayana Socialista (PGS) represented the culmination of the efforts made during the government of Hugo Chávez to follow a path that would dismantle the neoliberal policies of previous decades and advance the definition of anti-capitalist productive models (Comisión de Sistematización 2013). From the outset, this plan met with resistance and sabotage, from both the bureaucracy embedded in the structures of the state (companies and ministries) and the trade unions (Pérez Borges 2010: 64).[17] Both sectors reflected, to some extent, the interests of the large iron and aluminium multinationals that had been affected by the nationalizations, who were intent on recovering the business that the revolution had taken away from them (Carcione & Poliak 2010: 58).

REFLECTION

Hugo Chávez's period of government contributed to the relative improvement of workers' incomes and living conditions by introducing the social missions, conceived as "social wages". Health programmes in the neighbourhoods, construction of popular housing, school feeding programmes, access to vehicles and household appliances through pricing initiatives, expansion of the public university system, expansion of the pension system to housewives and non-contributing workers, among others, all made it possible to improve the general living conditions of the working class. That improvement is particularly remarkable when we take account of the fact that, while real wages increased

16. The Amazonia Consortium, in which the Techint Group of Argentina held a majority stake. Other companies participating in the consortium were: Siderar (Argentina), Tamsa (Mexico), Hylsa (Mexico), Sivensa (Venezuela) and Usiminas (Brazil).
17. The trade union most closely aligned with the anti-Chávez government bureaucracy throughout the Chávez-Maduro period was the FSBT, or FBT (Fuerza Socialista Bolivariana de Trabajadores), which followed in the steps of the old CTV and the Trade Union Bureau of Acción Democrática.

between 1999–2001 and 2003–06, there was an overall decrease of 20 per cent over the first decade of Chavismo (1999–2010) (Mateo Tomé 2010: 44).

On the international front, Chávez moved away from the position of his predecessors who had, historically, acted in subordination to the US government. He distanced himself from the so-called Western Bloc (the US and the European Union), moving closer to emerging powers such as China, Russia, Iran and Turkey. He maintained a strong relationship with the communist government of Fidel Castro in Cuba. He confronted the traditional US hegemony in Latin America, challenging the Organization of American States (OAS) and promoting the creation of alternative integration organizations such as CELAC (Community of Latin American and Caribbean States) and ALBA (Bolivarian Alternative for the Americas). A highlight of his international actions was his opposition to the Free Trade Area of the Americas (FTAA) project, a US proposal to reduce or eliminate the trade barriers among all countries in the Americas, excluding Cuba. It was defeated at the IV Summit of the Americas in Mar de Plata (November 2005), with the prominent participation of the presidents of the Mercosur countries,[18] who joined with Chávez to reject the US proposal and deliver a historic defeat to US interests, represented at the summit by both President George Bush and Condoleezza Rice (Karg & Lewit 2015).

During the Chávez term of office, there was a rise of left-wing forces throughout Latin America, leading to a radical change in the entire Latin American political landscape. The anti-imperialist discourse, confronting the US government and its traditional influence in the continent, was strengthened as never before in history. This radical shift resulted in the electoral triumphs of Luiz Inácio Lula da Silva (2003–10) and Dilma Rousseff (2011–16)[19] in Brazil; Néstor Kirchner (2003–07) and Cristina Fernández de Kirchner (2007–15) in Argentina; Rafael Correa in Ecuador (2007–17); Evo Morales in Bolivia (2006–19); Tabaré Vazquez (2005–10) and José "Pepe" Mujica (2010–15) in Uruguay; Fernando Lugo in Paraguay (2008–12);[20] Michelle Bachelet in Chile (2006–10); Daniel Ortega in Nicaragua (2007–21); Mauricio Funes in El Salvador (2009–14); Manuel Zelaya in Honduras (2006–09); [21] and Ollanta Humala in Peru (2011–16).

The main accusation against Chávez was not that he was a "populist" but that he was a "communist". The influence of Chavismo throughout Latin America revived in the mouths of US government spokespersons and allied forces across the continent the discourse of the old Cold War, which ended in 1991 after the collapse of the Soviet Union. The campaign waged by the US

18. Néstor Kirchner, Luiz Inácio Lula da Silva and Tabaré Vásquez.
19. Impeached by the legislative branch in her second presidential term.
20. Impeached by the legislative branch in 2012.
21. Overthrown by a military coup in 2009.

government against Chávez and the influence of Chavismo in the continent meant resurrecting in the twenty-first century the fight against "communist expansion" as carried out in the 1960s, 1970s and 1980s.

Chávez's illness in mid-2011 weakened the forces that were fighting for alternative paths to the old neoliberal recipe book, and in the course of 2012 the Guayana Socialist Plan (PGS) began to be dismantled and abandoned by the ministries and companies involved (García 2011; Rivero 2010). His death in 2013, and the inauguration of Nicolás Maduro as president in 2013, meant the almost total abandonment of the anti-neoliberal programme, and the return of the same economic policies implemented in the last decade of the twentieth century. Maduro maintained the same radical discourse as his predecessor and presented his government as a genuinely "workerist"[22] and "socialist"[23] one, which had the backing of the ruling class. However, in office, he has implemented a real change of economic course, opening the doors to neoliberal policies, in a framework of growing authoritarianism (Alarcón 2017; Luna 2019; Vivas Santana 2019; Sutherland 2020).

THE RETURN TO THE NEOLIBERAL AND AUTHORITARIAN PAST UNDER THE GOVERNMENT OF NICOLÁS MADURO

The reality of the Venezuelan economy more than eight years into Nicolás Maduro's rule ranks as the worst performance in the world, and one of the five worst performers in the history of capitalism over the past 70 years (Bermúdez 2016; Vera 2018). A contraction of more than 50 per cent of GDP in seven years; closure of 60 per cent of existing factories; a minimum wage of less than US$3 a month in the context of a monthly food basket of US$300; a society that had received a trillion dollars in the oil boom between 2004 and 2008 that, without having gone through a war, has today a totally destroyed economy (Straka 2019). All of this highlights the absence of a coherent economic plan, and the adoption of measures that contradict each other and that deepen the collapse of the Venezuelan economy every day (Sutherland 2018).

22. Maduro was a union activist in the Caracas Metro, where he worked as a bus driver in the 1980s. In the dispute staged within the Chavista trade union forces from 2003 onwards, the FBT tendency prevailed, thanks to the backing given by Chávez to its main leader, Nicolás Maduro. The formation of the Central Bolivariana Socialista de Trabajadores (CBST) in November 2011 took place under almost total control of the FSBT, with the more radical tendencies being completely displaced.

23. Maduro's first militancy was in the Socialist League party, a Marxist-Leninist organization that existed from the 1970s until its integration into the PSUV when the latter was formed by Chávez in 2007. The Socialist League sent Maduro to Cuba sometime in the 1980s for political training.

The failure of endogenous development projects, due to state mismanagement of nationalized companies, combined with the fall in oil prices over the 2012–22 decade, has generated a drop in production and an increase in foreign borrowing to fund the state apparatus and the importation of manufactured goods and foodstuffs. This is the background to the current scenario of hyperinflation, over-indebtedness and falling oil production (Vera 2018). It is important to note that this economic crisis has been exacerbated to the point of collapse, as a result of the blockade of assets, and the economic and financial sanctions, applied by the United States and its international allies in the course of 2017–19 (Ayala 2019: 23).

The decision to grant a license to the Arco Minero del Orinoco (AMO) project is perhaps the starkest example of the return to neoliberal economics. It involved the approval of the extraction of minerals in the states of Bolívar and Amazonas, on a surface equivalent to 12.2 per cent of the national territory, inhabited by 54,686 indigenous people and with significant ecological biodiversity. This territory was handed over to multinational companies for the exploitation of gold, copper, diamonds, coltan, iron bauxite and other minerals (Lander 2016). The approval of the AMO did not comply with the constitutional requirement to consult the indigenous communities living in the territory. The project also subordinates any disputes that may exist between the Venezuelan state and the contracting companies to international tribunals (ICSID), despite express constitutional provisions that reject any interference by foreign courts in the national economy[24] (El Estímulo 2016; Aporrea 2016). Similar to the maquiladora regions of traditional neoliberalism, the AMO does not recognize the validity of labour rights as laid out in the Constitution and the LOTTT in areas subject to mining concessions.

As Edgardo Lander puts it:

> The Venezuelan government is secretly taking strategic decisions that could be defining the future of the country for the rest of the century .... Through the presidential decree of the AMO, it was decided to create a ... mining free zone, under military control, where many of the constitutional rights, among others, the rights of indigenous peoples, are pre-emptively suspended.
>
> (Lander 2016: n.p.)

24. During the 1998 election campaign, Chávez emphasized that such clauses in the oil opening contracts (allowing disputes to be arbitrated in foreign courts) were tantamount to an act of treason. Later he ignored the concession made by the Caldera government to the Canadian mining company Gold Reserve and refused to pay ICSID compensation when the company appealed to the tribunal. Maduro, acting in reverse, contracted again with Gold Reserve and paid the compensation that Chávez had refused.

In terms of wage policy, the performance of wages during the period 1999–2020 shows an upward curve in the first half of the period (1999–2007) and a downward curve in the following years (2008–20). The fall in wages in recent years reaches levels not seen in any other neoliberal administration on the continent. Real wages in 2020 have fallen by 96 per cent since the period 2006–07 (Sutherland 2020). The Federation of Associations of University Professors of Venezuela (FAPUV) puts the fall in salaries in the period 2001–20 at 99 per cent (FAPUV 2020). This total collapse of real wages by 99 per cent is what explains the enormous migration of more than four million people from Venezuela since 2015. Biardeau points out the wage regression of Venezuelan workers is so pronounced that, in 2020, a Venezuelan worker's monthly salary was almost equivalent to that earned by an oil worker in a day's work 84 years earlier[25] at the time of the great oil strike of 1936 (5 bolivars a day equivalent to $1.57 a day) (Biardeau 2020).

Maduro's government, with memorandum 2792 of the Ministry of Labour of October 2018 (La Izquierda Diario 2018a), ignored all the collective bargaining agreements in force in the public administration and in the private sector, sweeping away, in a single act, all that had been achieved under Hugo Chávez. As the class-conscious trade union leader Orlando Chirino states: "In the labour relations of the last 30 years a government had not produced a legal instrument as reactionary and anti-worker as Memorandum 2792" (Chirino 2019: n.p.). The government's policy has been to "flatten" the wage tables, establishing minimal differences between starting salaries and the highest pay scales, violating the constitutional principle of progressivity in labour rights, ignoring seniority, professional and technical training, degrees of responsibility and the meritocracy of workers (La Izquierda Diario 2018a).

As can be seen from above, similar to the neoliberal programmes implemented by the governments of Carlos Andrés Pérez and Rafael Caldera between 1989 and 1999, Nicolás Maduro's government is following a neoliberal path in the design and implementation of its programmes. Below are details of just some of these programmes and their effects:

- Liberation of exchange control and free floating of the currency against the dollar. Since 2017 the bolivar has been devalued at the rate of hyperinflation.
- Import of food and other products free of tariffs. Import permits have been granted to businesses sympathetic to the government.
- Price liberalization of foodstuffs and other products from the basic food basket. When price regulations are established for a specific list of products, the amount needed to purchase that list is more than 20 times the official minimum wage (Aporrea 2020).

25. The minimum wage in Venezuela was, as of 4 July 2020, 400,000 Bs. per month. At the official exchange rate of 202,000 bolivars to the dollar, this is equivalent to US$1.98 per month.

- Pulverization of real wages, which in relation to the dollar have been reduced by between 96 per cent and 99 per cent in 20 years.
- Maintenance of VAT as a regressive tax that penalizes consumers.
- Privatization processes in major branches of industries such as oil, iron, aluminium, gold and diamonds and, in services such as petrol distribution, which by law is a function reserved to the state. The "unregulated" price of gasoline was set by the government at $0.50 per litre, introducing the dollar as the country's official currency (Vázquez Heredia 2020).
- Almost total labour flexibilization, with Memorandum 2792, which ignores the labour rights enshrined in the Constitution itself and in the LOTTT (Ministerio del Trabajo 2018).
- Limitations of the "missions" social policies, which are most effective in the capital Caracas, and are almost non-existent in the rest of the cities and towns (Transparencia Venezuela 2020). In recent years, the food box delivery service CLAP[26] has been added to the social missions as has the *carnet de la patria* (Aula Abierta 2018), which is random and irregular.[27]

At the same time, Maduro's government has developed a significant authoritarian profile, manifested in the following:

- The government has suspended the validity of the National Constitution through the so-called "Anti-Lockout Law"[28] (LAB), approved by the unconstitutional Constituent Assembly (2017–20), which allows the president of the republic to relax and suspend legal and constitutional regulations and norms to advance a reorganization and restructuring of public entities and state-owned companies, including the modification of the business regime, business model and the state's shareholding in mixed and public companies, in the context of a policy of opening up the economy to national and international capital (Márquez 2021).
- The LAB also empowers the president to negotiate the assets and liabilities of the republic in order to generate income, which, in plain language, is an open-ended authorization to liquidate the republic's assets through a process of privatization and renegotiation of financial liabilities. All of this, without being subject to legal and constitutional controls (Márquez 2021).

26. Food box provided by the government to workers and families through the Local Supply and Production Committees (Comités Locales de Abastecimiento y Producción). In major cities in the province, CLAPs arrive about twice a year.
27. The vouchers distributed through the *carnet de la patria* are not regular in their delivery, nor do they have fixed amounts. They do not provide any kind of stability to working families. Generally, the amount is between $1 and $2. A *carnet* holder can go several months without receiving a bonus.
28. The justification for passing this law has been the economic sanctions imposed by the US government against Venezuela.

- The LAB establishes exceptional contracting mechanisms, a regime of confidentiality for all economic decisions of the executive and submits disputes with foreign investors to foreign courts. All of this violates express provisions of the Constitution, annuls the National Assembly's oversight functions and ends up, effectively, abolishing the rule of law in Venezuela (Márquez 2021).
- The Regionalization Law (decree-law of 2014) and the Special Economic Zones Law (draft of 2021) aim at a reorganization of the territory of the republic, outside the territorial division enshrined in the Constitution. This is characterized by "maquila zones" and extractivist enclaves, typical of neoliberal "savage" capitalism, which involves the suppression of taxes, and the absence of labour and environmental regulations.
- The "Law Against Hatred" of 2017 established penalties that can include 20 years in jail, media shutdown, and fines to companies and electronic media. It has served to imprison dozens of opposition activists for merely criticizing the actions of the government (La Izquierda Diario 2018b; Crónica Uno 2020; Provea 2021).
- Finally, there has been an indefinite suspension of all trade union elections, non-recognition of the majority of workers' federations, and the use of small trade union organizations sympathetic to the government to simulate a non-existent "workers' democracy".

CONCLUSIONS

Despite many major mistakes made in his economic policy, the Chávez government made significant attempts to transcend neoliberalism and promote a productive economy, based on economic independence and popular participation. During the first decade of the twenty-first century, government policies enacted in Venezuela sought to leave behind oil rentierism and move towards a socialist economy.

After Chávez's death in 2013, neoliberalism and authoritarianism returned under the government of Nicolás Maduro. Economist Pasqualina Curcio (2020), a prominent supporter of Nicolás Maduro's government, recognizes how the distribution of gross domestic product (GDP) has changed regressively between 2014 and 2017.[29] Using a didactic example, Curcio explains that in 2014 "the cake of the Venezuelan economy", was

29. It only goes to 2017 because that is the last year in which the Central Bank of Venezuela (BCV) published statistics.

divided into 16, distributed in portions of: seven for the bourgeoisie, seven for wage earners, and two for the state (Curcio 2020). In 2017, with a cake one third smaller than in 2014 (according to the BCV, the economy shrank 34 per cent between 2014 and 2017), the distribution was: ten portions for the bourgeoisie, five for the wage earners, and one for the state. In terms of prices and wages, between 2014 and 2017 prices increased by 10.013 per cent and wages by only 6.436 per cent (Curcio 2020). Curcio herself recognizes that this distributional regression of GDP was further accentuated between 2017 and 2020.

Some direct consequences of this regression are detailed in a recent Caritas study, "Child Nutrition and Food Security" of April 2020 (Caritas 2020), which found that severe malnutrition in children under five years of age grew by 5.78 per cent in just six months, from 11.5 per cent in November 2019 to 17.3 per cent in April 2020. In the same period, the number of households with access to state-subsidized food through the "cajas CLAP" decreased by almost a third, from 73 per cent to 41 per cent, while numbers suffering from food insecurity grew from 32.2 per cent to 40 per cent, of which 21 per cent suffer from severe food insecurity (PCDC 2020).

The self-styled anti-imperialist character of Maduro's government,[30] has aligned itself with the Eastern Bloc made up mainly of China and Russia. However, it has simultaneously executed a neoliberal plan of privatizations, labour flexibilization and political repression against its own people. Despite this, the Maduro administration is seen as suspect by the governments of the United States (and its allies in the European Union), which has interfered in the internal affairs of Venezuela. This interference explicitly seeks the removal of Maduro from power, and the assumption of a political leadership docile to the interests of the Western powers.

In reality, Nicolás Maduro's government is one with similarities to the populist regimes of the twentieth century in Latin America, due to the predominance of an extremely radical demagogic discourse that is not inconsistent with an authoritarian and neoliberal bent, but with an orientation to the people and in the interests of national development. A complex and contradictory reality, which shows how the interests of big multinational capital have no ideological boundaries and how the neoliberal economic programme can be implemented by governments that formally declare themselves to be enemies of this same neoliberalism.

30. Anti-imperialist in relation to the West but aligned with China and Russia, which, in economic terms, is not distanced from the neoliberal philosophy. In fact, some analysts such as Hernández Parra (2020) point to China as the new model that inspires the International Monetary Fund.

REFERENCES

Adarfio, A. 2011. "El Control Obrero en el Nuevo Modelo Productivo". *Revista Comuna* 3: 43–56.

Alarcón, J. 2017. "Maduro y su "socialismo" neoliberal". www.aporrea.org/actualidad/a254516.html.

Alayón, R. 2007. *La rebelión latinoamericana a la globalización neoliberal*. Caracas: Instituto de Altos Estudios "Pedro Gual".

Aporrea 2016. "Venezuela indemnizará a Gold Reserve por $759 millones". www.aporrea.org/economia/n295027.html.

Aporrea 2020. "Conozca el precio en dólares que impuso el gobierno a 27 productos regulados". www.aporrea.org/economia/n354661.html.

Aula Abierta 2018. "Carnet de la Patria: Discriminación para el control político". http://aulaabiertavenezuela.org/index.php/2018/08/31/carne-de-la-patria-discriminacion-para-el-control-politico/.

Ayala, M. 2019. "Estructura y coyuntura en la crisis venezolana". *Cuadernos de Coyuntura* 4: 21–30. https://revistas.unc.edu.ar/index.php/CuadernosConyuntura/issue/view/1980.

Barrios-Ferrer, G. 1990. "Los sucesos del 27 y 28 de febrero de 1989". *Argos* 11: 55–88.

Bermúdez, A. 2016. "Cómo Venezuela pasó de la bonanza petrolera a la emergencia económica". BBC Mundo. www.bbc.com/mundo/noticias/2016/02/160219_venezuela_bonanza_petroleo_crisis_economica_ab.

Biardeau, J. 2015. "Hugo Chávez y la Declaración del "Socialismo". www.aporrea.org/internacionales/a209620.html.

Biardeau, J. 2020. "Estructura de repetición del rentismo y conciencia sumisa-enajenada". www.aporrea.org/ideologia/a291706.html.

Carcione, C. 2009. "Lo que fue privatizado, nacionalícese". *Comuna* 1: 13–19.

Carcione, C. 2010. "Experiencias de Democracia Obrera en la Venezuela Bolivariana". *Comuna* 2: 56–71.

Carcione, C. & M. Poliak 2010. "El Plan Guayana Socialista en la encrucijada". *Comuna* 3: 57–62.

Caritas Venezuela 2020. "Nutrición infantil y seguridad alimentaria". http://caritasvenezuela.org/wp-content/uploads/2020/06/Caritas-Informe-de-Desnutricion-Abril-2020.pdf.

Carvallo, G. & M. López Maya. 1989. "Crisis en el sistema político venezolano". *Cuadernos del Cendes* 10: 47–53.

Chirino, O. 2005. *Orlando Chirino responde*. Caracas: Equipo Editorial Aporrea.org.

Chirino, O. 2019. "El memorándum 2792 es una reforma laboral antiobrera y reaccionaria". http://deslinde2011.blogspot.com/2019/05/orlando-chirino-el-memorandum-2792-es.html.

Comisión de Sistematización Plan Guayana Socialista 2013. "Sistematización del Balance del Plan Guayana Socialista". www.aporrea.org/trabajadores/a175676.html.

Crónica Uno 2020. "Luego de 8 días presos, fueron liberados los tres sindicalistas de Sucre". https://cronica.uno/luego-de-8-dias-presos-fueron-liberados-los-tres-sindicalistas-de-sucre/.

Curcio, P. 2020. "La economía: números imposibles de manipular y no para insultar". Últimas Noticias. https://ultimasnoticias.com.ve/noticias/opinion/abrebrecha-la-economia-numeros-imposibles-de-manipular-y-no-para-insultar/.

Ellner, S. 2009. "Las reformas neoliberales y la crisis política venezolana, 1989–1999". In M. Ayala & P. Quintero (eds), *Diez años de revolución en Venezuela: Historia, balance y perspectivas (1999–2009)*. Buenos Aires: Editorial Maipue.

El Estímulo 2016. "Venezuela indemnizará a Gold Reserve con $769 millones por expropiación". https://elestimulo.com/venezuela-indemnizara-a-gold-reserve-con-769-millones-por-toma-de-activos/.

España, L. 1989. "Un estallido social no esperado". *SIC* 513: 118–19.

FAPUV 2020. "Significado y alcance de la recuperación del salario y la seguridad social de los profesores universitarios de Venezuela". Federación de Asociaciones de Profesores Universitarios de Venezuela. https://infofapuv.com/2020/06/10/significado-y-alcance-de-la-recuperacion-del-salario-y-la-seguridad-social-de-los-profesores-universitarios-de-venezuela/.

García, A. 2011. "La contrarrevolución obrera: FBT". www.aporrea.org/endogeno/a125298.html.

Giacalone, R. 2003. "Privatización del acero en Argentina, México y Venezuela". *Nordic Journal of Latin American and Caribbean Studies* 33: 53–87. www.iberoamericana.se/articles/abstract/10.16993/ibero.380/.

Hernández Parra, P. 2020. "Sr Trump: la suerte está echada. O cruza el Rubicon o muere en el intento". www.aporrea.org/internacionales/a291537.html.

Karg, J. & Lewit, A. 2015. "Del No al ALCA a Unasur. Diez años después de Mar del Plata". *Idelcoop* 217. www.idelcoop.org.ar/sites/www.idelcoop.org.ar/files/revista/articulos/pdf/revista-217-web-resenas-01.pdf.

Lander, E. 1994: "El impacto del ajuste neoliberal (1989–1993)". In E. Lander (ed.), *Neoliberalismo, Sociedad Civil y Democracia. Ensayos Sobre América Latina y Venezuela*, 107–51. Caracas: Universidad Central de Venezuela.

Lander, E. 2016. "Comentarios sobre el acuerdo con la Gold Reserve". www.aporrea.org/contraloria/a232524.html.

La Izquierda Diario 2018a. "Trabajadores marcharon en Caracas contra el plan de ajuste de Maduro y los empresarios". www.laizquierdadiario.com.ve/Trabajadores-marcharon-en-Caracas-contra-el-plan-de-ajuste-de-Maduro-y-los-empresarios.

La Izquierda Diario 2018b. "Detienen al dirigente sindical Rubén González". www.laizquierdadiario.com.ve/Detienen-al-dirigente-sindical-Ruben-Gonzalez-regresando-de-la-marcha-convocada-por-la.

López Maya, M. 1994. "Venezuela: El impacto de sus reformas políticas durante el lapso crítico de 1989–1993". *Cuadernos del Cendes* 26: 27–54.

López Sánchez, R. 2017a. "El movimiento de trabajadores durante el gobierno de Hugo Chávez (1999–2012)". *Notas Históricas y Geográficas*. 19: 34–50. http://revistanhyg.cl/articulos/category/num-19-sep-dic-2017/.

López Sánchez, R. 2017b. *El movimiento de trabajadores en Venezuela durante la revolución bolivariana: 1999–2012.* Caracas: Fundación Editorial El perro y la rana.

López Sánchez, R. & C. Hernández. 2016. "Control obrero y consejos de trabajadores, nuevas formas de gestión productiva". *Opción* 32(80): 184–214. www.redalyc.org/pdf/310/31047691009.pdf.

Luna, M. 2019. "El paquetazo de Moreno nos distrae del paquetazo de Maduro". www.aporrea.org/economia/a283224.html.

Márquez, G. 2021. "El gobierno de Maduro construye un Régimen Autoritario Neoliberal Periférico y Extractivista Ampliado". www.aporrea.org/economia/a304634.html.

Martínez, I. 2018. "Chávez, Maduro y la Tercera Vía". *El País*, 20 August. https://elpais.com/internacional/2018/08/20/america/1534802084_511115.html

Mateo Tomé, J. 2010. "La evolución de los salarios en Venezuela". *Boletín Económico de Información Comercial Española* 2994: 43–57.

Ministerio del Trabajo 2018. Memorando-circular nº 2792. www.laizquierdadiario.com.ve/IMG/pdf/lineamiento_para_las_negociaciones_colectivas-2.pdf.

PCDC 2020. "Acuerdo pre-electoral para atender la emergencia social". *Plataforma Ciudadana en Defensa de la Constitución*. www.aporrea.org/actualidad/a292368.html.

Pérez Borges, S. 2010. "Hacia un nuevo modelo sindical". *Comuna* 3: 63–97.

Pérez Borges, S. *et al.* 2009. "La nacionalización de Sidor" *Comuna* 1: 23–51.

Prato Barbosa, N. 1994. "Crisis y desobediencia social en Venezuela". *Cuadernos del CENDES* 11(26).

Provea 2021. "Provea reclamó libertad para trabajadores petroleros presos". www.elnacional.com/venezuela/provea-reclamo-libertad-para-los-trabajadores-petroleros-presos/.

Rengifo, S. and J. Medina. 2019. "El populismo en Amèrica Latina: debate en torno a una vaguedad conceptual". *Revista Tecnologia e Sociedade* 15(36): 235–53.

Rivero, A. 2010. "La coherencia de la FBT en Guayana". www.aporrea.org/trabajadores/a112509.html.

Rodríguez Rojas, P. 2010. "Venezuela: del neoliberalismo al socialismo del siglo XXI". *Política y cultura* 34: 187–211.

Stanley, M. 2000. "El populismo en América Latina". *Anuario del Departamento de Ciencias de la Comunicación* 5. https://docer.com.ar/doc/xvec85v.

Straka, T. 2019. "20 años de chavismo: El quiebre del estado mágico". *Nueva Sociedad* 280. https://nuso.org/articulo/20-anos-de-chavismo-el-quiebre-del-estado-magico/.

Sutherland, M. 2018. "¿Nicolás Maduro tiene un plan?". *Nueva Sociedad*. www.nuso.org/articulo/nicolas-maduro-tiene-un-plan/.

Sutherland, M. 2020. "Venezuela: Salario Cero". www.aporrea.org/economia/a290026.html.

Toussaint, E. 2009. "Latinoamérica: en pro de una integración regional y una desvinculación parcial del mercado capitalista mundial". In *Respuestas del Sur a la crisis económica mundial*. Caracas: Centro Internacional Miranda. www.cadtm.org/Latinoamerica-en-pro-de-una?debut_tous_articles_auteur=340.

Transparencia Venezuela 2020. "Clap llega a su cuarto aniversario marcado por la corrupción y la improvisación". https://transparencia.org.ve/clap-llega-a-su-cuarto-aniversario-marcado-por-la-corrupcion-y-la-improvisacion/.

Vásquez Heredia, O. 2020. "Maduro anunció privatización y liberalización de facto del mercado interno de gasolina". www.aporrea.org/energia/a291164.html.

Vera, L. 2018. "¿Cómo explicar la catástrofe económica venezolana?". *Nueva Sociedad* 274 . https://nuso.org/articulo/como-explicar-la-catastrofe-economica-venezolana/.

Vilas, C. 1988. "El populismo latinoamericano: un enfoque estructural". *Desarrollo Económico* 28(111).

Vivas Santana, J. 2019. "Maduro aplica disimulado y tardío plan de ajuste neoliberal". www.aporrea.org/actualidad/a279339.html.

CHAPTER 8

POPULIST RESPONSES TO CRISES OF MARKET DEMOCRACY: THE CASE OF BOLIVIA'S EVO MORALES

John Brown

Populist movements emerge as responses to crises of representation whereby elites are incapable/refuse to respond to people's grievances (Arditi 2007: 56). Populism may thus be understood as a regular feature of politics, representing a subversive challenge to the status quo, and as a launching point for a reconstruction of a new order when the previous one has lost legitimacy (Laclau 2005: 177). Indeed, populism may be understood as part of a process of social transformation, a protective movement of society in response to the excessive expansion of the free market (Polanyi 1944).

Where the interests of the wealthiest sectors of society are organized into politics, while issues concerning popular classes are organized out, democracy loses legitimacy. Where left/right party-party differences narrow, popular indifference and distrust of parties and institutions grows (Mair 2013). Mistrust in the political system, alongside withdrawal from participation, opens space for a movement of opposition (Schmitter 2019: 152). As parties/politicians become detached from their traditional social bases, while inequality and socioeconomic precarity become entrenched, democracy is viewed by excluded sectors as a facade for the maintenance of elite privilege. Appealing to a sense of personal danger and a shared sense of political exclusion, populists may portray the political class as having failed, and likely to continue to fail, effectively barring citizens from any realistic prospect of a better life (Dunn 2019: 56).

Such a decomposition of legitimacy of the prevailing model of democracy occurred in several Latin American states around the turn of the millennium. Anti-system outsiders emerged where labour-based and centre-left parties were at the forefront of advancing neoliberal policies, a configuration found in Bolivia, Ecuador and Venezuela (Roberts 2015). The adoption of neoliberal policies by centre-left parties caused party systems to converge around variants of market orthodoxy, programmatically de-aligning partisan competition and channelling societal opposition into extra-systemic forms of social and electoral protest, thereby opening vacant political space for outsiders on the left flank of mainstream parties (*ibid.*)

Traditional parties "were perceived as instruments of local and foreign elites that implemented neoliberal policies and thereby increased social inequality" (de la Torre 2016: 64). As satisfaction with the economically and politically exclusionary market model of democracy sagged, waves of anti-neoliberal mobilization erupted. Protests represented a struggle for reincorporation, whereby excluded segments of society sought to (re)connect with state institutions, so as to gain access to rights the state failed to provide (Rossi & Silva 2018). Populist leaders successfully bound sectorial and group interests together by framing the grievances of women, Afro-Latinos, indigenous groups, urban and rural popular groups, informal workers and landless peasants, among others, as issues of democratic citizenship that the neoliberal-inspired market-democracy denied (Silva 2009). The populist nature of Latin America's outsiders refers to challenging political-economic elites, whose insider status is founded on the exclusion of other sectors of the national community (Roberts 2019). Populism in the Andes, then, should be understood as a response to a *crisis of too little democracy* (Brown 2020b), with popular blocs and populist leaders challenging the status quo of incorporation for a minority elite bloc and political and socioeconomic exclusion for the majority.

Unsurprisingly, such populist challengers triggered intense resistance from those sectors of society who had commanded, and benefited from, the market model. While left-led governments faced opposition blocs who demanded pro-market orthodoxy and a protection of pre-existing political/economic power distribution, they simultaneously faced pressure from organized popular sectors via social movements/unions/neighbourhood organizations for greater participation and improved living conditions. It is by grasping the nature of these varied and evolving power struggles that one can understand the advances and limitations of the reform processes. Moreover, analysing populist performance via such a relative power lens helps to shed light on the realities of actually existing populism, whereby processes may entail simultaneous democratizing and de-democratizing features.

Scholars from the liberal tradition describe how populist leaders such as Hugo Chávez, Evo Morales and Rafael Correa threatened democracy by challenging liberal norms. For example, Weyland (2013) outlines the ways these leaders eroded institutional checks and balances and marginalized the opposition through "discriminatory legalism". Levitsky and Loxton (2013: 109) describe these cases as being "competitive authoritarian", whereby democratic institutions exist and are used as the primary routes to power, but incumbents then abuse state powers to skew electoral competition in their favour, to such an extent that an opposition's ability to compete is seriously compromised. Leaders in these cases were said to rely on "populist rhetoric" to build their political hegemony, before riding roughshod over democratic norms by boosting the power of the executive.

While liberal scholars decry the "hyper-presidential" nature of the "radical" left cases, anti-system outsiders in the Andes emphasized that entrenched political-economic elites blocked programmes for change, and hence they argued for a strong president who relied on "plebiscitarian appeals for popular support" so as to "counter the bias toward the status quo" (Munck 2015: 374). Illiberal populist responses to exclusionary, elite-dominated market democracy resonate with Slater's (2013) notion that democracies will careen between oligarchic forms and domineering populist forms as intense conflicts between partisan actors, deploying competing visions of democratic accountability, emerge. Populists will call for more substantial inclusivity or vertical accountability, while opponents will defend democracy for the constraints against excessive concentration of unaccountable power in the executive – that is, horizontal accountability. Such competing visions speak to the democratizing potentials and dangers of populism. While many theorists condemn populism as a threat to liberal democracy, Berman notes that "although it is certainly true that democracy unchecked by liberalism can slide into excessive majoritarianism or oppressive populism, liberalism unchecked by democracy can easily deteriorate into oligarchy" (Berman 2017: 30). It is useful, therefore, to appraise the impact of populists on democratic quality, not only in terms of respect for liberal norms, but also in terms of their success, or otherwise, of deepening and extending democratic quality by boosting the participatory and substantive incorporation of erstwhile excluded groups. The remainder of this chapter examines the emergence, development and potential legacy of the process headed by Evo Morales in Bolivia.

ANTECEDENT ERA: MARKET DEMOCRACY AND POPULAR RESISTANCE

A New Economic Policy was designed by the IMF and implemented under decree by Bolivian president Víctor Paz Estenssoro (1985–89). Currency devaluation, free-floating exchange rates and interest rate liberalization were adopted. Public sector spending declined, and state lending and subsidies to the mining and traditional agricultural sector were restricted. The "imposition of the New Economic Policy by 'shock treatment' caused profound economic and political exclusion of the popular sectors, deeply threatening their livelihood and leaving them without defences within established political institutions" (Silva 2009: 109).

In 1993, Gonzalo Sánchez de Lozada became president (1993–97) and adopted further neoliberal reforms that eroded the quality of political and socioeconomic citizenship for popular sectors. A privatization drive saw the majority of shares of publicly owned companies in energy, telecommunications and transport transferred to multinational corporations (Trujillo & Spronk 2018: 135). Massive job losses, subcontracting of work to non-unionized labour, the atomization of workers as factories were replaced by smaller workshops, and informalization all followed privatization. A shift in agricultural policy witnessed transnational corporations (TNCs) and large domestic agricultural enterprises, based in the *media luna*[1] departments, lead a drive to insertion in the global economy. Peasants lost land, credit and markets for their crops, fostering an urbanization of rural labour. Reductions or eliminations of subsidies to staple foodstuffs, utilities, fuel and transport worsened the economic exclusion of swathes of society, where poverty levels remained above 50 per cent in urban areas and 77 in rural zones. Policymaking was dominated by the interests of capital, guided by supranational agencies, and decisions were taken in a technocratic and unaccountable manner. Excessive use of presidential decrees, scant legislative debate and a lack of consideration for the interests, demands and priorities of subordinate social groups became the norm.

A wave of protest erupted during the presidencies of Hugo Banzer (1997–2002), de Lozada (2002–03), and Carlos Mesa (2003–05), as the presidents adopted economically exclusionary reforms without popular sector inclusion in decision making. During the Cochabamba Water War – a series of massive protests over a water privatization scheme in the city – popular protest movements began to forge links with political parties, particularly the Movimiento al Socialismo (MAS) party headed by Evo Morales. MAS was a movement party in that it engaged in electoral politics and competed for office, while at the same time it engaged in extra-parliamentary struggles and bargaining in pursuit of a programmatic agenda. The MAS used the context of the Water War to adopt a "plural popular" (Albro 2005) strategy of coalition building, in which "indigenous issues became the framing plank for successful political articulation" (Anria 2013: 27). Morales, via the MAS, played a key role in coordinating among multiple groups – peasant organizations, cocaleros, urban labour unions, and urban neighbourhood organizations – by framing specific group or organization grievances as issues that emerged due to Bolivia's market democracy.

1. The term *media luna* (half moon) refers to the crescent shape formed by the boundaries of the departments of Santa Cruz, Beni, Pando and Tarija, where the most conservative sectors of the political and economic elite opposition are located.

Following the 2002 election of de Lozada, under IMF-direction the government implemented economic stabilization policies, including income tax rises and a moratorium on public sector pay rises. In October 2003 residents in the city of El Alto coordinated enormous demonstrations when de Lozada's plans to give TNCs concessions to pipe Bolivia's natural gas to Chilean ports, for export to the US, were unveiled. The "terms of the concession to foreign capital, framed as a giveaway, turned the issue into a symbol of the popular sector's exclusion from market society" (Silva 2009: 134–5) and the wave of protests that engulfed El Alto and then spread across the country became known as the 2003 Gas War.

The government ordered the military to break up marches, with troops killing scores of civilians. The repression backfired. Mass protests erupted across the country calling for the president's resignation, with miners and protesters from Oruro and Potosí, coca growers from Chapare and peasants from the highlands converging in La Paz. A set of demands emerged, calling for the ousting of the president and his neoliberal model, as well as the nationalization of gas. With an estimated 500,000 people in the streets, de Lozada fled the country for exile in the US with vice-president Carlos Mesa taking over.

Mesa initially sought to appease mobilized popular sectors but, as economic elites increased pressure on him, and with the TNCs, IMF and US embassy allying behind the domestic elites, Mesa dropped any pretence of supporting popular demands (Gustafson 2020: 113; Webber 2010: 54). However, popular organizations at the local, regional and national levels coordinated protests, mobilizing hundreds of thousands of protesters, effectively shutting down the cities of La Paz and El Alto and forcing Mesa to resign.

During Mesa's presidency, "Bolivia was characterized by a deepening political polarization along the axes of class, race, and region" (Webber 2010: 52). Two social blocs emerged. First was a left-indigenous bloc, comprised predominantly of indigenous urban proletarian and peasant forces. The second bloc, which consolidated between October 2003 and June 2005, "was an eastern-bourgeois bloc led by the regional bourgeoisies of the hydrocarbons-rich departments of the *media luna*" (*ibid.*).

The convergence around structural adjustment policies by all the mainstream parties – including supposed leftist parties – and the backtracking on campaign promises by elected officials, meant that popular sector anger and aspirations were funnelled into extra-systemic forms of social and electoral protest. The MAS filled the void created by the decline of the traditional parties who were associated with neoliberalism. Morales and the MAS easily won the 2005 elections in the first round, setting the stage for new struggles between the competing social blocs around competing notions of democracy.

CONSTRUCTING POST-NEOLIBERAL DEMOCRACY AND THE CONSTITUENT ASSEMBLY PROCESS (2006–09)

Following the collapse of the traditional party system and the delegitimation of the market model of democracy, in conjunction with the waves of anti-neoliberal protests coordinated by powerful popular organizations, Morales was elected to office with the ideological scope and popular backing to advance an alternative, post-neoliberal democracy. However, an opposition bloc cleaved around protection of the status quo and market democracy. In the political sphere, despite winning the presidential election and a simple majority in the Chamber of Deputies, the MAS did not control the senate or the conservative judiciary. Furthermore, opposition bloc politicians won control of the majority of departmental governments, including those regions where key sources of economic power lay (finance, agro-industry and hydrocarbons). They also dominated the ideological sources of power (media, churches), and wielded control over fascistic mobs (a form of military power) who engaged in violent repression of government supporters.

In June 2006 the government presented the National Development Plan (NDP) 2007 that called for a deepening and extending of democracy. The plan offered an alternative vision to that of market democracy and called for *buen vivir*, an indigenous vision based on communitarian forms of living together. The plan outlined that the state needed to intervene as "promoter and protagonist of national development", whereby the state would act to transform society and the economy, but only if "all peoples and cultures are present in the economic and political decisions of the state".

The plan was based around developing two sectors of the economy. The first comprised surplus-generating activities such as hydrocarbons, electricity, mining and natural resources, and the second was made up of employment- and income-generating sectors such as tourism, agriculture, manufacturing, transport and services. The plan called for revenues, generated through increased state control over the surplus-generating sectors, to be redirected toward the transformation of the employment-/revenue-generating sectors via state spending and redistribution, boosting internal demand and supporting social equality. Nationalization of primary commodity sectors was also to be used to develop the industrialization of primary materials (Arze 2016).

In May 2006, Morales declared that Bolivia's hydrocarbon sector was to be nationalized, so as to allow the state to increase the price of, and rents from, its natural gas exports. Via decree 28701, "the Morales administration recovered the state's right to commercialize its hydrocarbons and increased the prices it received from the sale of its natural gas" (Kaup 2010: 129).

As discussed in detail below, while the "nationalization" was in fact moderate, the changes represented a fundamental shift in the state's role in the hydrocarbon sector and boosted the fiscal capacity of the government.

The NDP plan to deepen popular sector voices in decision-making and to extend democratic quality, via increased state control over the economy and redistributive social policies, as well as indications that there would be a reform of land ownership, directly challenged elite interests. In response to the NDP, elites in the *media luna* engaged in a legal (via a supportive judiciary) and (often violent) extra-institutional struggle for regional autonomy, with the backing of allied media, in a bid to avoid the proposed changes to the status of private property rights, land reform and redistribution of state revenue.

While the opposition bloc pressurized the MAS from the right, powerful popular organizations pushed the MAS from below to advance the process. It is crucial to highlight that the MAS had both a core social coalition and a more autonomous bloc of movement organizations that engaged with it in a strategic alliance. The core was composed of an "inner circle" that included: the cocaleros; the Six Federations of the Tropics unions; the Bartolina Sisa National Confederation of Campesino, Indigenous, and Native Women of Bolivia (CNMCIOB-BS); and the Unitary Syndical Confederation of Peasant Workers of Bolivia (CSUTCB). The second strategic bloc included: the principal labour union, the Bolivian Workers Central (COB); public sector unions; urban informal sector workers organized in neighbourhood associations called the Federation of Neighbourhood Associations (FEJUVE) especially in El Alto; informal sector miners' unions, the so-called *cooperativistas*; and the National Council of Ayllus and Markas of Qullasuyu (CONAMAQ).

In the tug-of-war between the opposition bloc and popular demands, with the government located in between, MAS was heavily reliant on defensive mobilization by the popular base to prevent elite destabilization tactics from succeeding. Having been elected on an anti-neoliberal mandate, with large-scale popular backing, and with powerful movements pushing the government from below, yet confronting a recalcitrant opposition bloc determined to block the post-neoliberal agenda, the Morales government justified bending liberal norms as necessary to weaken/overcome opposition.

For example, to combat the conservative bias in the judiciary, the MAS pressurized some sitting judges, including the chief justice of the Supreme Court, by filing criminal charges against them. According to Sánchez-Sibony (2021), the MAS-government denounced the judiciary publicly, claiming it was corrupt, and mobilized supporters to demand the resignation of members of the Constitutional Tribunal and the Supreme Court. There were also frequent confrontations with the traditional media who were linked to the elite landowning families of the *media luna*, with Morales describing them as a principal enemy of the post-neoliberal project.

Such illiberal behaviour retained popular support, as it was considered part of the struggle against a pro-neoliberal opposition bloc intent on restraining the MAS's attempts to adhere to electoral promises to move toward a post-neoliberal model of democracy that deepened and extended the quality of citizenship for long-excluded groups. Facing a common enemy, an ally-type, party-base relationship developed. Indeed, during this first stage of the post-neoliberal process, via the Unity Pact,[2] CONALCAM,[3] the Constituent Assembly process, the promulgation of a new Constitution and the appointment of movement/organization leaders to ministry positions, the quality of democracy for popular sectors who had been excluded in the preceding market democracy era was deepened and extended.

In January 2009 voters approved a new Constitution by 61.4 per cent to 38.6 per cent. The Constitution outlines various mechanisms that seek to deepen and extend democracy. Adhering to Unity Pact demands, the Constitution redefined the nation as "plurinational and communitarian". Bolivia's democracy is described in article 1.1 as "participatory, representative and communitarian". In addition to standard liberal representative democracy, mechanisms of direct and participatory democracy include referendum, recall of public servants, prior consultation and legislative initiatives of citizens. Furthermore, members of the judiciary, after pre-selection by the legislative, are to be elected by the populace. Organized civil society is to participate in the design of public politics, and to execute social control at all levels of the state. In terms of extending democracy, the 2009 Constitution supports economic, social, and cultural rights for underprivileged groups, proclaiming its primary goal as to achieve *buen vivir*. To achieve this, the Constitution calls for the distribution of the surplus from non-renewable resource extraction to all citizens.

Despite the forging of ally-type relations between MAS and popular organizations, the 2009–14 period would witness the emergence of party-base tensions. To understand why, it is necessary to outline the nature of government–TNC relations post-2010 and how these shaped state autonomy.

2. The Unity Pact was a coalition of popular movements, who came together in order to fight first for the realization of the Constituent Assembly and, after that process had begun, to articulate and promote campesino and indigenous interests in the assembly (Zuazo 2010: 129).
3. In response to opposition bloc destabilizing tactics, and stemming from the Unity Pact, Morales organized supporters from the top down into the Coordinadora Nacional por el Cambio (CONALCAM).

TENSIONS IN THE POST-NEOLIBERAL PROCESS (2009–14)

Before Morales's re-election in 2009, "Bolivian politics was characterized by sharp polarization between the opposition on the right and the government and its allies on the left" (Ellner 2013: 17). However, with the promulgation of the new constitution and the retreat of the erstwhile secessionists into institutional channels of opposition, the MAS was no longer able to rally the base against a common enemy (Fontana 2013). In fact, after the secessionist drive was defeated, tensions escalated between party and base.

To fulfil the promises to boost social citizenship, Morales depended on revenues from the country's natural-resource industries. However, he had inherited an extractive industry with path-dependencies that imbued TNCs with high levels of structural power (Kaup 2010). The state gas company, YPFB, and the hydrocarbon sector in general, had received very little investment since the late 1990s. Furthermore, the gas industry was dominated by Petrobras and Repsol, which had long-term contracts giving them access to hydrocarbon reserves that bi- and multilateral trade agreements legally guaranteed (Kaup 2013).

Morales was elected promising to eliminate the worst excesses of economic exclusion, but this was not an easily fulfilled promise. The Bolivian economy was underdeveloped and reliant on commodity exports; the state extraction company was underfunded and outdated; and transnational extractive firms were contractually and infrastructurally embedded in the economy and had the extractive capacity and capital to invest in new explorations. In this context, Morales could not push for wholesale nationalization (Kaup 2010: 135). However, taxes and royalties on transnational corporations were increased, boosting state income from gas exports, from US$673 million in 2005, to more than US$5 billion in 2013. YPFB increased its role, both operationally and as an auditor, while it had a greater voice in determining the destination of investments (Paz & Ramírez-Cendero 2021: 138, 144). Despite these advances, the state sought only to regain control of previously capitalized assets, and the firms holding these assets extracted a small percentage of Bolivia's gas (Kaup 2010). Hence, most of the hydrocarbon value chain was not nationalized.

Public expenditure, underpinned by a commodities boom and the increased taxes and royalties on hydrocarbon exports, increased by 500 per cent between 2006 and 2013 (Arteaga 2015). There were significant investments in education and health. Transfers such as the Bono Juancito Pinto, which aimed at incentivizing school attendance, covered 1.8 million children; all of the population were eligible for Renta Dignidad, an old-age pension; and the Bono Juana Azurduy aimed to lower maternal-infant mortality rates and chronic child malnutrition. From 1999 to 2011, average income rose 45 per cent, and 182 per cent among rural populations (*ibid.*)

The real minimum wage increased by 87.7 per cent from 2005–14 (Johnson & Lefebvre 2014). Inequality decreased, with the income of poorer sectors of the population growing much faster since 2006 than that of the higher-income households. Poverty was reduced between 2005 and 2011 from 59.6 per cent to 45 per cent, and extreme poverty fell from 36.7 per cent to 20.9 per cent (*ibid.*).

There was a clear movement toward a post-neoliberal model of development and democracy, and Morales and the MAS presented their project as a radical alternative to neoliberalism, involving a diversification of the economy away from primary export-based development, accompanied by a nationalization of Bolivia's natural resources. However, neither of these goals was fully achieved. Bolivia became more dependent on primary exports than before, with primary goods increasing from 89 per cent of total export value in 2005 to 95 per cent in 2012 (ECLAC 2013: 111). Hydrocarbons, as a share of total export value, increased from 35 per cent before Morales's first election to 51 per cent in the 2011–14 period (Arze 2016). Furthermore, Petrobras and Repsol, two transnational companies, retained control over 75 per cent of natural gas production. Such compromise, while allowing Morales to govern, restricted the space for a more radical agenda. Despite popular sector support for a radical-substantive democratization project, the moderation of the project, in the face of the structural power of economic opposition, triggered a recalibration of party–base relations.

Leaders from those organizations that were part of the original core of the MAS tended to gain access to ministries more than non-core organizations who strategically supported and allied with the MAS. Core organizations' choices for MAS candidates to fill representative roles in the legislature were accepted more often, and their voices carried more weight in participatory spaces, such as CONALCAM. For strategic organizations, however, the post-neoliberal project contained regressive elements of top-down meddling. Those organizations who sought to challenge the MAS's development plan – either because it was considered too moderate and ceded too much ground to domestic and transnational economic elites, or because it relied on a continual encroachment into indigenous lands – faced an increasingly hostile environment. The MAS leadership sought to weaken contestatory organizations via a divide-and-conquer strategy. By incorporating militant leaders into the party structure, MAS leaders sought to ensure a calm governing environment. Co-opted organization leaders were required to show political loyalty if they wished to receive a cut of the public funds, which they required in order to respond to the demands of their base (Tapia 2011; Lazar 2008).

In conjunction with co-opting, the MAS fostered *paralelismo*, that is, the creating of parallel organizations to existing contestatory organizations. Factions of popular organization leaderships who would support the MAS and refrain from contestatory mobilization against MAS policies were identified and funded, while critical voices were side-lined. If confrontations emerged with core-allies, the government framed these as "creative tensions" but, where strategic groups' mobilizations directly challenged the underpinning development model and government–business relations, they were labelled "counterrevolutionary" (Trujillo & Spronk 2018). The outcome was a divided and confused base, whose collective power was diminished, while social movements, indigenous communities and former allies turned against each other. These processes of co-optation, division and *paralelismo* were also evidenced, among others – the CONAMAQ, CIDOB, urban popular organizations such as the FEJUVEs, and the Assembly of Guaraní People (APG) (Brown 2020a; Schilling-Vacaflor 2017; Morales 2013).

RE-ELECTION REFERENDUM, CONTESTED ELECTIONS, COUP AND A NEW MAS-LED ERA (2014–21)

In the 2014 presidential elections Morales won 61 per cent of the vote. At the inauguration of his third term, he outlined a ten-year development plan – the Patriotic Agenda 2025. The Agenda outlined plans to continue using extraction to finance development. As vice-president García-Linera stated in August 2016, "we are going to use extractivism for at least two decades more" in order to develop and protect society. Moreover, with "no other strong national leadership in the wings, MAS party logic held that a fourth presidential term for Morales was critical to accomplish this mission" (Achtenberg 2016: 374–5). Thus, Morales sought a referendum on modifying the Constitution to allow a third re-election. A "No" coalition formed around traditional right-wing politicians. In addition, "ex-MASistas" and representatives of alienated left-popular sectors, seeking to rehabilitate what they perceived as a stagnating "process of change", constituted themselves as the "popular No" bloc, and rejected the referendum process (*ibid.*).

The referendum was narrowly defeated by 51.3 per cent, thereby blocking the possibility of re-election for Morales. However, the MAS asked the Constitutional Tribunal to rescind limits on elected authorities seeking re-election, arguing that they violate human rights. The Constitutional Tribunal ruled that all elected officials could run for office indefinitely. The illiberal use of presidential power to meddle in judicial affairs, alongside the court's decision to allow re-election, galvanized the divided political opposition, while further de-legitimizing Morales in the eyes of some former allies.

The referendum defeat reignited the dispute over the meaning of democracy, with opposition protests focusing on the defence of liberal norms, such as alternation of leaders, pluralism, and the rule of law. As Mayorga (2020: 6) states, the MAS responded to such critiques of its democratic credentials by focusing on the participative and substantive components of democracy, highlighting that there is an equivalence between democracy and justice.

Following the "no" vote in the 2016 referendum, and the judicial decision to allow Morales to run, in the lead up to the 2019 elections the opposition bloc pushed the narrative that an authoritarian, illiberal MAS would do anything to stay in power. According to early polling, Morales's main rival was former president Carlos Mesa. To avoid a second-round run-off required winning a simple majority or more than 40 per cent of the vote plus a 10 per cent margin of victory over the nearest rival. With almost 84 per cent of the votes counted, and with Morales leading with 45.3 per cent to Mesa's 38.2 per cent, the unofficial online counting system (*trep*) stopped live transmission of the quick-count ballots. The following day, following a request from the Organization of American States (OAS) for a resumption of the *trep*, updated results were presented, reflecting 95 per cent of tally sheets. Morales' margin of victory had narrowly exceeded the 10 per cent required to avoid a second-round run-off. The OAS immediately stated their "deep concern" about the "change in trend", creating the impression that fraud had taken place. However, a report by researchers at MIT's Election Data and Science Lab suggests that:

> Morales's victory can be explained by his voter support before the preliminary vote count halted ... We find the final result can be explained by a pattern in the vote count prior to the cut-off of the *trep*. Therefore, we cannot find quantitative evidence of an irregular trend as claimed by the OAS.
>
> (Williams & Curiel 2020: n.p.)

Following the Electoral Court's announcement of the results in favour of Morales, with the OAS casting doubts over their legitimacy and with opposition-bloc media stoking beliefs that fraud had occurred, large-scale protests erupted in urban areas. While the initial protesters were middle-class voters angered by perceived fraud, there was a belief among diverse social classes that the government would use power illiberally to remain in power. Formerly allied groups, who had faced co-optive efforts, rejected the electoral results. These included: lowland indigenous groups; coca growers in the Yungas who felt Morales favoured core-organization cocaleros in the Chapare; cooperative miners in Potosí; CONAMAQ; and factory-worker unions in Cochabamba. They later demanded Morales's renunciation (Schneider 2019).

While middle-class and some former strategically allied popular organizations protested, the moment was ultimately captured by far-right conservative elements of the opposition bloc. Since April 2019, Luis Camacho had taken control of the Civic Committee of Santa Cruz and had vehemently opposed Morales's re-election bid. Camacho reached out to the president of the Civic Committee of the Potosí region (Comico) headed by Marco Pumari. Representing urban civil society interests in the city, Comico had been mobilizing against the Morales government since 2016, demanding that the central state give the department a greater share of revenues earned from extracting lithium in the region. The powerful Potosí miners openly rejected Morales. This was crucial because the miners had a strong voice in the powerful COB. Juan Carlos Huarachi, head of the COB, called on Morales to "reflect" on his position. The COB's withdrawal of support greatly weakened Morales's position.

With Camacho and allied racist figures inciting violence, and with protests continuing across the country, Camacho called on the police to "stand on the side of the people". Police mutinies followed in Cochabamba, Santa Cruz and Sucre while the police mingled with protesters in La Paz. General Williams Kaliman "suggested" Morales step aside. With a loss of military power; with ideological powers in the form of church leaderships, the OAS, and traditional and social media aligned against him; with business associations withdrawing their support; with a re-emerging political opposition; and with a popular base that was divided and unwilling to engage in mass-defensive mobilization, Morales and MAS representatives were forced from office.

Following the ousting of Morales, Jeanine Áñez, former deputy leader of the senate (also former TV host and long-time critic of Morales from the *media luna*), with a Bible in her hands, was declared caretaker president. When Áñez was named interim president, she immediately received the backing of major business organizations who stated their support for the "return to democracy" (Wolff 2020). The interim government's constitutional role was to convene new elections. However, instead, it recognized right-wing leader Juan Guaidó as legitimate president of Venezuela; persecuted MAS leaders and intimidated supporters; arbitrarily detained outspoken critics of the coup government; shut down critical media outlets and arrested journalists; called members of the MAS "animals"; and deployed the armed forces to repress indigenous anti-coup protesters at Sacaba and Senkata, killing at least 22 and injuring several hundred (IHRC & University Network for Human Rights 2019; Achtenberg 2020).

With the interim government postponing elections, indigenous and campesino groups in the Unity Pact began organizing their bases, first to demand new elections, and then to vote for the MAS presidential and vice-presidential ticket of Luis Arce and David Choquehuanca. The COB, whose leader Juan Carlos Huarachi had suggested Morales step aside to pacify the country, apologized for failing to defend the president and gave the interim government an ultimatum: fresh elections or "social upheaval". While there had been tensions between the MAS and sectors of its constituent base around 2018–19, as well as tensions *within* popular organizations, the extreme actions of the interim government provided a common enemy which acted as a spur to reunify divided organizations.

When the elections were finally held in October 2020, the MAS ticket of Arce and Choquehuanca won more than 55 per cent of the vote, with Carlos Mesa winning 28.5 per cent and Fernando Camacho just 14 per cent. In the first elections without Morales, and without state powers which critics had long-accused the MAS of abusing to help guarantee success, the party easily defeated the opposition candidates. Moreover, the MAS candidates won more of the vote share nationally than Morales had achieved in the 2019 elections, while winning in six of nine departments. The MAS also won a majority in both chambers of the legislature, although not a two-thirds majority as they had achieved in the 2014 elections. The results dispelled any notions that the MAS was simply a party whose success depended on Morales. Indeed, it appears that, while Morales's candidacy may have been unacceptable for some voters, the MAS, and the post-neoliberal model it advocated, retained legitimacy. It is important to stress, however, that part of the 2020 success for the MAS was based on its status as the only party capable of competing on a national level and defeating the pro-neoliberal, racist opposition parties. Tensions between the MAS and constituent organizations that had been simmering under Morales's presidencies, while pushed aside to confront a common enemy, had not disappeared. For example, local elections in March 2021 witnessed further tensions between the MAS and new popular parties that received the backing of former strategically allied organizations. The new parties, and their bases, demanded that the MAS end efforts at controlling popular contestatory mobilization via co-optive practices and support for parallel organizations.

POPULISM AND DEMOCRACY: LESSONS FROM BOLIVIA

The emergence of outsider populist Evo Morales at the head of the MAS was a direct response to a crisis of representation for popular sectors. An exclusionary market model of democracy organized the interests of white elites into politics, while indigenous-popular voices were excluded from policymaking. Rising socioeconomic exclusion triggered a Polanyian defensive movement by society. A myriad of groups such as cocaleros, urban labour, lowland indigenous groups and women's groups, among others, faced dual political and socioeconomic exclusion, under the neoliberal-infused market model of democracy. Although each group had specific grievances, Morales successfully framed their issues under a common banner of anti-neoliberalism and called on organizations to unite in social and electoral protest against market democracy. Morales' populist framing mechanism, and dual street/electoral protest tactics, thus directly challenged the status quo and called for a reconstruction of the social order, whereby the state would act as a guarantor of societal well-being (with society now broadened to incorporate popular sectors rather than just a white elite). Two distinct social blocs thus emerged – a popular bloc which backed Morales's project and an elite-led bloc, with ties to US capital who had benefitted under the neoliberal era.

Populism, understood as a defensive movement that challenges an exclusionary, delegitimized status quo, will foster opposition. As the Bolivian process highlights, democratization processes will inherently entail tensions and pushback from those who have long enjoyed dominant status. As these struggles advance, it is highly likely there will be episodes of (simultaneous) democratization and de-democratization: liberal norms may be bent so as to bypass opposition to a project founded on promises to deepen participation and extend substantive citizenship rights to formerly excluded sectors. In fact, there is "ample reason to believe that elected executives seeking to broaden substantive democratic inclusion might clash with elites who prize democracy's constraints on absolute power more than its promise to empower the many" (Slater 2013: 732–3). Indeed, as Cameron (2021: 786) notes,

> without denying populism's potentially deleterious effects on democracy, the focus is partially misplaced because oligarchic modes of rule and populist mobilization are co-constitutive ... Populism is both a typical reaction to oligarchic modes of rule and an endemic feature of democratic politics in unequal societies.

Understanding these power struggles, between anti-neoliberal populists elected to respond to oligarchic domination of democracy and the elites who seek to defend their domination of the political system, requires that theorists move beyond a narrow institutionalist appraisal of populist-led projects. The sole focus of analysis should not only be on the "illiberal populist" or "competitive authoritarian", but on how anti-neoliberal outsiders interact with oligarchic opposition. As the Bolivian case demonstrates, to grasp the actions of newly elected anti-neoliberal governments, including willingness to engage in illiberal behaviours, and to comprehend popular sector support or rejection for government actions, it is essential to view the post-neoliberal process via a historic lens, that encapsulates the market democracy era. By grasping who was incorporated, and who was excluded under market democracy (political and socioeconomic inclusion of middle classes and elites, exclusion of popular and indigenous sectors), and taking account of the preceding domination of ideological, economic, military and political sources of power by a select elite bloc, we can better comprehend why governments may bend liberal norms, and why they retain popular backing for doing so. That is, "measuring" the impact of populist outsider-led projects on democratic quality can only be meaningful if we analyse the preceding status quo that triggered the populist response in the first place.

In addition to highlighting potential tensions between liberal and radical-substantive democracy, the Bolivian case demonstrates how populist projects that unify multiple groups under a common framing mechanism (for example anti-neoliberal democracy) may lead to internal tensions in the popular bloc, or the *pueblo*. While a broad frame is essential to garner the electoral (and street) backing of multiple groups (especially where the populist is an outsider candidate lacking an institutionalized party structure), over time specific group grievances may become a source of party–base tension. Moreover, as the populist project challenging the status quo must work within confines set by the very elites whose interests are challenged, it is inevitable that a populist project will fail to adhere to all pre-electoral promises to all groups. For example, as the Morales-led project confronted the confines set by a path-dependent reliance on primary commodity exportation, the MAS clashed with sectors of the popular bloc, leading to issues of co-optation and *paralelismo*. Hence, a full grasp of the impacts of populist-led processes on democratic quality entails broadening our conceptualization of democracy, from a narrow liberal perspective to one that incorporates liberal, participative and substantive criteria. Second, it is necessary to evaluate the nature and evolution of party–base relations.

Finally, while populist projects may be passing fads; brief moments of rage that are soon dispersed when the populist outsider fails to achieve promises once in office, this is not necessarily the case. The post-neoliberal project in Bolivia demonstrated that a more substantive model of democracy and citizenship could be achieved if a populist outsider won election. Despite all the frictions, and the moderation of the project in the face of opposition bloc powers, the post-neoliberal model of democracy, outlined in the Constitution, retains high levels of legitimacy. Spaces of participation, such as the Unity Pact that brought together the leaders of major popular organizations to guide the MAS from below, were reforged during the 2019–20 period of confrontation with the coup government, and the MAS candidate easily won presidential elections on a mandate to deepen and advance the post-neoliberal project. There is a highly politicized and powerful organized popular bloc who have seen both the possibilities and dangers of a progressive populist in office. Bolivia's populist moment has thus altered the status quo irrevocably and a wholesale return to exclusionary market democracy is now off the table.

REFERENCES

Achtenberg, E. 2016. "Evo's Bolivia at a political crossroads: taking stock of Bolivia's changing political environment after Evo Morales' 2016 referendum defeat". *NACLA Report on the Americas* 48(4): 372–80.

Achtenberg, E. 2020. "MAS party under threat as Bolivia moves towards new elections (without Evo)". *NACLA Rebel Currents*, 10 January. https://nacla.org/blog/2020/01/10/mas-party-under-threat-bolivia-new-elections-without-evo.

Albro, R. 2005. "The water is ours, ¡*Carajo*! Deep citizenship in Bolivia's water war". In J. Nash (ed.), *Social Movements: An Anthropological Reader*, 249–71. Oxford: Basil Blackwell.

Anria, S. 2013. "Social movements, party organization, and populism: insights from the Bolivian MAS". *Latin American Politics and Society* 55(3): 19–46.

Arditi, B. 2007. *Politics on the Edges of Liberalism: Difference, Populism, Revolution, Agitation*. Edinburgh: Edinburgh University Press.

Arteaga, W. 2015. Building citizenship in the context of the debate on the post-2015 agenda in Bolivia. *Community Development Journal* 50(4): 571–88.

Arze, C. 2016. *Una Década de Gobierno. ¿Construyente el Vivir Bien o un Capitalsimo Salvaje*. La Paz: CEDLA.

Berman, S. 2017. "The pipe dream of undemocratic liberalism". *Journal of Democracy* 28(3): 29–38.

Brown, J. 2020a. "Party-base linkages and contestatory mobilization in Bolivia's El Alto: subduing the Ciudad Rebelde". *Latin American Perspectives* 47(4): 40–57.

Brown, J. 2020b. "Neoliberalization, de-democratization, and populist responses in Western Europe, the US, and Latin America". *Critical Sociology 46*(7–8): 1173–87.

Cameron, M. 2021. "The return of oligarchy? Threats to representative democracy in Latin America". *Third World Quarterly* 42(4): 775–92.

de la Torre, C. 2016. "Left-wing populism: inclusion and authoritarianism in Venezuela, Bolivia, and Ecuador". *Brown Journal of World Affairs* 23: 61–76

Dunn, J. 2019. "The challenge of populism: why populist politics spreads in the world". *Populism* 2(1): 53–67.

ECLAC 2013. *Statistical Yearbook for Latin America and the Caribbean*. Santiago: United Nations.

Ellner, S. 2013. "Latin America's radical left in power: complexities and challenges in the twenty-first century." *Latin American Perspectives* 40(3): 5–25.

Fontana, L. 2013. "On the perils and potentialities of revolution: conflict and collective action in contemporary Bolivia." *Latin American Perspectives* 40(3): 26–42.

Gustafson, B. 2020. *Bolivia in the Age of Gas*. Durham, NC: Duke University Press.

IHRC & University Network for Human Rights 2019. "They shot us like animals: Black November and Bolivia's interim government". www.humanrightsnetwork.org/bolivia.

Johnson, J. & Lefebvre, S. 2014. "Bolivia's economy under Evo in 10 graphs". *CEPR*, 8 October. http://cepr.net/blogs/the-americas-blog/bolivias-economy-under-evo-in-10-graphs.

Kaup, B. 2010. "A neoliberal nationalization? The constraints on natural-gas-led development in Bolivia". *Latin American Perspectives* 37(3): 123–38.

Kaup, B. 2013. "Transnational class formation and spatialities of power: the case of elite competition in Bolivia". *Global Networks* 13(1): 101–19.

Laclau, E. 2005. *On Populist Reason*. London: Verso.

Lazar, S. 2008. *El Alto, Rebel City: Self and Citizenship in Andean Bolivia*. Durham, NC: Duke University Press.

Levitsky, S. & J. Loxton 2013. "Populism and competitive authoritarianism in the Andes". *Democratization* 20(1): 107–36.

Mair, P. 2013. *Ruling the Void: The Hollowing of Western Democracy*. New York: Verso.

Mayorga, F. 2020. "El MAS-IPSP ante un Nuevo Contexto Político: De 'Partido de Gobierno' a 'Instumento Político' de las Organizaciones Populares". In J. Souverein and J. Rodríguez (eds), *Nuevo Mapa de Actores en Bolivia*, 1–34. La Paz: FES.

Morales, W. 2013. "The TIPNIS crisis and the meaning of Bolivian democracy under Evo Morales". *The Latin Americanist* 57(1): 79–90.

Munck, G. 2015. "Building democracy ... which democracy? Ideology and models of democracy in post-transition Latin America". *Government and Opposition* 50(3): 364–93.

Paz, M. & J. Ramírez-Cendrero 2021. "Extractivism and resource nationalism in Bolivia: foreign direct investment policy and development under Evo Morales". In A. Ellner (ed.), *Latin American Extractivism: Dependency, Resource Nationalism, and Resistance in Broad Perspective*, 129–47. Lanham, MD: Rowman & Littlefield.

Polanyi, K. 1944. *The Great Transformation: The Political and Economic Origins of Our Time*. New York: Farrar & Rinehart.

Roberts, K. 2015. *Changing Course: Party Systems in Latin America's Neoliberal Era*. New York: Cambridge University Press.

Roberts, K. 2019. "Bipolar disorders: varieties of capitalism and populist outflanking on the left and right". *Polity* 54(4): 641–53.

Rossi, F. & E. Silva 2018. "Introduction: reshaping the political arena". In E. Silva & F. Rossi (eds), *Reshaping the Political Arena in Latin America: From Resisting Neoliberalism to the Second Incorporation*, 3–22. Pittsburgh, PA: University of Pittsburgh Press.

Sánchez-Sibony, O. 2021. "Competitive authoritarianism in Morales's Bolivia: skewing arenas of competition". *Latin American Politics and Society* 63(1): 118–44.

Schilling-Vacaflor, A. 2017. "'If the company belongs to you, how can you be against it?' Limiting participation and taming dissent in neo-extractivist Bolivia". *The Journal of Peasant Studies* 44(3): 658–76.

Schmitter, P. 2019. "'Real-existing' democracy and its discontents: sources, conditions, causes, symptoms, and prospects". *Chinese Political Science Review* 4(2): 149–63.

Schneider, A. 2019. "Algunos Elementos para Comprender el Golpe de Estado en Bolivia". *CEDLA Blog*, 13 November. https://cedla.org/cedla-en-los-medios/47243/.

Silva, S. 2009. *Challenging Neoliberalism in Latin America*. New York: Cambridge University Press.

Slater, D. 2013. "Democratic careening". *World Politics* 65(4): 729–63.

Tapia, L. 2011. *El Estado de Derecho como Tiranía*. La Paz: CIDES-UMSA.

Trujillo, J. & S. Spronk 2018. "Socialism without workers? Trade unions and the new left in Bolivia and Ecuador". In E. Silva and F. Rossi (eds), *Reshaping the Political Arena in Latin America: From Resisting Neoliberalism to the Second Incorporation*, 129–56. Pittsburgh, PA: University of Pittsburgh Press.

Webber, J. 2010. "Carlos Mesa, Evo Morales, and a divided Bolivia (2003–2005)". *Latin American Perspectives* 37(3): 51–70.
Weyland, K. 2013. "Latin America's authoritarian drift: the threat from the populist left". *Journal of Democracy* 24(3): 18–32.
Williams, J. & J. Curiel 2020. "Analysis of the 2019 Bolivia Election". *CEPR*, 27 February. https://cepr.net/report/analysis-of-the-2019-bolivia-election/.
Wolff, J. 2020. "Las Élites Económicas en la Bolivia Contemporánea." In J. Souverein & J. Rodríguez (eds), *Nuevo Mapa de Actores en Bolivia*, 139–63. La Paz: FES.
Zuazo, M. 2010. '¿Los Movimientos Sociales en el Poder?" *Nueva Sociedad* 227: 120–36.

CHAPTER 9

ECUADOR: POPULISM AND THE 2007–17 POLITICAL CYCLE

Pablo Dávalos

INTRODUCTION

In the international debate on populism, the Argentine political philosopher, Ernesto Laclau, achieved a key epistemological shift, when he ascribed populism to the ways of constructing the political within a logic of articulations, in a dynamic of equivalences and heterogeneities (Laclau 2005). Thus, for Laclau "populism is simply a way of constructing the political", and the political is always populist (Laclau 2005: 11). In this way, he counteracts the type of consensus that presented populism as a threat to liberal democracy, as well as broadening the field of possible theorists for the debate on populism.

Laclau's epistemological turn is based on the theoretical weaknesses of the concept of populism, and its inability to generate a canonical definition. The resistance to granting a strong epistemological support to this notion of populism is due to a position of principle, with respect to the theorization of liberal democracy, that is universal and teleological, and with a political subject that is essentially grounded. That is why, from this point of view, populism is considered as a syndrome of liberal democracy (Wiles 1969), or as a pathology of societies in full economic development and political modernization, that would prevent such development and economic growth (Edwards 2019).

The presence of the charismatic leader who turned the people against the oligarchies and polarized the political system within a Manichean strategy, takes up Carl Schmitt's friend/enemy notion. While this can somehow describe populism, in reality, it does not explain it epistemologically (Tushnet 2019). The *aporia* of liberalism that prevents that conceptualization is that, without the construction of the "people", there is no populism, but neither is there democracy (Laclau 2005: 213). Precisely because of this, Laclau proposes to change strategy and not to ask what populism is (because there is still no epistemologically convincing answer on its definition), but rather to ask: "to what social and political reality does populism refer? … of what reality or social situation is populism an expression" (Laclau 2005: 31). In this way, and as Peruzzotti puts it, Laclau "turned the debate on populism on its head" (Peruzzotti 2019: 33). Populism would no longer be a supposed pathology of liberal democracy, but rather another way of constructing politics in terms of the political. Perhaps this is why Laclau's text formed part of the *doxa* of some leftist parties, such as Podemos in Spain, or neo-Peronism in Argentina (de la Torre 2019).

In this *terra incognita*, as Arditi (2004) defines populism, it is important to understand its conditions of possibility and its conditions of existence. That is, the ontological, political and historical framework that makes it possible, because, in short, populism accompanies liberal democracy like a shadow (Canovan 1999). However, if populism is the shadow of liberal democracy, as Canovan puts it, then why does liberal democracy resist recognizing itself in its own shadow? What numinous contours can be seen in this shadow that liberal democracy chooses to cover up or deny? If populism is a kind of numinous shadow of liberal democracy, it is because it shows contours that belong to it and that are only expressed in populism. De la Torre is not incorrect, when he points out that populists "politicize exclusions, point out the malfunctioning of democracies and demand better forms of representation and democratic participation" (de la Torre 2019: 24).

In rationally assumed politics there are no enemies but antagonists. The dimension of antagonism, writes Chantal Mouffe, is "inherent to human relations, antagonism that can take many forms and arise in different types of social relations" (Mouffe 2007: 15). However, antagonism is "external to society" and establishes the limits that would prevent society from fully constituting itself, because they start from, and are defined by, the heterogeneity of the social (Laclau & Mouffe 2006: 169). The incomplete and open character of the social is one in which no articulation can suture the field and, therefore, the notion of people is not exhausted by any ontic content or class articulation (Sánchez Díaz 2016).

According to Laclau, the *plebs* assume, and claim to be, the legitimate universal of the social totality. It becomes *populus*, through a chain of equivalences, and in a field of contingencies of the political. It is in the political territory that Laclau situates populism: "Does this mean that the political has become synonymous with populism?" Yes, Laclau answers, "in the sense in which we conceive the latter notion" (Laclau 2005: 195). If populism is inscribed in the political, then there is a direct convergence with post-foundational thought.

Post-foundational thought starts from the difference between being and entity as established by Heidegger. Being is the empty universal that acts as the constituent moment of the political. Being is the concrete particular that fills this void, through an *entification* of being and a permanent and contingent ontic actualization of being. Therefore, the epistemological critique of post-foundational thought relates to any principle or essence that allows making politics intelligible outside society. For example, the liberal universalism of the modern rational subject, or the dialectical totality of Marxism and the articulation of social conflict in class struggle, is produced from this ontological difference. This means that those transcendental foundations that explain politics lose the possibility of constituting and closing society within those principles, or essences, of the social. Thus is generated a distance from economic determinism, behaviourism, positivism, sociologism, among others, for a more contingent understanding of politics (Marchat 2007).

For example, the most positive view of liberalism would consider liberal democracy subject to a universalist paradigm that becomes a discourse of order. This is the only way to understand what Edwards calls "good economic policy" (Edwards 2019: 77). Thegood economic policy is that which comes from the neoliberal mainstream and which, finally, coincides with John Williamson's Washington Consensus (Williamson 2004). This is precisely the *entification* of being that post-foundationalism claims. It is to present the particular as the universal. It is, in Laclau and Mouffe's terms, hegemony; that is, the way in which "a certain particularity becomes the name of a universality that is entirely incommensurable to it" (Laclau 2008: 15).

Following the path set by Laclau, it is a matter of understanding the social and political reality and populism as an expression of it; that is to say, it is necessary to discern the conditions of possibility and existence of the populist phenomenon, from a prudent distance of the essentiality and positivity of the liberal discourse, because it is the only theoretical way to avoid redundancy in the conceptualization of populism.

If Laclau is right and populism is "simply a way of constructing the political", and if the political expresses both the ontological difference between being and entity, as well as the process by which being is actualized and manifested in the entity, then we must ask ourselves about the excess of the political of which populism is an expression. Indeed, populism cannot be explained without explaining, determining and constructing the concept of "the people" (*populus*). But if this concept is constructed, populism is legitimized, and democracy appears only as one form of the concept. Laclau is right, without the *populus*, populism is unthinkable, but so also is democracy. This is where the *aporia* between form and content of the political in modern societies arises.

The modern political form of political systems, supposedly rational and plural, cannot absorb its own political content, and the emergence, appeal and conformation of populism is the expression of *aporia*; it is the case that the content exceeds its form, and that there is no way to discipline and subdue it, nor to suppress it, because there is no possible dialectic. By betting on the ontological abyss, it is impossible to theoretically close the notion of populism. Consequently, the *aporia* of defining it emerges, which would require extending the category of populism to all behaviour of the political system. Why is there this fundamental asymmetry between form and content in modern democracies? What are the signs of this *aporia*? If populism is the expression of a social reality, what is this reality? It can be hypothesized that populism is the expression of the radical caesura in modern societies between economics, politics and law (in addition to other caesuras such as those stemming from affections and emotions, or from ludic, aesthetic or erotic visions).

Thus, there can be a political democracy, but never an economic democracy. One can vote for the president of the republic or the congress, but never for the head of the office or the factory. Law can guarantee law and order, but not the redistribution of wealth. Affections and emotions may be present in the political campaign, but not in the exercise of government. Playfulness is suppressed for the sake of competitiveness and productivity. The modern subject can be rational but not erotic. There would be no libido in politics.

Liberalism decontaminates the economy of all its human and social features. It cleanses the economy, politics and law of all social contradictions. Thus, it separates them and studies them as pure and rational forms. When these supposedly pure and rational forms evidence the contamination of the human, then the theory of political liberalism proceeds to further close the field of its prescriptions. Populism would be the attempt of societies to overcome these radical caesuras of modernity and liberalism and to bring about a suture between politics and economics, between law and politics. As Canovan (1999) suggests, it is the redemptive face of democracy. Populism would be something more than a "political logic" (Laclau 2005: 150). It would be a symptom, an indicator of what is failing in the structure itself that is threatened by "pathological" outbursts (Žižek 2006: 556). The supposed pathology of liberalism, which is expressed in this apparent suture in populism, is the expression of reification, as the process that separates human beings from their own conditions of existence and possibility as humans (Lukácks 1985).

By excluding reification from his theoretical analysis, Laclau succeeded in giving populism a dignity that had been denied to it in liberal analysis. However, it could not account for those radical caesuras of capitalism. The stark reality of capitalism, in its "solipsistic dance" that "pursues its goal of profitability in blissful indifference to how its movement will affect society"

(Žižek 2006: 566), does not match theoretical notions about populism. The problems inherent in the processes of capital accumulation, and its political forms of domination, slip through his fingers like sand.

THE EXHAUSTION OF NEOLIBERALISM (1982–2005) AND THE RISE OF "POPULISM"

The three-term presidency of Rafael Correa of Ecuador, from 2007 to 2017, has been pointed to by some theorists as a populist cycle (Edwards 2019; de la Torre 2013a; Mazzolini 2021). This political process is also identified as "Citizen Revolution" (Dávalos 2014; Muñoz Jaramillo *et al.* 2014). Edwards qualifies the theory of the 2007–17 process as "populism without fiscal dominance", due to the dollarization of the economy that prevents inflationary processes and limits the margin of manoeuvre of economic policy (Edwards 2019: 89). Carlos de la Torre calls it "Technopopulism" (de la Torre 2013b). Most authors agree in locating him within the currents of left-wing populism, together with Hugo Chávez in Venezuela, Evo Morales in Bolivia, Luiz Inácio Lula da Silva in Brazil, Daniel Ortega in Nicaragua, and Néstor Kirchner in Argentina (de la Torre 2013b).

If Laclau's thesis is to explain populism on the basis of the social, historical and political conditions that make it possible, it can be stated that this political cycle of the citizen revolution corresponds to the exhaustion of a longer political cycle that began in 1982, with the Latin American foreign debt crisis. In Ecuador, this corresponds to the adjustment and structural reform policies of the IMF and the World Bank, which were imposed from 1983 to 2005. In 1999–2000, the country's most important economic crisis occurred, leading to the dollarization of the economy in 2000. The year 2005 saw the fall of former President Lucio Gutiérrez, who had declared himself a strong supporter of IMF adjustment policies (Páez 2004).

Indeed, from 1982 to 2005, Ecuador was subject to the prescriptions of the Washington Consensus, in successive agreements with the IMF (Dávalos 2011). While it is true that, within the neoliberal economic and political cycle, there were populist governments, such as that of Abdalá Bucaram, who only lasted half a year in office in 1997, it is also true that these were modalities in the political system that did not alter the longer-term neoliberal cycle. In contrast, the new political cycle, that began in 2007 and ended in 2017, corresponds to a radical break with, and criticism of, neoliberalism, the IMF, the World Bank, and the policies of the Washington Consensus (Dávalos 2014).

The first hypothesis which can be established is that the political cycle of the citizen revolution, that began in 2007, is the result of the exhaustion of the political cycle of neoliberalism. What were the reasons for this exhaustion?

One of the main reasons was the 1999–2000 crisis, brought about by the deregulation of the banking and financial system, that began in 1994 under the government of Sixto Durán Ballén (1994–98). The deregulation of the banking system caused a distortion in the country's savings-investment circuits and created the conditions for a speculative financial bubble. This bubble burst in 1999, following the decision in 1998 to transfer the responsibility for bank liabilities with public money from the international monetary reserves. This law also created the Deposit Guarantee Agency (AGD) as the institution that backed private liabilities with public funds (Cantos Molina 2020). At this juncture, the political system turned to private banks to create a protective cover against the crisis and citizens' claims. A later audit of the process would show that the private banks created Ponzi schemes for credits and, in addition, created a file of credits with advantageous conditions for the banks' shareholders in a dynamic that was known as "linked credits" (Páez 2004).

RAFAEL CORREA'S ELECTORAL TRIUMPH AND THE BEGINNING OF A NEW POLITICAL CYCLE

When Lucio Gutiérrez was ousted in 2005, his vice-president, Alfredo Palacio, took over. He decided to be more prudent in terms of economic policy and suspended the agreements with the IMF. The decision to suspend these agreements was made by his then Minister of Economy, Rafael Correa. The population applauded this decision and decided to support it politically.

The rupture with the IMF and the criticism of the neoliberal discourse enhanced Correa's image. In fact, at the end of the following year, 2006, he would be elected president of Ecuador with a political movement, the Citizen Revolution Movement, behind him (Tibocha & Jassir 2008). In his electoral campaign, Correa took up the anti-political themes of Gutiérrez, and subscribed to the slogan, "*Que se vayan todos*" ("Let them all go") to such an extent that he did not present candidates for parliament and, announced that, if he won, he would immediately call for a constitutional assembly. This convinced voters to support him politically. Indeed, in 2007, on the very day of his inauguration, the second executive decree signed by Correa called for a "Constituent Assembly" with full powers. Barely ten years after the promulgation of the 1998 Constitution, Ecuador began to write a new constitutional text, this time moving away from all the prescriptions of neoliberalism and the rule of law (Paz y Miño Cepeda *et al.* 2007).

The process of social mobilization around the Constituent Assembly was stimulated by the radical criticism of neoliberalism, the IMF, and so on, and a view that there was a need to recover the country from the corruption of the traditional political parties, referred to as "partyocracy". The slogan of "getting out of the long neoliberal night", which Correa took up from the World Social Forum of Porto Alegre, mobilized society and was expressed in wide support for the candidates of the Citizen Revolution. At that point, there was a deployment of symbolic universes appealing to the people to mobilize them, but it was still too early in the process for this to qualify as populism. These symbolic universes corresponded to the anti-political sentiment of the society that needed a catharsis, with respect to the 1999–2000 crisis. Since Correa's governing party, Alianza País, was still to be constituted, the call for the Constituent Assembly and the electoral process that was correlative to it served to create *ex nihilo* that political movement. Until then, it had been a motley rainbow of leftist social and political organizations that had been constituted as an electoral registry in order to register the candidacy of Correa (Dávalos 2014).

The Constituent Assembly process of 2007–08 in Ecuador not only changed the constitutional rules of the game in a transcendental manner, making it possible to move from the rule of law to the constitutional rule of rights and justice, but also served to create the governing party, Alianza País. With an enormous political capital, the nascent government had a wide margin in which to manoeuvre, and it used the elections that endorsed the confirmation of the Constituent Assembly to structure and define the party. However, the Assembly not only functioned as a political process to create the governing party, but it was also a process of social catharsis that eliminated the electoral possibilities of the political opposition and reduced it to acting on the margins of the political system. The new Constitution reflected the need for a radical refoundation of the political system and its institutions while, at the same time, providing the new government with the levers of power to allow it to ensure its own conditions of political domination.

One of the key issues for society, the culpability of the private bankers and the power elites in creating the 1999–2000 crisis, became the subject of constitutional treatment and public debate. The Washington Consensus was demonized by public opinion. Institutions perceived as intrinsically linked to neoliberalism were distrusted and the IMF and the World Bank were expelled from the country in 2007 (La Voz de América 2007). Correa had become one of the most radical and implacable critics of these international financial institutions. The Constitution, approved in 2008 by referendum, also created a legal framework that would make economic adjustment under the terms of the Washington Consensus impossible. It regulated the fiscal rule, that established a relationship of accounting equality between permanent revenues and permanent expenditures of the state, in such a way that current spending was separated from the calculation of the fiscal deficit. Thus, current spending had no relationship with the fiscal deficit by constitutional prescription (Asamblea Nacional del Ecuador 2008: Art. 286).

The global and specific geographic context was also favourable to the new government. It was surrounded by a series of Latin American governments that subscribed to and supported Ecuador's redistribution and sovereignty proposals and that made up a regional environment critical of the Washington Consensus.

THE EFFICIENT POLITICAL MACHINERY OF THE CITIZEN REVOLUTION

Populism was a facade of a model of political domination, highly effective in the use of the tools and technologies of modern political communication. With ample resources at its disposal, the government of Rafael Correa built an institutional architecture for the technocratic management of national politics in an unprecedented exercise in the Ecuadorian political system. The Citizen Revolution developed a dashboard with permanent indicators of the mood of the population, so that the recourse to populism was calculated in an extreme and rigorous way. This process involved ongoing measurement of the public mood through surveys, opinion polls and sophisticated political research. Following on from this, the government tailored and refined its message, actions and public policies to take account of/reflect public opinion. Thus, the government appeared to be perfectly in tune with the population.

When impasses with the social and political opposition could not be solved with populist initiatives, the government was quick to create the conditions for plebiscites. Within a few months, that way of doing politics turned the government of Correa into the most effective political machine in the entire history of Ecuador's modern democracy. In the period 2007–17, Correa won ten elections in a row (Ortiz 2018: 555), and his power within the political system was overwhelming. The opposition, in this context, had little room for manoeuvre, with both the right-wing and left-wing oppositions made, effectively, irrelevant. It was impossible to win elections against the governing party. One of its critics from the right, César Montúfar, called the Citizen Revolution an "electoral authoritarian regime" (Montúfar 2016: 85). Former President Osvaldo Hurtado (1982–84), who had started the neoliberal adjustment programmes in Ecuador, called the Citizen Revolution an autocratic dictatorship that concentrated power against basic rights (Hurtado 2012). All political parties, and the entire political class, were surprised and overwhelmed by this unprecedented way of doing politics. However, it is the case that the government's methods to "concentrate power" were all liberal and democratic. What Correa and Alianza País did that was different was to apply them within a framework of political efficiency and technocratic rationality.

In addition to its ability to control politics in all its facets from the institutionality created specifically for this purpose, the governing party of Rafael Correa built an impressive media apparatus that began to rival and displace the mainstream media. During his entire period of power, 2007–17, Correa turned the mass media, long linked to the economic elites and to the traditional political parties, into his real political interlocutors. It was the first time in Ecuador's recent history where a government pushed opposition political parties and movements to the margins of the political system, while placing the traditional mass media at the centre of the political game. This political strategy was mistakenly seen as an attack on the rights of freedom of expression. It was, in fact, never considered a political strategy with a precise objective. This confusion was functional to the hegemonic power construction of Alianza País, in that it created a political *aporia* for the traditional media. Their position as interlocuters and the fourth pillar of democracy was undermined as they tried to reposition themselves in relation to both government and opposition.

Likewise, public policies were placed within this political strategy of hegemonic construction. No public policy was adopted without first passing through the filter of this matrix of political domination. Public investment was a correlate that reinforced the hegemony of the ruling party. The impressive network of roads and highways built during this political cycle, as well as the hydroelectric plants, and the public infrastructure of hospitals, universities and other developments, served to reinforce the social imaginary of a government that invested directly in the people and that had to fight against the media and the "partyocracy" to do so.

It was a political process that went beyond any framework of interpretation that could be defined as populism. The political cycle that began in 2007 was something much more complex, vast and profound than a mere populist cycle, at least in the traditional sense. Ecuador's political system had never seen the construction of such an efficient and effective political machine as the Alianza País movement.

THE MIDDLE CLASSES: THE POLITICAL FOUNDATIONS OF THE CITIZEN REVOLUTION

It is within this matrix of hegemony construction, that Correa's governing party created its social base, but unlike the process in Venezuela or Bolivia, which have popular sectors as their main axis of reference, the social base of Ecuador's governing party was not the popular sectors but the middle class. A middle class was created from the redistribution of the commodity surplus directly by the state. It was a process that allowed the governing party to garner loyalty for its political project because the labour, and financial, stability of these middle sectors depended on the stability of the government. It was not necessary for them to become militants *a fortiori*, but to create a logic in which the personal destiny of public officials was directly linked to the destiny of the governing party.

The expansion of the middle class was significant, and poverty was reduced to such levels that, even Sebastián Edwards, a proponent of the "good economics" of the neoliberal mainstream, acknowledged it. In the 2007–17 cycle, the Gini index measure of inequality in Ecuador, found that it had reduced from 53.4 in 2006 to 44.7 in 2017, "a significant achievement that has not been matched by any Latin American country in modern times" (Edwards 2019: 94).

Finally, while the salaries of public sector employees grew faster than those in the private sector, at the same time their stability became fragile. One small political slip and they were out. The incentive of meritocracy was used to attract and retain talented people to the governing party and, ultimately, turn them into powerful political cadres.

POLITICAL CONFLICT AS A RESOURCE FOR THE CONSTRUCTION OF HEGEMONY

Something that characterized this 2007–17 political cycle was not populism, which in reality was just a tool in the government's repertoire, but political tension and conflict. It was a period in which, at the same time that the political indicators and variables were positive, an atmosphere of permanent tension and confrontation was created.

This arose as a result of the creation of fear as a heuristic of power. However, unlike other political processes in which fear is exercised directly on the population, this was the strategic use of fear as a resource for social mobilization and political cohesion. It involved creating a fear of the loss of all that had been achieved by the Correa government, and of the threat of the "partyocracy" regaining power and dismantling the new populist institutionality and revoking the benefits. It was about creating fear of a future without Alianza País and without Rafael Correa. Perhaps the best metaphor for this strategy is the phrase that Correa took from Ignacio de Loyola, which he applied in times of political tension: "In a besieged fortress, any dissidence is treason" (Representaciones diplomáticas de Cuba en el exterior 2016: n.p.).

This atmosphere of tension, insecurity and direct conflict with enemies, was built week after week in the speeches of Correa, copied from his counterpart, Hugo Chávez of Venezuela. But Chávez addressed the popular sectors and politicized them. Correa addressed the militants of his own party and disciplined them. He never admitted the slightest dissidence within his movement. The political tension, which at times replicated Carl Schmitt's friend/enemy logic, facilitated the construction of a disciplined, loyal and always ready party. It was a machine that was greased every day. It was the epitome of a Leninist party (Dávalos 2014).

The concept of populism may be able to describe some of the traditional forms of political construction, but it prevents us from understanding what was most important in Ecuador: the technocratic construction of power. Carlos de la Torre identified the process to an extent (de la Torre 2013b), but he was unable to discern the complexity of what the dynamic meant, in terms of the construction of political hegemony, perhaps because of his adherence to his own underlying theoretical assumptions.

EXTRACTIVISM AND THE END OF THE POLITICAL CYCLE

A process of the magnitude of Correa's construction of power required significant resources. The fact that his government had not adopted a belligerent position in tax matters with those classes of economic means, in order to keep them onside, meant that those resources could only come from extractive income. But this extractive profit depended on the volatility of international markets and the expansion of its frontier.

Correa's period in power was further characterized by its radical commitment to extractivism, summarized in a phrase of his as: "We cannot be beggars sitting on a sack of gold" (Dávalos 2013: 213). The "sack of gold" in question was the mineral resources to be found in Ecuador's indigenous territories. By betting on extractivism, the Citizen Revolution process moved into direct conflict with indigenous organizations, involving a direct dispute over their territories. In order to realize the income from extractivism, the regime of the Citizen Revolution had to enter into direct conflict with indigenous peoples, especially in the Amazon.

Thus, a significant feature of the 2007–17 political cycle was the harsh confrontation with indigenous organizations and the dynamic of violence and dispossession that ensued. The defence of their territories and, in particular, water, became the focus of confrontation between the government and the indigenous peoples. It began as early as 2007, when the government ordered the army to quell unrest among the Amazonian population of the Dayuma community in the province of Orellana. The people had threatened to close the oil pipeline if their demands were not met. The deployment of substantial forces by the state against a poor indigenous community heralded a campaign of suppression against the indigenous peoples who opposed the extractive drifts. For the indigenous organizations, this constituted more of the same; it was just a continuation of their resistance against extractivism under previous neoliberal cycles. Therefore, the anti-neoliberal and anti-Washington Consensus discourse had no relevance for the indigenous organizations.

For them, Correa's government was the continuation of neoliberalism by other means.

The government of the Citizen Revolution proceeded to politically neutralize the indigenous movements and their capacity for mobilization by isolating them from the rest of society, while disconnecting their representative organizations from their international networks. In this way, the political capacity of the indigenous movements was reduced while, at the same time, they were ostensibly supported by the state through specific social assistance programmes. Many of these programmes were directed by the then vice-president, Lenín Moreno. These programmes created an impression internationally, of a progressive government that used the extractive income to carry out social work for the direct benefit of the poor of the regions. It was not understood how it was possible for these sectors to oppose the government and many saw it as a political naivety that played into the hands of the right wing.

Ultimately, extractivism produced an irremissible fracture between the Citizen Revolution project and the indigenous movement. The indigenous people viewed everything that came from Alianza País and Rafael Correa with suspicion. Correa and the Alianza País were never able to overcome this suspicion, which surfaced years later, when they tried to form an electoral alliance to prevent the return of the right in the elections of 2021. For the indigenous organizations that endured a more aggressive dispossession dynamic than that of the neoliberal period, the Citizen Revolution had nothing to offer. It was this resistance that little by little weakened the Correa political machinery.

CONCLUSIONS

Several conclusions can be drawn from the above analysis:

- In the period 2007–17, there was never a construction of a *populus* from the Citizen Revolution. Its social base was the middle classes, not the popular sectors; hence its political weaknesses. The middle classes sectors were the first to abandon this political project when they considered that it no longer represented them. The popular sectors were indirect beneficiaries, via the spillover effect, but they were not part of the real political substratum of the citizen revolution. Therefore, it can be said that one of the basic requirements of any populist proposal were not met in this case
- There was not so much a "Manichean" relationship between people and oligarchies, but rather between citizens and the "partyocracy". The political system existed prior to the arrival to power of the citizen revolution.

Therefore, the other basic requirement to qualify it as populism is not fulfilled either.

- The construction of political hegemony was never a contingent process and never universalized particular contents. Instead, it remained within a dialectical tension in which universalization was not of specific contingent contents, but of an *ethos*, that of the revolution of the citizens who moralize public policy and in which any dissidence is seen as betrayal.
- There was never a disorder in public finances. On the contrary, the Citizen Revolution created an order and a structure for public finances that had not existed until then; that is, instead of excessive public spending, there was a strategic use of public spending.
- Income redistribution was aimed at creating a system of political loyalties and was basically focused on the middle classes; the popular sectors benefited from this redistribution due to the spillover effect of the policy.
- The "populist strategy" was never improvised or spontaneous, but rather the opposite. It was subjected to rigorous analysis and exact measurement that was always validated in terms of precise indicators, born of political communication and modern research techniques. The Citizen Revolution built an impressive institutional architecture to support, consolidate and sustain itself in this technical way of doing politics.
- The Citizen Revolution never affected in any way the economic power groups or their strategic interests. When it had to resort to new fiscal resources to finance its political project it did not use fiscal policy such as a tax on the wealth of large economic groups, for example, or a better fiscal determination of their income and taxation. It chose instead to expand and deepen extractivism, at the risk of confronting the indigenous organizations that defended, with legitimate rights, their territories.
- The political conflicts during the 2007–17 political cycle were never inscribed within the coordinates of antagonism, but within a friend/enemy logic that surpassed antagonism and led directly to the neutralization of the opposition through direct state violence. However, that violence was never used against the dominant economic powers but, rather, against the indigenous movement. Indigenous leaders were accused of terrorism and were relentlessly persecuted. The Citizen Revolution never recognized them as legitimate interlocutors and therefore felt free to apply both laws and forces of the state against them.
- Can the notion of populism help us to understand the efficient political machine that once was Alianza País? Was the charismatic leadership of Rafael Correa sufficient argument to qualify that process as populist? The answer to both questions must be no. The period 2007–17 was never populist one, at least not in traditional terms. What happened in Ecuador over this period was a process of greater depth. Alianza País was

the first political organization in the country that modernized political domination, using a process of strategic and rational mechanisms and instruments of political communication. Never before had a government technified politics to such an extent. The very construction of Correa's leadership was as much a technical achievement as it was a political one. The Citizen Revolution reduced the contingencies of politics to the minimum possible and subjected them to a regime of calculation, foresight and opportunity. All other political parties appeared shoddy and amateur in the face of the perfectly oiled and highly efficient Alianza País machine. It ensured that the party never lost an election until 2017, when it suffered a betrayal from within.

- Was the Citizen Revolution a leftist process? Again, the answer here is no. In fact, the protagonists assumed themselves as "progressives". Their main leader, Rafael Correa, has always been characterized by his conservative and ultramontane positions. His political movement was not supportive of the feminist, labour, indigenous, youth and student movements. Instead, he wanted to control them and turn them into cogs in his machine, and he dedicated himself to dividing, persecuting and destroying them when they resisted this co-optation.
- The negative position taken against the traditional media, perceived as being too close to the former political system and political class, was not a fight for the right to freedom of expression, but rather a strategy aimed at turning the media into the only valid political subjects of the political opposition recognized by the citizen revolution.

Perhaps we might look to the work of Jean Baudrillard and his "simulacrum" theory to help us understand the process of hegemonic construction of Rafael Correa and his Alianza País movement during the period 2007–17. Baudrillard's simulacrum is defined as: "something that replaces reality with its representation". Thus, Correa's ascription to the left and his definition of his political philosophy as "progressivism" and "socialism of the twenty-first century" were, in reality, simulacra. His appeal to populism was another simulacrum. His charismatic leadership was, in fact, a construct, created and maintained by the party electoral and political machinery. Without that machinery in place, the power of the leadership and the party evaporated, as indeed happened in 2017 with the election of Lenín Moreno as president as anointed successor but one who supposedly "betrayed" Correa. Since that 2017 crisis, Alianza País has not been able to win another election. It needed access to the state machinery to do so. The "Citizen Revolution" proclaimed by Correa was the name for the most efficient political machinery ever generated in Ecuador's political system in all its republican history.

REFERENCES

Arditi, B. 2004. "El populismo como espectro de la democracia: una respuesta a Canovan". *Revista Mexicana de Ciencias Políticas y Sociales* 47(191): 86–99.

Asamblea Nacional del Ecuador 2008. *Constitución 2008*. Quito: Asamblea Nacional.

Canovan, M. 1999. "Trust the people! Populism and the two faces of democracy". *Political Studies* 47(1): 2–16.

Cantos Molina, A. 2020. *AGD de la estafa a la impunidad*. Quito: El Conejo.

Dávalos, P. 2011. *La Democracia Disciplinaria: El proyecto posneoliberal para América Latina*. Bogotá: Desde Abajo.

Dávalos, P. 2013. "'No podemos ser mendigos sentados en un saco de oro'. Las falacias del discurso extractivista". In F. Alvarez *et al.* (eds), *El Correísmo al desnudo, de VVAA*, 190–215. Quito: Montecristi Vive.

Dávalos, P. 2014. *Alianza PAIS o la reinvención del poder. Siete ensayos sobre el posneoliberalismo en el Ecuador*. Bogotá: Desde Abajo.

de la Torre, C. 2007. "The resurgence of radical populism in Latin America." *Constellations* 14(7): 384–97. DOI: 10.1111/J.1467-8675.2007.00453.X.

de la Torre, C. 2008. "Protesta y democracia en Ecuador: la caída de Lucio Gutiérrez." In M. Lopéz Maya, N. Iñigo Carrera & P. Calveiro (eds), *Luchas contrahegemónicas y cambios políticos recientes de América Latina, de VVAA*, 197–227. Buenos Aires: CLACSO, 2008.

de la Torre, C. 2013a. "In the name of the people: democratization, popular organizations, and populism in Venezuela, Bolivia, and Ecuador." *European Review of Latin American and Caribbean Studies* 95: 27–48.

de la Torre, C. 2013b. "Technocratic populism in Ecuador." *Journal of Democracy* 24(3): 33–46.

de la Torre, C. 2019. "Global populism histories, trajectories, problems, and challenges". In C. De la Torre (ed.), *Routledge Handbook of Global Populism*, 1–28. London: Routledge.

Edwards, S. 2019. "On Latin American populism, and its echoes around the world". *Journal of Economic Perspectives* 33(4): 76–99.

Hurtado, O. 2012. *Dictaduras del Siglo XXI*. Quito: Paraíso Editores.

La Voz de América 2007. "Ecuador expulsa a representante del Banco Mundial", 26 April. www.vozdeamerica.com/a/article-2007-04-27-voa4/28024.html.

Laclau, E. & C. Mouffe. 2006. *Hegemonía y estrategia socialista. Hacia una radicalización de la democracia*. Argentina: FCE.

Laclau, E. 2005. *La razón populista*. Mexico: FCE.

Laclau, E. 2008. *Debates y combates: Por un nuevo horizonte de la política*. Buenos Aires: FCE.

Lukácks, G. 1985. *Historia y conciencia de clase*. Barcelona: Orbis.

Marchat, O. 2007. *Post-Foundational Political Thought: Political Difference in Nancy, Lefort, Badiou and Laclau*. Edinburgh: Edinburgh University Press.

Mazzolini, S. 2021. "Rafael Correa and the citizen's revolution in Ecuador: a case of left-wing non-hegemonic populism". In P. Ostiguy, F. Panizza & B. Moffitt (eds), *Populism in Global Perspective: A Performative and Discursive Approach*. New York: Routledge.

Montúfar, C. 2016. *¿Vivimos en democracia? Análisis conceptual del régimen político de la revolución ciudadana*. Quito: UASB-Corporación Editora Nacional.

Mouffe, C. 2007. *En torno a lo político*. Buenos Aires: FCE.
Muñoz Jaramillo, F. *et al.* (eds) 2014. *Balance Crítico del gobierno de Rafael Correa*. Quito: Universidad Central del Ecuador.
Ortiz, R. 2018. "Los problemas estructurales de la Constitución ecuatoriana de 2008 y el hiperpresidencialismo autoritario". *Estudios Constitucionales* 16(2): 527–66.
Páez, P. 2004. "Liberalización financiera, crisis y destrucción de la moneda nacional en Ecuador". *Cuestiones Económicas* 20(1): 5–71.
Paz y Miño Cepeda, J., P. Dávalos & C. De la Torre Muñoz 2007. *Asamblea Constituyente y Economía: Constituciones en Ecuador*. Quito: Abya Yala.
Peruzzotti, E. 2019. "Laclau's theory of populism: a critical review". In C. De la Torre (ed.), *Routledge Handbook of Global Populism*, 33–43. London: Routledge.
Representaciones diplomáticas de Cuba en el exterior 2016. "Discurso de Rafael Correa Delgado, presidente de Ecuador", 29 November. http://misiones.minrex.gob.cu/es/articulo/discurso-de-rafael-correa-delgado-presidente-de-ecuador.
Sánchez Díaz, A. 2016. *Hegemonía y antagonismo: Análisis crítico de la teoría política de Ernesto Laclau y Chantal Mouffe*. Tesis de Maestría, Mexico: UNAM.
Tibocha, A. & M. Jassir 2008. "La Revolución Democrática de Rafael Correa". *Análisis Político* 64: 22–39.
Tushnet, M. 2019. "Varieties of populism". *German Law Journal* 20(3): 382–9.
Wiles, P. 1969. "A syndrome, not a doctrine: some elementary theses on Populism". In G. Ionescu & E. Gellner (eds), *Populism: Its Meaning and National Characteristics*, 163–79. London: Macmillan.
Williamson, J. 2004. "The Washington Consensus as policy prescription for development", 13 January. www.piie.com/publications/papers/williamson0204.pdf.
Žižek, S. 2006. "Against the populist temptation". *Critical Inquiry* 32(3): 551–74.

CHAPTER 10

THE NICARAGUAN CRISIS AND THE MIRAGE OF LEFT POPULISM

William I. Robinson

Nicaraguan president Daniel Ortega began a fourth consecutive term in office in January 2022, in the midst of a political and economic crisis that portends protracted instability in the Central American country. Since returning to office in 2007, Ortega and his wife, and vice-president, Rosario Murillo have dressed in a quasi-leftist discourse of "Christian, Socialist, and Solidarity", their programme of constructing a populist multiclass alliance under the firm hegemony of capital and Sandinista state elites. This alliance began to unravel in the second decade of the century, and then collapsed entirely in the aftermath of the government's violent repression of a 2018 mass popular uprising. The repression – which according to Amnesty International involved excessive use of force, extrajudicial executions, control of the media and the deployment of pro-government paramilitary squads against protesters (Amnesty International 2018) – left several hundred dead and sent tens of thousands more into exile.

With seven opposition presidential candidates imprisoned and held incommunicado in the months leading up to the November 2021 vote, and all the remaining contenders but one coming from small parties allied with Ortega and Murillo and his Sandinista National Liberation Front (FSLN), the results of the presidential elections were a foregone conclusion. In a complete breakdown of the rule of law, Ortega carried out a wave of repression from May to October, arresting, and detaining without trial, under various draconian national security laws, several dozen opposition figures. Among them were presidential candidates; peasant, labour and student leaders; journalists; and environmentalists. Several hundred others were forced into exile or underground.

Those arrested or forced underground in the pre-electoral crackdown included a number of historical revolutionary leaders, among them legendary guerrilla commanders Dora María Téllez and Hugo Torres. Both had participated in the 1978 raid on the National Palace that forced the Somoza dictatorship to free 60 political prisoners, and Torres had also participated in the daring 1974 Christmas party raid that forced Somoza to release Daniel Ortega from prison. Among those exiled were celebrated novelist, and Ortega's vice-president during the 1980s revolution, Sergio Ramirez. While the government charged Ramirez with "conspiracy to undermine national integrity", his actual crime was to have provoked the ire of the regime by publishing his latest novel, *Tongolele No Sabía Bailar* (*Tongolele Did Not Know How to Dance)*, a fictionalized account of the 2018 mass protests that marked the onset of the political crisis and the degeneration of the regime into dictatorship. The book was promptly banned in the country, with customs authorities ordered to block shipments at ports of entry (Manso de Lucas 2021).

The November 2021 vote took place in a climate of fear and intimidation, and in the complete absence of safeguards against fraud. The opposition issued a joint statement on 7 October calling for a boycott of the election. The government declared, after polls closed, that Ortega had won 75 per cent of the vote and that 65 per cent of voters cast ballots, whereas the independent Urnas Abiertas (Open Ballots) voting rights organization reported an abstention rate of approximately 80 per cent and widespread irregularities at polling stations around the country (*Heraldo Internacional* 2021). It was impossible to get accurate figures for the results of the vote, given that the Sandinistas exercise total control of the Supreme Electoral Council and near absolute control over reporting of the results, that independent foreign observers were banned and that journalists and civic organizations have been cowed from speaking out on the vote by the threat of repression (Miranda 2021).

If the 1980s revolution, led by the FLSN, inspired progressives the world over, the crisis is now generating deep fissures within the international left. As in the wake of the 2018 protests, significant portions of the left continue to insist that Nicaragua is experiencing a renewed revolutionary process, under the leadership of Ortega-Murillo and that the United States is bent on overthrowing the regime. These accounts point to social programmes, introduced by Ortega once he resumed power in 2007, and to US funding for a number of Nicaraguan organizations associated with the anti-Sandinista opposition.

WHAT IS LEFT IN NICARAGUA?

Relentless US intervention throughout the 1980s, including a counterrevolutionary military campaign, an economic embargo and internal political interference, eventually led to the Sandinistas being voted out of office in 1990. This electoral defeat plunged the Sandinista party into a sharp internal crisis over programmes, ideological orientation and strategy. Through the early 1990s, the Sandinista grassroots engaged in sustained resistance to the neoliberal programme, imposed on the country by the United States and the international financial agencies, in consort with the local capitalist class and conservative politicians. At the same time, however, a new Sandinista elite emerged among those who had acquired substantial properties during the 1990 regime change by privatizing and allocating to themselves – in what is known in Nicaragua as "the piñata" – the state assets, public property and Sandinista party resources that constituted the collective patrimony of the revolution.

As the 1990s progressed, new Sandinista landlords and businessmen began to develop an affinity of class interests and to ally themselves with the traditional bourgeoisie (Robinson 2003). Throughout that decade, and the next one, hundreds of historical Sandinista leaders, along with thousands of party members, left or were forced out of the FSLN as the Ortega faction gained an iron-clad control over the party machinery, and suppressed all attempts to renovate and democratize the party. This reduced the FSLN to a shell of the historical party. The new Sandinista elite gradually moved, from leading the popular classes in their resistance to the neoliberal programme of capitalist reconstruction, to using the party's dwindling authority to contain those classes and control their mobilization. If the Ortega inner circle had hacked its way into the ranks of the country's elite in the aftermath of the 1980s revolution, upon its return to power in 2007, the Sandinista bourgeoisie set about vastly expanding its wealth (*El País* 2009). Leading Sandinistas, grouped around Ortega, have heavily invested in tourism, agro-industry, finance, import-export and subcontracting for the *maquiladoras*.

Ortega has proved to be remarkably adroit at using radical-sounding language and anti-imperialist rhetoric to strike a reflexive chord of support among the international left. The FSLN leadership continued to legitimate itself with a revolutionary, and left populist, discourse that no longer corresponded to any political programme or conduct, other than that of furthering its own group interests and securing a place among the dominant bloc in the new neoliberal order. But it is hard to see what, if anything, would qualify the regime as revolutionary or socialist. Ortega returned to power in 2007 through a pact with the country's traditional right-wing oligarchy, the former members of the armed counterrevolution (known as the contras) and the conservative Catholic Church hierarchy and Evangelical sects. Promising absolute respect for private property and unrestricted freedom for capital, he then proceeded to co-govern with the capitalist class, organized into the Superior Council of Private Enterprise (COSEP), until the latter broke with Ortega in the wake of the 2018 protests.

After re-entering office, Ortega's government increased spending on public health and education, invested in infrastructure and introduced other welfare projects (to be doled out through FSLN patronage networks). These social programmes were welcome and important gains for the popular classes after years of relentless privatization and austerity. But they did not alter the essential neoliberal model put in place by the three governments that preceded Ortega's return to power (Robinson 2018). On the contrary, the Ortega-Murillo administration vigorously and violently defended existing class and property relations, receiving praise from the International Monetary Fund (IMF) and the World Bank for its pro-capitalist, pro-transnational corporate policies, as well as acclaim from the United States for its cooperation with the US Southern Command, the Drug Enforcement Agency and US immigration policies. Meanwhile, the nepotistic inner circle of the regime enriched itself through plunder of state resources, in particular through its control over Albanisa (Olivares 2016), the shadowy financial and oil conglomerate, established with several billion dollars in Venezuelan subsidies. The eight Ortega-Murillo children serve as advisors to the presidency, own or control an empire of private and, ostensibly, public television, radio and internet news outlets, manage public investment funds, and run a network of family businesses (Jorgic & López 2020).

Social indicators improved in the early years of Ortega's return to power, so long as commodity prices were high, the influx of foreign investment continued, international credits remained abundant, and the spigot of several billion dollars in the Venezuelan petro-dollar subsidy stayed open. Notwithstanding this, it is difficult to get any independent confirmation of the government's claim, echoed by its defenders abroad, that poverty has been cut in half. This is because the typical source for this data is the World Bank (2021) which, in turn, relies on official Nicaraguan government data. Accounts that report a startling improvement in living standards, such as one issued by the pro-Ortega Council on Hemispheric Affairs in Washington, DC, either rely solely on Nicaraguan government claims or simply do not provide sources for such data at all.

The Managua-based independent research institute, the International Foundation for Global Economic Challenge (FIDEG) has conducted annual household surveys since 2009. These surveys are considered by poverty researchers to be a more reliable assessment of poverty rates, than GDP-per capita, and other forms of aggregate data. According to the 2020 FIDEG report (FIDEG 2020), poverty rates declined slightly, from 44.8 per cent in 2009 to 39 per cent of the total population in 2014. But then poverty rates started to climb in 2015 – three years before the 2018 crisis that the government claims is responsible for rising poverty rates – reaching nearly 45 per cent of the total population by 2019, and essentially wiping out the mild gains registered in the early years of the Ortega-Murillo regime.

THE BONANZA FOR TRANSNATIONAL CAPITAL

The regime has not developed any of the policies typically associated with a socialist-oriented agenda. In the countryside, the agricultural sector is dominated by transnational agribusiness. In the early years of its return to power, the Sandinista government provided limited support to the peasant sector through a clientelist model of handouts. But land reform was never on the agenda. Instead, the capitalist development strategy subordinated the peasantry to the agribusiness sector. Displaced peasants were encouraged to push into and colonize what remained of the agricultural frontier in the less populated eastern side of the country. In the course of capitalist development in Latin America, this is the well-known pattern of rural capital accumulation. By the mid-2010s, settler colonization further penetrated into the Atlantic region, where the indigenous and Afro-descendent populations are concentrated, encroaching on and violating their communal lands, disrupting local autonomy and sparking an escalation of ethnic conflict that has led to numerous killings and displacement of these populations.

Banking, agriculture, industry, imports and exports are all controlled by local and transnational capitalist conglomerates: 96 per cent of the country's property is in the hands of the private sector (Baltodano 2018). There are no capital controls, no progressive tax policies (on the contrary, tax policies are regressive) and no tolerance for autonomous mobilization by the popular sectors. The regime has routinely deployed the army, police and paramilitary forces to violently repress these mobilizations (Robinson 2018) when they have taken place, including attempts: by maquiladora sweatshop workers to form independent unions and to fight for higher wages; by peasants resisting the environmentally disastrous plan to construct a canal through the country; and by mine workers and community activists protesting concessions to transnational mining companies and environmentally damaging development policies.

Meanwhile, corporate tax receipts plummeted from 2010 onwards (World Bank 2019). These corporate tax receipts are the second lowest in Central America, after El Salvador, according to World Bank data. Generous investment incentives, and concessions to transnational corporations, include ten-year across-the-board tax holidays (Healy Consultants 2021). Law 480, that authorized the Nicaraguan Canal Development Project, granted a Hong-Kong based company "exclusive concessions [that] will last for 50 years from the beginning of operations" and are extendable for another 50 years (Amnesty International 2017: 11). Nicaragua became a haven for transnational capital precisely because the government generated ideal conditions for the corporate bonanza, including establishing internal labour discipline and stability, and the lowest wages in all of Latin America outside of Cuba. In this regard, the Ortega-Murillo model is akin to the tripartite corporativism developed by the Partido Revolucionario Institucional (PRI) that long ruled Mexico. In this model, clientelist networks draw in sectors from the popular classes, while the leadership of official trade unions, peasant associations and community organizations is integrated into the ruling apparatus and acts to tightly control any independent mobilization from the grassroots.

The model worked in Nicaragua until the economic crisis hit in 2014. That crisis must be placed in the context of the contradictions of capitalist development in Nicaragua and worldwide, in this age of globalization (Robinson 2020). Along with the rest of Latin America – under left and right governments alike – from the 1990s right through into the second half of the 2010s, Nicaragua experienced a vast expansion of local and transnational corporate investment in mining operations, logging, agribusiness, tourism and maquiladora industrial production. As economic difficulties mounted, and growth rates dropped, starting in the mid-2010s, the government reached agreements with international financial agencies to deepen neoliberal austerity measures, one of which – a cut in pensions and an increase in pension contributions by workers and employers – was the spark that initially triggered the April 2018 protests.

IS THE UNITED STATES TRYING TO OVERTHROW THE ORTEGA-MURILLO REGIME?

The 1979 Sandinista Revolution that overthrew the Somoza dictatorship won the broad solidarity of progressives and the left all over the world. But the ongoing crisis is generating deep fissures within the international left. The regime has justified its escalating repression, with the claim that those detained are foreign agents who are part of a US conspiracy to carry out a *coup d'état*. In support of this claim, significant portions of the international left point to US funding for Nicaraguan opposition organizations. While the United States is indeed supplying funding to some opposition groups, there is a peculiar Manichean absence in these left accounts of any focus on the internal contradictions in Nicaragua, that have given rise to the crisis in the first place.

Along with several hundred other US citizens and several thousand *internacionalistas* from around the world, I participated in the 1980s in the revolutionary process. And in early July 2021, I joined more than 500 Nicaragua solidarity workers in the United States in signing a petition (Open Letter to the Nicaraguan Government 2021) that declared: "the crimes of the U.S. government – past and present – are not the cause of, nor do they justify or excuse, the crimes against humanity committed by the current regime of Daniel Ortega and Rosario Murillo". The letter called on the Nicaraguan government "to release more than 130 political prisoners, to rescind and make null and void the draconian national security law under which these individuals were arrested, and to negotiate electoral reforms to ensure free and fair elections".

Those who claim that the US government is promoting counterrevolutionary "regime change" in Nicaragua, point to multimillion-dollar funding (Harris 2021) from the US Agency for International Development (USAID), channelled through the National Endowment for Democracy (NED), and allocated to non-governmental organizations, media outlets and business associations associated with the opposition. In my view, NED activity anywhere in the world should be condemned by progressives, and there is nothing positive about what the United States is doing in Nicaragua. Nonetheless, this NED funding is taken by some on the left as a sign of a regime change operation, without any understanding or analysis of what it seeks to achieve. NED funding in Nicaragua started in the mid-1980s and has never ceased. It is not new to the Ortega-Murillo period. In the 1980s it was part of the counterrevolutionary strategy (Robinson 1992). From 1990 on, it has sought to bolster pro-neoliberal/capitalist forces, to help these forces to achieve hegemony in civil society, to promote the transnational capitalist agenda in the country and to prevent any radicalization of the grassroots (Robinson 1996). The charge that this funding has been aimed at overthrowing the government is hard to sustain, given that Ortega has co-governed with these same forces, bolstered by the NED. The NED programme in Nicaragua is distinct from those in such countries as Cuba, Venezuela or Iran, where they form one component of an all-out destabilization campaign.

In the early 1990s I wrote the first two books exposing the origins and *modus operandi* around the world of what was then, a little-known agency attached to USAID (Robinson 1992, 1996). I showed that the NED seeks distinct objectives in different countries, depending on Washington's overall foreign policy objectives in each country. In some countries, NED programes have been part of larger campaigns to overthrow established governments, as with the so-called "coloured revolutions" in Eastern Europe and former Soviet republics, in Nicaragua in the 1980s, or in Venezuela today. In other countries where popular forces are struggling against dictatorships and authoritarian regimes, such as South Africa until the fall of apartheid in 1994, Egypt during the Arab Spring or Honduras currently, NED programmes seek to bolster elite hegemony within these mass movements for democratization in order to prevent any radicalization of the grassroots and to secure outcomes compatible with the global capitalist order.

The NED runs programes in some 100 countries around the world, the majority of which are US allies, such as the other Central American republics. According to the NED databases (see NED n.d.) its programmes in Nicaragua totalled a little under US$6 million over the past five years. The NED spent a similar amount during the five-year period in Colombia, its closest ally in South America, and in Guatemala and Honduras. In this same period, it disbursed: US$12 million to Kenya, its close ally in East Africa; some US$8.5 million to its ally, Egypt; US$8 million to the Philippines; US$8.5 million to Mexico; and so on. In contrast, during this period, spending in Cuba – part of an explicitly counterrevolutionary programme – was US$25 million.

Unlike Washington's devastating destabilization campaign against Venezuela and Cuba, which involves all-out economic blockades and sanctions, Nicaragua, to date, remains part of the Central America Free Trade Agreement (CAFTA) and the United States is Nicaragua's main supplier of petroleum. The incoming Ortega government welcomed the CAFTA pact in 2006, at a time when social movements throughout the Isthmus were mounting large-scale protests against it. Nicaragua does not face trade sanctions, and commerce with the United States, the country's principal trading partner, is booming, amounting to over US$5billion in 2020 (United States Census). Despite the 2018 Nicaraguan Investment and Conditionality Act (NICA) that threatened to oppose loans to Nicaragua from the international financial institutions (United States Congress 2017–18), the spigot of international aid has remained wide open. On the eve of the November 2021 election in Nicaragua, the US Congress passed the RENACER Act (United States Senate 2021), which was a virtual carbon copy of the earlier NICA Act.

To date, the only sanctions that the US government has applied is on the personal assets, held in the United States, of several dozen top Nicaraguan government officials from the Ortega inner circle. Otherwise, it has not enforced the NICA or RENACER Acts. Charges by the regime, and its supporters among the international left, that Nicaragua suffers from "crippling US sanctions" (Perry 2021) are patently false. From 2017 to 2021, it received a whopping US$2.2 billion in aid from the Central American Bank of Economic Integration (BCIE) (*Confidencial* 2021a, 2021b), and in 2020–21 it received several hundred million in credits from the Inter-American Development Bank, the World Bank and the International Monetary Fund (*La Prensa* 2021). Also, Nicaragua does not face military or paramilitary aggression from Washington.

While some among the international left condemn calls for sanctions on Ortega, both the US and international left, in fact, had broadly mobilized (unsuccessfully) in 1978 and 1979 to force Washington to impose sanctions on the Somoza dictatorship, and to block international financing to it, because of its gross human rights violations. The worldwide left, similarly, demanded sanctions against apartheid South Africa, sought to block US and international financing for the Pinochet dictatorship and currently calls for "boycott, divestment, sanctions" against Israel. (For the record, I personally do not support trade sanctions on Nicaragua, or recognize that the United States has the right to unilaterally impose sanctions on other countries. Here I wish to highlight the hypocrisy and double standards of some among the international left.)

In my analysis, Washington's principal concern is not that of getting rid of Ortega. It is instead about preserving, in the face of a crisis that sprung from internal contradictions, the interests of transnational capital in the country, and the hegemony of capital over any post-Ortega political project. What the United States most fears is an unstable and unpredictable vacuum of power that could threaten capitalist interests in the country, and US policy objectives towards the region. But the problem with this is, that that the traditional political right in Nicaragua lacks any coherent strategy and is in a state of political disorganization, which leaves it to the business sector, and its corporate forms of organization, to put together some sort of transition process. This business sector – its agencies and its think tanks – has received most of the US funding and, in the wake of the 2021 elections, set out to search for some rapprochement with Ortega-Murillo that could preserve its economic interests.

Depending on how events unfold on the ground, US policy may change as the crisis deepens and as US-Nicaraguan political tensions heighten. In 2021 the USAID, as part of its Central American Regional Security Initiative (CARSI), which allocates funds for governments, private sector, and non-governmental organizations, set aside an additional $3 million for Nicaraguan civil society organizations, according to a USAID congressional notification on CARSI appropriations (USAID 2021). However, it should be noted that beyond the NED, USAID funding for Nicaragua during the first 13 years of the Ortega government, from 2007 to 2020, amounted to hundreds of millions of dollars (ForeignAssistance.Gov n.d.). The vast majority of this sum went to the government itself – to health and educational programmes, export-import support, food aid and commodities support, counter-narcotics operations, technical assistance for government development programmes, and so on. It is simply not tenable to claim, therefore, that USAID programmes in Nicaragua seek "regime change".

Right-wing forces and traditional conservative elites have gained hegemony over the opposition. The popular sectors have been caught, since 2018, between the corrupt and repressive Ortega government and the traditional oligarchy, backed by international right-wing forces, that has never conformed to the Sandinista monopoly of political power and that set about to take advantage of the popular revolt, to more directly return that power to itself. Hence, grassroots opponents of the Ortega-Murillo regime find themselves between the rock of an Ortega-Murillo dictatorship, and the hard place of the capitalist class and its political agents among the traditional conservative parties. The right – just as disturbed as Ortega by the outburst of popular protest from below in the 2018 uprising – tried to hitch mass discontent to its own agenda, of recovering direct political power and assuring there would be no threat to its control over the Nicaraguan economy.

It is both ironic and tragic that the young people who took to the streets to protest in 2018, were mostly the sons and daughters of an earlier generation of Sandinistas who participated in the 1980s revolution – ironic because they were condemned by the regime as counterrevolutionary pawns of a failed "US *coup d'état*", and tragic because the repression against them helped pave the way for conservative hegemony over the opposition. The mass of Nicaraguans, beyond the Sandinistas' secure base in some 20 percent of the population, have not shown any enthusiasm for the traditional conservative parties and businessmen that dominate the opposition and have no real political representation. A CID-Gallup poll, conducted on the eve of the November 2021 elections, found that 77 per cent of the country's electorate does not feel represented by any political party.

REFERENCES

Amnesty International 2017. "Nicaragua: danger: rights for sale: the interoceanic grand canal project in Nicaragua and the erosion of human rights", 3 August. www.amnesty.org/en/documents/amr43/6515/2017/en/.

Amnesty International 2018. "Nicaragua: authorities unleashed a lethal strategy of repression against protesters". www.amnesty.org/en/latest/news/2018/05/nicaragua-authorities-unleashed-a-lethal-strategy-of-repression-against-protesters/.

Baltodano, M. 2018. "La Rebelión del Pueblo de Nicaragua", *Nueva Sociedad*. https://nuso.org/articulo/la-rebelion-del-pueblo-de-nicaragua/.

Confidencial 2021a. "CID-Gallup Candidato Opositor Barrería a Orega el 7 de Noviembre: 65 per cent vs. 19 per cent", 13 October. www.confidencial.com.ni/politica/cid-gallup-candidato-opositor-barreria-a-ortega-el-7-de-noviembre-65-vs-19/.

Confidencial 2021b. "BCIE Entregó 2289 Millones de Dólares al Régimen de Ortega Desde 2017", 19 October. www.confidencial.com.ni/economia/bcie-entrego-2289-millones-de-dolares-al-regimen-de-ortega-desde-2017/.

El País 2009. "La Oligarquía Orteguista", 25 August. https://elpais.com/internacional/2009/08/26/actualidad/1251237603_850215.html.

ForeignAssistance.Gov n.d. https://foreignassistance.gov/.

Fundación Internacional para el Desafío Económico Global (FIDEG) 2020. "Encuesta de Hogares para Medir la Pobreza en Nicaragua". Managua: FIDEG. http://fideg.org/wp-content/uploads/2020/12/Informe-Pobreza-FIDEG-2019.pdf.

Heraldo Internacional 2021. "Urnas Abiertas Señala Irregularidades y Abstención en la Jornada Electoral en Nicaragua", 8 November. www.heraldo.es/noticias/internacional/2021/11/08/urnas-abiertas-senala-irregularidades-y-abstencion-en-la-jornada-electoral-en-nicaragua-1532155.html?autoref=true.

Harris, R. 2021. "US targets Nicaraguan presidential election: former solidarity activists echo imperial talking points". *Counterpunch*, 16 July. www.counterpunch.org/2021/07/16/us-targets-nicaraguan-presidential-election-former-solidarity-activists-echo-imperial-talking-points/.

Healy Consultants 2021. "Accounting and tax in 2021". www.healyconsultants.com/nicaragua-company-registration/accounting-legal/.

Jorgic, D. & I. López 2020. "Como Ortega Levantó un Imperio Mediático que Enriquece a su Famila y Afianza su Poder en Nicaragua". *Reuters*, 23 November. www.reuters.com/article/politica-nicaragua-ortega-idESKBN2831EF.

La Prensa 2021. "FMI, BCIE, Banco Mundial y BID Desembolsan al Gobierno Casi US$900 Millones de Dólares en Menos de un Año, Cifra Histórica", 3 November. www.laprensa.com.ni/2021/11/03/economia/2903897-fmi-bcie-banco-mundial-y-bid-desembolsan-al-gobierno-casi-us900-millones-de-dolares-cifra-historica.

Manso de Lucas, M. 2021. "Sergio Ramírez: 'Mi Novel Prohibida Se Lee en Nicaragua Como un Acto de Resistencia". *NIUS*, 9 September. www.niusdiario.es/cultura/libros/sergio-ramirez-tongolele-no-sabia-bailar-novela-lee-acto-resistencia-nicaragua-contra-daniel-ortega_18_3204348629.html.

Miranda, W. 2021. "El Periodismo Nicaraguense, Arrinconado Entre las 'Leyes del Silencio' y el Exilio". *El País*, 3 November. https://elpais.com/internacional/2021-11-04/el-periodismo-nicaraguense-arrinconado-entre-las-leyes-del-silencio-y-el-exilio.html.

National Endowment for Democracy (NED) n.d. www.ned.org/.

Olivares, I. 2016. "La 'Alcancía' de Albanisa'". *Confidencial*, 9 April. www.confidencial.com.ni/especiales/la-alcancia-de-albanisa/.

Open Letter to the Nicaraguan Government 2021. https://zcomm.org/znetarticle/open-letter-to-the-nicaraguan-government-from-u-s-solidarity-workers-1979-1990/.

Perry, J. 2021. "Sanctions may impoverish Nicaraguans, but likely will not change their vote". NACLA, 6 August. https://nacla.org/sanctions-may-impoverish-nicaraguans-will-not-change-their-vote.

Robinson, W. 1992. *A Faustian Bargain: US Intervention in the Nicaraguan Elections and American Foreign Policy in the Post-Cold War Era*. Boulder, CO: Westview Press.

Robinson, W. 1996. *Promoting Polyarchy: Globalization, US Intervention, and Hegemony*. Cambridge: Cambridge University Press.

Robinson, W. 2003. *Transnational Conflicts: Central America, Social Change, and Globalization*. London: Verso Press.

Robinson, W. 2018. "Capitalist development in Nicaragua and the mirage of the left". *Truthout*, 18 May. https://truthout.org/articles/capitalist-development-in-nicaragua-and-the-mirage-of-the-left/.

Robinson, W. 2020. "Don't cry for me, Latin America". *Human Geography* 12(1): 91–4. https://journals.sagepub.com/doi/pdf/10.1177/1942778620910941.

United States Agency for International Development (USAID) 2021. *CN #129, 23 February: Central America Regional Security Initiative (CARSI)*. Washington, DC: USAID.

United States Census. Various Years. www.census.gov/foreign-trade/balance/c2190.html.

United States Congress, H.R. 1918 – 115th Congress 2017–18. *Congress.Gov*. www.congress.gov/bill/115th-congress/house-bill/1918.

United States Senate, Committee on Foreign Relations 2021. "Chairman Menendez Lauds Senate Approval of Updated RENACER Act to Secure Passage in House of Representatives", 2 November. www.foreign.senate.gov/press/chair/release/chairman-menendez-lauds-senate-approval-of-updated-renacer-act-to-secure-passage-in-house-of-representatives.

World Bank 2019. "Profit tax (per cent of commercial profits) – Nicaragua." https://data.worldbank.org/indicator/IC.TAX.PRFT.CP.ZS?locations=NI.

World Bank 2021. "Nicaragua – poverty headcount ratio at national poverty line (per cent of population)". https://tradingeconomics.com/nicaragua/poverty-headcount-ratio-at-national-poverty-line-percent-of-population-wb-data.html.

CHAPTER 11

POPULISM AND THE RIGHT IN LATIN AMERICA

Barry Cannon

INTRODUCTION

Populism is a slippery concept, not least due to its use as a catch-all term for widely distinct political projects, extinguishing many of their differences. In the past I have argued (Cannon 2018) that we need to view populism as an academic analytical tradition rather than empirical fact, emphasizing instead the left/right dichotomy as the essential conceptual tool to help order, understand and explain political phenomena. In this chapter I develop this work further, using Bobbio's (1996) conception of the left/right dichotomy as a dyad, shaped by historical consensus and rupture centred on (in)equality. As Noël and Thérien (2008) argue, consensuses emerged between left and right on state development and welfare regimes in the post-Second World War period, and more recently, I argue here, around "progressive neoliberalism" (Fraser 2017) in the post-Cold War period. These global consensuses between left and right can be loosely mapped onto the Latin American experience, as respectively the postwar "state developmentalist" or classic "populist" phase, and the more recent phase of left-oriented "pink tide" governments. These have both been contested by right-oriented administrations, viewed in the dominant literature as respectively "neo-populism" in the 1990s (Weyland 1996, 2003; Roberts 1995), associated with figures such as Menem in Argentina, Collor in Brazil and most notably, Fujimori in Peru, and a more recent radical right populism, associated primarily with Jair Bolsonaro in Brazil. In both these literatures, there is strong emphasis on the autonomy of the political from ideology, allowing the concept to "travel" temporally and spatially. In this chapter, I review both these instances of right-wing populism in Latin America consecutively, using a more contextually sensitive approach to these phenomena, which is best equipped to appreciate their distinctions, while emphasizing what they share. Such an approach needs to include, as

Munck recommends in the introduction to this volume, the problematics of "development, democracy and social transformation". Taken from this perspective, while each right-wing populist regime in the region is shaped by the distinct temporal and spatial circumstances in which it emerges, what they share is the right's central historical objective of maintaining and deepening social hierarchy, not just at the level of class, but also in gender, ethnicity and sexuality. Additionally, I argue that the main ideological and programmatic vehicle for this, in the contemporary period, is neoliberalism. In other words, political action cannot be divorced from ideology, as much of the mainstream literature on contemporary populism claims. From such a viewpoint, I conclude that what both these cases of populism point to is a wider "crisis of liberal hegemony" (el-Ojeili and Taylor 2020), with liberalism increasingly becoming split into three discrete strategic branches, pointing to a long period of dissensus in the near to medium term.

THE RIGHT IN THEORY

Most analysts accept Norberto Bobbio's (1996) by now classic approach to the right/left dichotomy, which places (in)equality as its central and constant defining feature. Throughout modern political history, Bobbio argues, the consistent theme differing left from right has been "the distinction between a horizontal or egalitarian principle of society and a vertical or inegalitarian perception of society" (Bobbio 1996: 58). The left, therefore, believes that human beings are more equal than unequal, that inequality therefore is social, and as a result can, and should, be eradicated through human action. The right believes the opposite: that inequality is natural, indeed beneficial, and so cannot, and indeed should not, be eradicated. This is not to say that the left wishes to eradicate all inequalities, nor that the right wishes to preserve all inequalities. As Noël and Thérien (2008: 18) point out, the right has a long liberal tradition in favour of legal equality, if not actual equality, of socioeconomic outcomes. Nevertheless, generally speaking, it can be argued, along with Bobbio (1996: 65), that "the [left] is more egalitarian, and the [right] more inegalitarian". From this perspective, the core meaning of the left/right distinction can be conceived as "whether one supports or opposes social change in an egalitarian direction" (Ronald Inglehart cited in Noël & Thérien 2008: 10), with equality ultimately meaning "a rotation in the seat of power" for everyone (Robin 2018: 9). Left or right policy options, then, have implicit and explicit outcomes favouring some classes over others – intersected with inequalities related to gender, race and sexuality.

Bobbio (1996: 10), moreover, conceptualizes the left/right dichotomy as a dyad, emerging from conflict and polarization, an antithetical "distinction covering the whole of the political universe". Left and right, however, "are not absolute concepts, but historically relative" that is, they can change over time and across space (*ibid.*: 46). Movements in the left – from being identified with liberalism, to democracy and then later socialism, for example – cause consequent shifts and movements within the right, and vice versa. Different consensuses are established as history unfolds (universal suffrage, for example, or the post-Second World War Keynesian settlement), which nevertheless generate new cleavages (Noël & Thérien 2008: 10). The right, from this perspective, can be viewed as "counterrevolutionary", constantly reacting against the left as well as consistently borrowing from it (Robin 2018: 29–30). Yet equality, or more accurately inequalities, remain the central issue around which these consensuses and cleavages revolve.

Left and right positioning around (in)equality, however, is no idle choice. Underlying it are long and deeply held attitudes to social hierarchy. For the conservative mind, as Robin (2018: 24) reminds us, "hierarchy is order", and disorder is the overturning of hierarchy and hence the latter's justification. "Conservatism" then, Robin insists (*ibid.*: 7), "is the animus against the agency of the subordinate classes". The left/right distinction, therefore, does not just mean greater equality or inequality in all, or some, of the areas identified, but an overturning or reinforcement of traditional hierarchies, especially within, what Robin (*ibid.*) calls, the "private life of power", which underpins and benefits from such inequalities. The right, therefore, seeks to maintain distinctions between elites and masses, whereas the left seeks to reduce them. This is not to claim that the right does not "accept the entrance of the masses onto the political stage" (*ibid.*: 30); conservatism is nothing if not adaptable to change. But the main aim of the right is to ensure that such change can be used to support the concept and practice of hierarchy. One means to achieve this is through the "private life of power", that is, allowing the masses "to locate themselves symbolically in the ruling class or be provided with real opportunities to become faux aristocrats in the family, the factory and the field" (*ibid.*).

Moreover, by the right here I do not just mean the "political" right, that is the parties and institutions embedded in institutional democracy. Rather, along with Robin (2018: 28–9): "I treat the Right as a unity, as a coherent body of theory and practice that transcends the divisions so often emphasised by scholars and pundits." The right, then goes beyond the political to straddle, what Michael Mann (1986) identifies as, the four arenas or networks of power which have consistently underpinned most organized governance since historical records began. These are ideological, economic, military and political (IEMP) power, all of which intersected with transnational factors (see Cannon 2016, 2019). This approach, while not neglecting the political, provides a more wide-angled view of the social ecology, which ensures the persistence and reproduction of right-wing ideas in social life, including in politics. In this sense, "the right" is not only collections of political parties, but rather can be approached from a type of Gramscian metapolitical viewpoint. This includes not just "war of manoeuvre" tactics, aimed at capturing state institutionality through, for example, electoral politics or military coups, but also "war of position" strategies in the realm of culture, aimed at capturing "hearts and minds" to construct a right-wing "common sense". The right-wing "war of position" then is, as Karl Ekeman (2018: n.p.) observes of the post-1968 French new right, "a cultural struggle aimed at changing perceptions, affections, and worldviews, so as to naturalize a politics from the right", a type of *Kulturkampf* which has increasingly become the hallmark of right-wing politics and, in particular, radical or far right politics in the contemporary period (Rydgren 2018: 26).

That said, since the 1980s, neoliberalism has become the dominant ideological frame by which social hierarchy has been maintained, largely due to its role in increasing and perpetuating socioeconomic inequality (Harvey 2005; Stiglitz 2012; Piketty 2014). It can be argued, then, that ideologically speaking (although not necessarily in terms of party identification) those who support and actively promote neoliberalism are on the right of the political spectrum while those who oppose it, or at least question it, are to the left. Since its initial roll-out, however, neoliberalism has become split into what Nancy Fraser (2017) has termed "progressive", "reactionary", and indeed, "hyper reactionary" forms. The first dominant variety pursues a meritocratic form of neoliberalism, which acknowledges inequalities of, at the very least, gender, sexuality and ethnicity, with class inequalities rebranded as "disadvantage", or simply poverty. This has allowed for a centrist left/right consensus around, what Sandel (2020: 13) has called, the "tyranny of merit", whereby through a pursuit of "equal opportunity" selective processes, society's "winners" can believe that they "have earned their success through their own talent and hard work", and not through their superior positioning in a hierarchical society. The latter two forms, on the other hand, emphasize an important social conservative ideological position with an extreme anti-egalitarian thrust, particularly on issues of recognition. However, this is, according to Brown (2019: 15), the logical outcome of neoliberalism's three core objectives: critiquing and dismantling society; attacking "democracy understood as popular sovereignty and shared political power"; and extending the personal protected sphere at the expense of the public.

POPULISM AND THE (LATIN AMERICAN) RIGHT

The contemporary right, then, can be conceptualized, as a class-based, elite-led project, at the national, regional, and transnational level, with neoliberalism at its ideological core (Cannon 2019). In this sense, the centre of politics, of both centre-right and centre-left, in its adoption of neoliberalism, has moved further to the right, making societies right-oriented in their general social ethos – the "extreme" centre, as British political theorist and activist Tariq Ali (2015) has labelled it. Such a wide-ranging view of the right, however, is somewhat at odds with dominant conceptions of populism, which currently can be situated between what Munck here has identified as the "populism as political strategy", and poststructuralist perspectives. Dominant literature on the subject tends to negatively counterpose populism with (liberal) democracy when in fact, as Munck here rightly points out, the relationship between the two is much more complex and nuanced. Part of the problem is a narrow view of what constitutes the political as being primarily national and electoral, when in fact it needs to be situated in the national and transnational, to include a wider range of actors beyond the strictly party political, and to be situated in more wide-ranging struggles over key issues, such as development, democracy and social transformation, as Munck here identifies. Most work on populism refutes this more wide-ranging ontological stance, in favour of the previously identified neoclassical viewpoint of the separation of politics from all other social spheres. Indeed, labelling a political phenomenon as populist could be seen as part of a wider, historically situated, contemporary discussion on inequalities, and the role of liberal democracy or polyarchy in their perpetuation (Cannon 2018: 480).

Populism in Latin America is usually associated by analysts with the left, be that the so-called "classic" populism of the early and mid-twentieth century, such as that of Juan Domingo Perón in Argentina, or more recent examples during the "pink tide" period of left-wing governments, such as Hugo Chávez in Venezuela (Mudde & Kaltwasser 2013). From this perspective, Latin America, is viewed as less prone to the emergence of right-wing populist phenomena. Nevertheless, while generally true, at least two periods of right-wing populism have been identified by analysts in the region. The first, labelled a "neo-populist", or "neoliberal populist", period can be identified in the late 1980s and 1990s, and includes figures such as Carlos Salinas de Gortari in Mexico (1988–94), Carlos Menem in Argentina (1989–99), Fernando Collor de Mello in Brazil (1990–92) and Alberto Fujimori in Peru (1990–2000), among others (Weyland 1996, 2003; Vilas 2004; Conniff 2020). The second, more recent, phase of radical right-wing populism (RRP) in the region is primarily associated with President Jair Bolsonaro of Brazil, elected in October 2018, as well as other right-wing leaders such as "interim" president of Bolivia, Jeanine Añez (2019–20), opposition politician José Antonio Kast in Chile, and in Peru, three times presidential candidate and daughter of former president Alberto Fujimori, Keiko Fujimori.

The following two sections will consider each of these instances of right-wing populism in turn, examining their characterization in the literature.

What we find is that the radical right populism of Bolsonaro seeks to regain some of the momentum of the initial neoliberal reform era ushered in by neo-populists However, it differs in its radical rejection of progressive neoliberal tenets around recognition, which neo-populists tentatively accepted as part of a wider emerging transnational left/right consensus on these issues.

(NEOLIBERAL) NEO-POPULISM, 1989–2001.

The context and immediate causes of populism, according to both Weyland (1996, 2003) and Roberts (1995: 113), the two most influential analysts of neo-populism, are structural. The processes of modernization which took place previously, during the military dictatorships (Weyland 1996: 7), but also in the immediate post-authoritarian democratic period, led to a "collapse of the developmentalist state" (Roberts 1995: 90), clearing the way for neo-liberalism (*ibid.*), and indeed making its acceptance inevitable (Weyland 1996: 9). The result is a political context where "populist leadership is likely to thrive" (Roberts 1995: 90), in the form of the above-mentioned presidents, Fujimori, Menem, Collor, etc. Thus, populism is seen by both these analysts as a political strategy, involving personalist, "outsider" leaders who organize an ostensibly unorganized mass of mostly poor or "subaltern" sectors (Roberts 1995: 88), in a "direct, unmediated, uninstitutionalized" manner (Weyland 2003: 1097). This populist project is "delinked from a socio-economic programme" (*ibid.*), instead having "an amorphous or eclectic ideology, characterized by a discourse that exalts subaltern sectors, or is anti-elitist and/or anti-establishment" (Roberts 1995: 88). A link is retained with previous developmentalist strategies, however, as these populists use "widespread redistributive or clientelistic methods to create a material foundation for popular sector support" (*ibid.*), motivated entirely by "the leader's insatiable quest for power" (Weyland 2003: 1102; see also Roberts 1995: 89).

While this characterization can be applied to any populist experience anywhere, what puts the "neo" into "neo-populism" is its neoliberal character. According to Roberts (1995: 113), the previously noted modernization processes and the crisis of the "developmentalist" state, not only provided a political context for populism, but also for neoliberalism, because "ultimately, the two phenomena are mutually reinforcing", having some "unexpected affinities" (Weyland 1996; see also Roberts 1995: 112). These are, according to Weyland (1996: 16): the use of special appeals to the informal sectors; distance from organized civil society associated with the previous "developmentalist" regime; branding the parties linked to it as the enemy; ruling in an autocratic manner, utilizing the state "as the decisive agent for effecting change"; and distributing whatever benefits are available, in a targeted manner, to the poorest rather than to more established working and middle classes. Under "neo-populism", the core of the anti-elitist message was a rejection of the previous, "populist", "developmentalist" state as being antiquated and inefficient, with neoliberal restructuring hailed as the only manner to modernize the economy and end the crisis. Yet the similarities between neo-populism and neoliberalism are fortuitous and contingent, rather than causal or organic, as "populism should be decoupled from any specific phase or model of socio-economic development" (Roberts 1995: 112).

These regimes, as most in the region at the time, beginning with Pinochet in Chile, were radical in their neoliberalism (Rodríguez 2021), although between these two analysts there are contradictory conclusions on their impact. For Weyland (2003), for example, the "unexpected" coupling of populism with neoliberalism has been positive, as neo-populists "promoted significant social democratisation" (*ibid.*: 1103), providing recognition and material benefits to the poor, pursuing "some elite turnover in government and state institutions" (*ibid.*), especially of women, and extending "significant political voice" to these sectors through the extended use of opinion polls, which he hails as the "scientific form of gauging 'the will of the people'" (*ibid.*: 1105). Consequently, Weyland concludes that neo-populists showed "greater compliance with the political norms of democracy" than did classic populists (*ibid.*: 1106). He insists that neo-populism has had beneficial impacts on poverty and inequality and hence is the "best bet for neopopulist leaders" (*ibid.*: 1110) and for the consolidation and quality of democracy in the region. Here Weyland is echoing the hopefulness of the post-Washington Consensus of the 1990s, which sought to make compatible neoliberal economic reforms with "the social and institutional agenda of the region" (Munck 2003: 500). Roberts (1995), on the other hand, is more sanguine in his conclusions on the impact of neo-populism on the region, arguing that it challenges both the left by proving that the right can attract "a broad base of political support" (*ibid.*: 115) among popular sectors, and neoliberals by reviving both populism and autocracy, both of which they claim to reject. This, he warns would make it even more difficult to develop the necessary institutionality, particularly within civil society, needed to consolidate democracy in the region at that time.

There were two important contexts in Latin America which critics contend are underdeveloped in this account: the role of the "state developmentalist" regime of "classic" populism in Latin America's democratization; and the onset of the so-called "transition" to democracy (Lynch 2017; Vilas 2004; Quijano 1998). First, "state developmentalism" under "classic populism" saw many Latin American states achieving a form of "peripheral modernity" (Munck 2013: 10), which saw "a strong commitment to the development of a robust national state" (*ibid.*: 75). Classic populism, as Lynch (2017), Vilas (2004) and Quijano (1998) point out, overturned economically dependent, oligarchic regimes, implanting in their place a national, popular, socio-economic one, which extended national and regional economic and political autonomy, as it deepened and extended citizenship rights for many of those previously denied them. "Neo-populist" theory under-emphasizes these democratic gains, and neoliberalism's aim of reversing and overturning them (Lynch 2017: 94). Moreover, "neo-populist" theory was reductionist in its abstracting one facet of historic Latin American populism – in this case leadership – and making it the sum of its characteristics. Such an approach is contrary to the complexity of political regimes which, as Vilas insists, "is much more than a set of specific elements susceptible to contingent combinations. It is a power structure oriented towards defined objectives based on interests" (Vilas 2004: 147–8). Rather, the abstraction of politics from, as Weyland (2003: 1097) claims, "specific socioeconomic policies or class bases of support ... [or] a specific socioeconomic context", is an ontological position which reflects, as Vilas (2004: 139) astutely points out, "the separation of politics and economics typical of neoclassical theory". This partial narrative allows for the elision of key political and economic causal factors which allowed these regime to emerge in the first place.

Second, much of Latin America was undergoing a process of democratization from the previous military dictatorships, which dominated the region during the 1970s. The dominant narrative characterizing this era was put forward by the "transitology" school of democratization theory, viewing this as a process, led by cost-benefit calculations on the part of elites, seeking to implant a narrow procedural and institutional version of democracy in the region (Cannon & Hume 2012: 1041). The theory was criticized for being inherently teleological in this assumption, leading to conceptual stretching in its attempts to explain why such a form of democracy did not emerge and consolidate as expected. As Lynch (2017: 94) explains, these theoretical suppositions and expectations clashed frontally with the impacts of the neoliberal model imposed in tandem with the so-called "transition" to democracy in the region. Rather than pluralist democracies based on elite bargaining, the neoliberal model produced a massive "expropriation of [citizens'] rights and public goods in favour of minorities who would supposedly initiate or re-initiate economic growth" (*ibid.*), as well as a transfer of political power from "trade unions, popular organizations, parties, and the State to ... large businesses, neoliberal technocrats, and security organisms" (*ibid.*). Branding these regimes (neo)populist, in a pejorative manner, both helped avoid "analysis of the crisis in the democracy of elites in the region ... [as well as] helping erase historic populism from the collective memory" (*ibid.*: 100). Moreover, in the case of Peru's Fujimori at least, massive human rights violations, such as massacres and forced sterilization programmes, affecting largely popular sectors and, in the second case, poor, mostly indigenous, women, cast serious doubt on Weyland's optimistic claims of social democratization for women, ethnic groups and the poor under Fujimori (Weyland 2003: 1112). This elision underlines, as Burt (2006: 44) rightly claims, neo-populism theory's failure to "adequately address the coercive dimensions of power". It is interesting to note additionally that, despite such human rights violations, Fujimori received strong financial and diplomatic support from the US, IFI's and aid agencies (Schady 2000; Gonzalez de Olarte 1993; McClintock 2000; Roberts & Peceny 1997).

From these perspectives then, "neo-populist" analysis downplays or ignores the fundamental right-wing nature of these political projects, and their role in extinguishing the democratic gains achieved under the previous historical populist projects in the region, and the essential role of neoliberalism in achieving that objective. Rather than providing "scientific" analysis, they obscure the social, hierarchical, restorationist ambitions at the heart of the neoliberal project. In this they point to the fundamental incompatibility between the twin aims of neoliberal restructuring, and recognition of minorities, at the heart of the so-called post-Washington Consensus. The core of the theory around neo-populism, and of neo-populists in general, was the rejection of "developmentalism", the Latin American version of the Keynesian left/right consensus, which now became almost exclusively associated with a redundant and increasingly irrelevant left.

THE "TRUMP OF THE TROPICS": RADICAL RIGHT POPULISM IN LATIN AMERICA

By the time Jair Bolsonaro became president of Brazil in January 2019, populism as an analytical frame had gone global. Contemporary populism now was no longer viewed as a largely Latin American, or even developing world, phenomenon. Rather it had come to refer largely to radical right parties and leaders who had begun to enter democratic institutions throughout Europe, especially in the aftermath of the attacks on the US on 11 September 2001, and even more so in the wake of the 2008 financial crisis and 2015's refugee "crisis" in Europe (Mudde 2019). Its most emblematic moment, however, came in the United States with the election of Donald J. Trump to the presidency in 2016. The dominant ideational frame, most closely associated with the work of Cas Mudde and Cristobal Rovira Kaltwasser, draws heavily on the political autonomy approach, pioneered by Weyland and Roberts in Latin America, but also on the poststructuralism of Laclau. Hence, while the populist analytical frame's emergence was perfected in Latin America, Latin American right-wing populism, whose most dominant figure is Jair Bolsonaro, is viewed from the global perspective of the rise of the radical (populist) right.

Mudde (2019) identifies the causes of radical right populism as a mixture of economic and cultural anxieties; the first around deindustrialization, inequality and economic stagnation, the latter around immigration, crime and family, with both linked to popular distrust of globalization dynamics. According to Mudde (*ibid.*) it has four main characteristics: nativism, authoritarianism, familialism and populism. In practice, this means that it is: racist; top-down and authoritarian in its approach to social issues, such as drug addiction, crime and family breakdown; anti-immigration and migrants; and hostile to feminism and feminists as well as LGBTQIA+ groups (*ibid.*: 151). Its populism is in its separation of society into "two homogenous and antagonistic groups – the pure people and the corrupt elite", with politics being viewed as ideally "an expression of the *volonté générale* [general will] of the people" (*ibid.*: 7–8).

Most mainstream commentary on Bolsonaro advances such a characterization, emphasizing dangers to liberal democratic institutionality and, through attacks on minorities, to pluralism. Finchelstein (2019: 102), for example, believes that Bolsonaro "clearly stands on the border between fascist dictatorship and the democratic form of populism". Weyland worries that Bolsonaro will gradually "hollow out democracy", as he believes happened in Venezuela under Chávez (Fanning & Cabrera 2018). For Fukuyama, Bolsonaro, like other populist leaders in the world, is "a threat to democracy" (cited in Goldstein 2019: 253). Yascha Mounk (2018: n.p.) worries that the election of Bolsonaro puts "the biggest democracy in Latin America ... in mortal danger". Such concerns place these commentaries in the "death of democracy" school of thought, brought into fashion in the wake of Donald J. Trump's election to the US presidency in 2016. One of the most famous examples of this is Levitsky and Ziblatt's (2018) best-selling *How Democracies Die*, as well as examples by Pulitzer Prize-winning journalist and historian, Anne Applebaum (2020) and President Bill Clinton's ex-secretary of state, Madeleine Albright (2018). In such analyses, the theatre of democratic crisis can be found squarely within existing political institutionality, the main concern is with the perceived decline of (negative) freedoms associated with liberal democracy, and the crisis is regarded as a global one that has now, however, become more pressing because it is affecting the so-called "core" of the democratic world, including the United States. The analyses are largely descriptive rather than analytical, and there is little attempt to identify the reasons why these institutional failings emerge. Levitsky and Ziblatt (2018), for example, do acknowledge the role of inequality to some extent, but that role is neither expanded nor interrogated. Nor is existing democratic institutionality critically examined as a source of such instability, particularly with regard to its role in creating the conditions for such inequality to grow in the first place. Rather, these aspects are minimized in favour of an agent-centred analytical frame, with the cause of, and solution to, the crisis falling solely within the purview of political actors, with the citizens (i.e., civil society) playing an important, but supporting, role. Similar to mainstream approaches to neo-populism as discussed above, the dominant political science analytical frame for RRP then, is essentially conservative and neoliberal, as it suggests "a version of democracy completely tied down to the concept of freedom, to the detriment of the other substantive value of democracy: equality" (Giannone 2010: 74).

What is overlooked, and indeed obscured, by such agent-centred analysis with regard to Bolsonaro, is the essentially right-wing and conservative nature of his programme, which instead is recast as simply "anti-liberal", or "illiberal". This project was already begun by PT President Dilma Rousseff's erstwhile vice-president, Michel Temer, on assuming the presidency in August 2016, after Rousseff's highly questioned impeachment. On assuming office, Temer immediately presented a series of standard neoliberal policies such as: a fire sale privatization of state assets, possibly including parts of Petrobras, the state-owned oil giant and areas of the defence industry (Adghirni 2016); a wide-ranging labour law eliminating many historical workers' rights (Goldstein 2019); cuts in public spending on social programmes; and increased autonomy for the central bank (Leahy & Pearson 2016). He also introduced a new law to set constitutional limits on spending for the next 20 years (Robinson 2016) hence: institutionalizing austerity for the foreseeable future; eliminating the minimum allocation for education and health; reducing access for the poor to these social goods; and making it much more difficult for any future, especially left-wing government, to increase social spending. Moreover, Temer was consistently criticized for a negative attitude to gender and other cultural rights. All of this was packaged in an anti-left narrative with socialism and "communism" blamed for all Brazil's ills (Goldstein 2019)

Bolsonaro, on becoming president, took up, and further radicalized, the Temer agenda (Rangel 2018). Economically, Bolsonaro aimed to further deepen neoliberalism as evidenced by his choice of Paulo Guedes, ex-Chicago School professor and acolyte of Milton Friedman, as minister for the economy, giving him free rein to choose his team (*Latin American Herald Tribune* 2019). Markets were cautiously optimistic at the news, with UBS chief economist (and former deputy governor for Brazil's Central Bank), Tony Volpon venturing that, if Guedes "can get the reforms right, Brazil could be poised for another virtuous cycle" (Leahy & Schipani 2018: n.p.). Guedes aimed to increase privatizations, with promises to privatize or liquidate 100 state run companies (Fonseca *et al.* 2019), including Electrobras, the state electricity giant, and many airports and seaports (Conley 2019). Equally, Bolsonaro showed his anti-state animus by closing the Labour Ministry (hence undermining state regulation of employment conditions), installing a federal hiring freeze on state employment, and promising to reduce state employment by 30 per cent (Lopes & Faiola 2019). Moreover, Guedes managed to pass a wide-ranging pension reform, affecting 76 million state and private sector workers, which will "progressively end retirement by contribution time, raise the minimum retirement age, and reduce the average benefit amount across the board [– hurting] the poor and the middle class without bringing effective, long-term relief to the system" (Silva 2019: n.p.). Guedes sought also to slash taxes for the rich, aiming at halving the tax take in GDP terms from 36 per cent to 20 per cent (Conley 2019). Not all these measures have been achieved to date, nor have those that have been achieved been within the desired timescale, nor to the liberalizing level desired (Harris 2021). However, their anti-equality orientations are quite clear and hence radically right wing. Yet in effect they are no more radical than those imposed by the neo-populists of the 1990s.

What is particularly novel in the current context is Bolsonaro's culturally conservative agenda, which has received a great deal of media and academic attention. Nevertheless, its anti-equalizing animus is important to note, particularly when placed within the long-range colonialist context of Latin America, which alerts us to continuities, rather than ruptures with that past (Stumpf González *et al.* 2020). For example, Bolsonaro embraced the US-led "war on drugs", adopting "iron fist" policies on drugs and crime, relaxing gun ownership laws and citizens' legal protection against shoot-to-kill policies on the part of security forces. The result has been soaring gun ownership, including of high calibre weapons (Phillips 2021), and a culture of impunity for police assassination of suspects in poor areas, with most victims being black or brown (Milhorance 2021). There is a pronounced rejection of previously instituted measures aimed at reducing class, gender, or racial inequalities, directly relating such measures to "communism" (Berrón 2018). Affirmative action policies to improve equality prospects for Afro-Brazilians, indigenous groups (Rios 2021), women (Rangel *et al.* 2021) and LGBTQIA+ (Corrales 2017) had relative success in Brazil under the PT governments of Luiz Inácio Lula da Silva and Dilma Rousseff. Bolsonaro, on the other hand, has aimed at "de-legalizing and delegitimizing" this agenda, most notably by the "emptying of portfolios, bodies, and councils focused on the issue of civil rights" (Rios 2021: 35). Rangel *et al.* (2021: 168) note that Bolsonaro's arrival to power, became a "critical juncture that initiated a series of regressions in social rights, criminalization of leftist activism, and increases in police violence... with discourses of hate ... legitimized, targeting historically marginalized social groups (women, African Brazilians, LGBTQI+, the working class, rural communities, and Indigenous populations)". Feltran (2020: 101) argues that such actions, in the economy, in security and in the area of minority rights, emerged out of and are fully supported by a powerful military and evangelical alliance, "governed by the conservative and neoliberal elite" and constituting around "30 per cent of the electorate", as well as having a growing influence in Congress (Hinz *et al.* 2020). A minority, Feltran (2020: 101) warns, that is still "sufficient to deliver an absolute political majority". Indeed Webber (2020: 10) notes that evangelicals "delivered 11 million votes to Bolsonaro [in the October 2018 elections], more than the difference separating him from [the PT candidate Fernando] Haddad". These moves are a radical repudiation of the progressive neoliberal tendencies of the post-Washington Consensus model, promulgated by most of the main multilateral agencies and IFIs, largely dominated by the US and the "West", since the 1990s.

What is missing then from populist institutionalist type readings of Bolsonaro, is the core conservative, right-wing nature of his project. As Heller (2020: 592) accurately points out Bolsonaro's "populism has been marked not only by democratic regression (assaults on civil liberties, civil society organizations and independent institutions) but also by concerted efforts at retrenchment". By "retrenchment" he means "policies and programs designed to specifically exclude designated groups from recognition and access to public goods", as part of "a relatively well-defined project of rolling back expansions of social rights and asserting traditional socio-cultural hierarchies" (*ibid.*). Citing Weber, Du Bois and Bourdieu, he reasserts the inextricability of the cultural and the economic, and one could add the political to that mix (*ibid.*: 602). He also draws our attention to the "overlapping of domestic and global political fields" (*ibid.*: 604), whereby since the 1990s, "international governance institutions. a new global human rights eco-system, an expanding global public sphere and transnational advocacy networks have universalized the legitimacy of human rights and provided domestic groups with significant points of global leverage to advance their claims" (*ibid.*). However, Heller misses here that these same "global governance institutions", such as the IMF, the World Bank and the WTO, have not only provided elite domestic groups with cover to implement neoliberal policies but have insisted on them. Right-wing populism in Latin America, or indeed in mature Western democracies, cannot therefore be properly understood without reference to the interactions between the cultural, the economic and the political, or between the global with the regional, national and local. In the current context, the dominant global left-right consensus is around what Fraser (2017) calls "progressive neoliberalism", a neoliberalism-lite, mixed with legal and meritocratic mechanisms, to compensate for the sexual, gender, ethnic and, to some extent, class inequalities, exacerbated by neoliberalism's implementation. Right-wing populism, such as that of Bolsonaro, can be viewed as the right's backlash against this consensus, seeking to destroy it, and so release capitalism, in all its hierarchical glory, from these legal and ethical chains. In this, it is celebrating, rather than contradicting, the right's core ideological mission.

CONCLUSION

In this chapter I have sought to argue the following with regard to right-wing populism in Latin America. First, the right must be seen as part of a left/right dyad with (in)equality at its centre. This is affected by periodic moments of consensus and dissensus around (in)equality, depending on the balance of power between social forces at specific moments. Second, while these periods of consensus/dissensus vary in terms of outcomes, what is constant is the right's central aim of the maintenance and extension, where possible, of social hierarchy in the areas of class, gender, race, and sexuality. Third, on reviewing two instances of right-wing populism in Latin America – the so-called "neo-populism" of the 1990s and the contemporary radical right populism of Jair Bolsonaro in Brazil, I find that mainstream analysis deliberately emphasizes and abstracts the political from the other analytical areas of ideology and economics, as well as the local from the global. This serves to obscure the essential right-wing objective of these governments, of maintaining and extending social hierarchy. On close examination, neo-populism and *Bolsonarista* radical right populism, share a policy preference for swift, deep and merciless neoliberal reform. But Bolsonaro violently rejects and repudiates the transnational consensus of a progressive neoliberalism reifying both recognition and neoliberalism, which neo-populists accepted when it was in its infancy, and which was indeed perfected by the left. I have argued here that in this rejection, Bolsonaro and other radical right populists are, in fact, returning to the core nature of the right and its historical allegiance to the maintenance and extension of social hierarchy.

A central problem in mainstream approaches to the phenomenon of populism, is viewing the attitudes and issue positions associated with it as pathological, that is problematic or even extreme. El-Ojeili and Taylor (2020) reject this position, as it can, as I have pointed out, obscure wider conjunctural and geostrategic explanatory factors, which profoundly affect the problematics of development, democracy and social transformation, as highlighted by this volume. Such a position, they argue, serves dominant interests and the status quo, while blocking utopian thinking, that is "imaginative constructions of other better ways of being" (*ibid.*: 1152). They note that qualifying a political phenomenon as "extreme", indicates that it is "outside of mainstream attitudes, violating common standards or conventions" (*ibid.*: 1143). They see this stance as having three problems: it is ahistorical, as it fails to appreciate how such standards or conventions can change over time; it endorses a majoritarian perspective, regardless of the moral or political content of that perspective; and it assumes an "unproblematic access to and measurement of middle-lying normative values" (*ibid.*: 1144). Moreover, it correlates liberalism with moderation, when in fact, following Losurdo (2014:1144), liberalism is "a tangle of both freedom and oppression, emancipation, and dis-emancipation" and cannot be reduced to such an imprecise term. Instead, populism (among other supposedly pathological political phenomena) must be viewed as both symptom and result of a global "crisis of liberal intellectual and moral leadership" within a fragmented "post-hegemonic liberalism" (*ibid.*: 1150) which nonetheless is united by a "shared suspicion of popular politics, the people or the masses" (*ibid.*: 1151).

El-Ojeili and Taylor further argue that contemporary liberalism is divided into three fragments, with none achieving hegemony: a "punitive" neoliberalism, as seen in the austerity turn of governments in the wake of the Great Financial Crisis (GFC) which is violent and literally unjustified, and which "seeks to reinforce extant power relations in authoritarian directions" (2020: 1151); a neo-Keynesianism found among liberal intellectuals and in some of the international financial institutions, which is "an elite-civilising project that urgently seeks a way of saving capitalism from itself" (*ibid.*); and, the "liberalism of fear", issuing "urgent dystopian warnings", of which populism is one, raising "the spectre of terrifying threats to anything that challenges global capitalism" (*ibid.*).

The analytical approaches to right-wing populism in Latin America examined here, I contend, belong to the "liberalism of fear" category. Populism, regardless of its content, is always ultimately considered negatively as a living dystopia which "we" must stop at all costs. Instead of such an approach, el-Ojeili and Taylor (*ibid.*: 1152) urge us to reconsider the phenomena from a more open-minded perspective, which may allow us to find "utopian tropes" within them, which el-Ojeili (2019: 1161) argues could "shed a different light on even the most immediately unpleasant of contemporary ideologies".

REFERENCES

Adghirni, S. 2016. "After oil industry shift, Brazil seeks to open up defense". *Bloomberg Markets*, 25 October. www.bloomberg.com/news/articles/2016-10-25/brazil-seeks-to-open-defense-industry-to-foreign-participation.

Albright, M. 2018. *Fascism: A Warning*. New York: Harper.

Ali, T. 2015. *The Extreme Centre: A Second Warning*. London: Verso.

Applebaum, A. 2020. *Twilight of Democracy: The Failure of Politics and the Parting of Friends*. London: Penguin Random House.

Berrón, G. 2018. "Odio, frustración, y valores reaccionarios: Jair Bolsonaro y la regresión política en Brasil". *Nueva Sociedad*, October. https://nuso.org/articulo/odio-frustracion-y-valores-reaccionarios/.

Bobbio, N. 1996. *Left and Right: the Significance of a Political Distinction*. Chicago, IL: University of Chicago Press.

Brown, W. 2019. *In the Ruins of Neoliberalism: The Rise of Anti-Democratic Politics in the West.* New York: Columbia University Press.

Burt, J. 2006 "'Quien habla es terrorista': The political use of fear in Fujimori's Peru". *Latin American Research Review* 41(3): 32–62.

Cannon, B. 2016. *The Right in Latin America: Elite Power, Hegemony and the Struggle for the State.* London: Routledge.

Cannon, B. 2018. "Must we talk about populism? Interrogating populism's conceptual utility in a context of crisis". *New Political Science* 40(3): 477–96. https://doi.org/10.1080/07393148.2018.1487187.

Cannon, B. 2019. "Characterization, strategies, and objectives of the Latin American right". In H. Vanden & G. Prevost (eds), *Oxford Encyclopedia of Latin American Politics.* https://oxfordre.com/politics/view/10.1093/acrefore/9780190228637.001.0001/acrefore-9780190228637-e-1717.

Cannon, B. & M. Hume 2012. "Central America, civil society and the 'pink tide': democratization or de-democratization?" *Democratization* 19(6): 1039–64. DOI: 10.1080/13510347.2011.619775.

Conley, J. 2019. "Bolsonaro unveils mass privatization plan for Brazil while slashing taxes for rich and wages for poor". *Common Dreams*, 4 January. www.commondreams.org/news/2019/01/04/bolsonaro-unveils-mass-privatization-plan-brazil-while-slashing-taxes-rich-and-wages.

Conniff, M. 2020. "A historiography of populism and neopopulism in Latin America". *History Compass* 18: 1–11. https://doi.org/10.1111/hic3.12621.

Corrales, J. 2017. "Understanding the uneven spread of LGBT rights in Latin America and the Caribbean, 1999–2013". *Journal of Research in Gender Studies* 7(1): 52–82.

Ekeman, K. 2018. "On Gramscianism of the right". *Critique and Praxis* 13(13). http://blogs.law.columbia.edu/praxis1313/karl-ekeman-on-gramscianism-of-the-right/.

el-Ojeili, C. 2019. "Reflecting on post-fascism: utopia and fear". *Critical Sociology* 45 (7–8): 1149–66.

el-Ojeili, C. & D. Taylor 2020. "The extremism industry: a political logic of post- hegemonic liberalism" *Critical Sociology* 46(7–8): 1141–55.

Fanning, R. & K. Cabrera 2018. "Why a 'hollowing out' of democracy could happen if Brazil elects Jair Bolsonaro", *Texas Standard.* www.texasstandard.org/stories/why-a-hollowing-out-of-democracy-could-happen-if-brazil-elects-jair-bolsonaro/.

Feltran, G. 2020. "Centripetal force: a totalitarian movement in contemporary Brazil". *Soundings* 75(16): 95–110

Finchelstein, F. 2019. *A Brief History of Fascist Lies.* Oakland, CA: University of California Press.

Fonseca, P., A. Mano & B. Baum. 2019. "Brazil plans to privatize or liquidate 100 state-run companies". *Reuters*, 8 January. www.reuters.com/article/us-brazil-infrastructure/brazil-plans-to-privatize-or-liquidate-100-state-run-companies-idUSKCN1P2197.

Fraser, N. 2017. "From progressive neoliberalism to Trump – and beyond". *American Affairs Journal* 1(4). https://americanaffairsjournal.org/2017/11/progressive-neoliberalism-trump-beyond/.

Giannone, D. 2010. "Political and ideological aspects in the measurement of democracy: the Freedom House case". *Democratization* 17(1): 68–97. DOI: 10.1080/13510340903453716.

Goldstein, A. 2019. "The new far-right in Brazil and the construction of a right-wing order". *Latin American Perspectives* 46(227): 245–62. https://doi.org/10.1177/0094582X19846900.

Gonzalez de Olarte, E. 1993. Economic stabilization and structural adjustment under Fujimori. *Journal of Interamerican Studies and World Affairs*, 35(2): 51–80.

Harris, B. 2021. "Brazilian leaders dash hopes for sweeping tax reform". *Financial Times*, 25 May. www.ft.com/content/3a53dfdb-86a8-47ff-846f-88475ac114a1.

Harvey, D. 2005. *A Brief History of Neoliberalism*. Oxford: Oxford University Press.

Heller, P. 2020. "The age of reaction: retrenchment populism in India and Brazil". *International Sociology* 35(6): 590–609.

Hinz, K., J. Vinuto & A. Coutinho 2020. "Por Dios y por las armas: el ascenso neopentecostal y securitario en Brasil (2003–2019)". *Revista CIDOB d'Afers Internacionals* 126: 185–213. DOI: doi.org/10.24241/rcai.2020.126.3.185.

Latin American Herald Tribune 2019. "Brazil's Bolsonaro leaves economy to free-market crusader". *Latin American Herald Tribune*, 9 January. http://laht.com/article.asp?ArticleId=2472752&CategoryId=14090.

Leahy, J. & S. Pearson. 2016. "Brazil to formally enshrine central bank's autonomy". *Financial Times*, 13 July. www.ft.com/content/ff464df6-4895-11e6-ab7c-840b4062e27c.

Leahy, J. & A. Schipani 2018. "Opponents fear 'wrecking ball' Bolsonaro poses threat to Brazilian democracy". *Financial Times*, 24 October. www.ft.com/content/a1ce1194-d6a6-11e8-ab8e-6be0dcf18713.

Levitsky, S. & D. Ziblatt 2018. *How Democracies Die: What History Reveals About Our Future*. London: Penguin Random House.

Lopes, M. & A. Faiola. 2019. "What the first days of Bolsonaro's presidency say about the direction he will take Brazil". *The Washington Post*, 5 January. www.washingtonpost.com/world/the_americas/what-the-first-days-of-bolsonaros-presidency-say-about-the-direction-hell-take-brazil2019/01/04/89d59e72-0ed7-11e9-8f0c-6f878a26288a_story.html.

Losurdo, D. 2014. *Liberalism: A Counter History, translated by Gregory Elliot*. London: Verso.

Lynch, N. 2017. *Populismo ¿dictadura o democracia?* Lima: Universidad Nacional Mayor de San Marcos.

McClintock, C. 2000. "The United States and Peru in the 1990s: cooperation with a critical caveat on democratic standards". www2.gwu.edu/~clai/docs/McClintock_Cynthia_06-00.pdf.

Mann, M. 1986. *A History of Power from the Beginning to AD 1760*. Cambridge: Cambridge University Press.

Milhorance, F. 2021. "Police killing hundreds in Rio de Janeiro despite court ban on favela raids". *The Guardian*, 18 April. www.theguardian.com/global-development/2021/apr/18/police-kill-hundreds-rio-de-janeiro-favela-raids-court-ban.

Mounk, Y. 2018. "Lessons from Brazil: a disturbing election shows that we can't count on the lessons of history – or multiculturalism – to save democracy". *Slate*, 29 October. https://slate.com/news-and-politics/2018/10/bolsonaro-brazil-election-lessons.html.

Mudde, C. 2019. *The Far Right Today*. Cambridge: Polity.

Mudde, C. & C. Kaltwasser 2013. "Exclusionary vs. inclusionary populism: comparing contemporary Europe and Latin America". *Government and Opposition* 48: 147–74. DOI: 10.1017/ gov.2012.11.

Munck, R. 2003. "Neoliberalism, necessitarianism and alternatives in Latin America: there is no alternative (TINA)?" *Third World Quarterly* 24(3): 495–511.

Munck, R. 2013. *Rethinking Latin America: Development, Hegemony and Social Transformation*. New York: Palgrave Macmillan.

Noël, A. & J.-P. Thérien. 2008. *Left and Right in Global Politics*. Cambridge: Cambridge University Press.

Phillips, T. 2021. "Anger as Bolsonaro moves to make guns easier to access: 'A threat to democracy'". *The Guardian*, 15 February, www.theguardian.com/world/2021/feb/15/jair-bolsonaro-brazil-guns-easier-to-acquire.

Piketty, T. 2014. *Capital in the Twenty-First Century*. Cambridge, MA: Harvard University Press.

Quijano, A. 1998. "Populismo y fujimorismo". In F. de Laro (ed.), *El fantasma del populismo. Aproximación a un tema [siempre] actual*, 171–207. Caracas: ILDIS-FLACSO-Nueva Sociedad.

Rangel, P. 2018. "Guinada conservadora em políticas de gênero na América Latina: reflexões iniciais". *Cadernos Adenauer* 19(1): 211–27. http://www.kas.de/wf/doc/25933-1442-5-30.pdf.

Rangel, P., E. Dultra & D. McCoy 2021. "De-democratization in Brazil and the new puzzle of women's political representation". In B. Bianchi *et al.* (eds), *Democracy and Brazil: Collapse and Regression*, 166–94. Abingdon: Routledge.

Rios, F. 2021. "Cycles of democracy and the racial issue in Brazil (1978–2019)". In B. Bianchi *et al.* (eds), *Democracy and Brazil: Collapse and Regression*, 26–41. Abingdon: Routledge.

Roberts, K. 1995. "Neoliberalism and the transformation of populism in Latin America: the Peruvian case". *World Politics* 48(1): 82–116.

Roberts, K. & M. Peceny 1997. "Human rights and United States policy towards Peru". In M. Cameron and P. Mauceri (eds), *The Peruvian Labyrinth: Polity, Society, Economy*, 195–222. University Park, PA: Pennsylvania State University Press.

Robin, C. 2018. *The Reactionary Mind: Conservatism from Edmund Burke to Donald Trump*. Second edition. New York: Oxford University Press.

Robinson, A. 2016. "Brazil for sale: how a legal coup set the stage for privatization". *The Nation*, 27 July. www.thenation.com/article/archive/brazil-for-sale-how-a-legal-coup-set-the-stage-for-privatization/.

Rodríguez, J. 2021. "The politics of neoliberalism in Latin America: dynamics of resilience and contestation", *Sociology Compass* 15. https://doi-org.jproxy.nuim.ie/10.1111/soc4.12854.

Rydgren, J. 2018. "The radical right: an introduction". In J. Rydgren (ed.), *The Oxford Handbook of the Radical Right*: 1–13. New York: Oxford University Press.

Sandel, M. 2020. *The Tyranny of Merit: What's Become of the Common Good*. London: Allen Lane.

Schady, N. 2000. "The political economy of expenditures by the Peruvian Social Fund (FONCODES), 1991–95". *The American Political Science Review* 94(2): 289–304.

Silva, N. 2019. "Bolsonaro's new chapter of neoliberalism in Brazil". *Jacobin*, 18 December. https://jacobinmag.com/2019/12/jair-bolsonaro-brazil-neoliberalism-guedes-carvalho.

Stiglitz, J. 2012. *The Price of Inequality: How Today's Divided Societies Endanger Our Future.* New York: W. W. Norton & Co.

Stumpf González, R., M. Baquero and L. Grohmann 2020. "¿Nueva derecha o vino viejo en odres nuevos? La trayectoria conservadora en Brasil en el último siglo". *Política y Sociedad* 57(3): 647–70

Vilas, C. 2004. "¿Populismos Reciclados O Neoliberalismo A Secas? El Mito Del 'Neopopulismo' Latinoamericano". *Revista de Sociologia Política* 22: 135–51.

Webber, J. 2020. "A great little man: the shadow of Jair Bolsonaro". *Historical Materialism* 28(1): 3–49.

Weyland, K. 1996. "Neopopulism and neoliberalism in Latin America: unexpected affinities". *Studies in Comparative International Development* 31(3): 3–31.

Weyland, K. 2003. "Latin American neopopulism". *Third World Quarterly* 24(6): 1095–115. DOI: 10.1080/01436590310001630080.

CHAPTER 12

POPULISM AND THE LEFT IN LATIN AMERICA

Mariana Mastrángelo and Pablo Pozzi

Are Latin America's populist movements complementary or inimical to the traditional left parties? Or, rather, are they a new type of left, more autochthonous, original and anchored in the subcontinent's realities, as opposed to those ideologies that arose in nineteenth-century Europe? These questions assume, on the one hand, an ahistorical perspective that implies not only a certain uniformity in these movements but also that there are similarities between those movements that arose in the 1930s and 1940s, and those progressive, post-2000, governments that were termed "the pink tide". On the other hand, there is a problem in defining the term "left". Are we referring to the many varieties of Marxist groups or do we include anarchists, left nationalists and movements such as the Third World Priests? In addition, the same movements, described by academics as "populist" would not consider themselves to be so. Here we will term "left" all those political movements who question capitalism as a social and economic system and will consider "populist" those movements that tend to consider themselves as a vehicle of the people and its aspirations, implying a progressive slant to their policies, and a challenge to established elites. As such, from a Latin American perspective, people like Brazil's Jair Bolsonaro would not be considered "populist", while Cuba's Fidel Castro would be placed within the camp of the "left".

These issues become even more complex if we consider that many of the initial populist movements, in the 1930s and 1940s, joined conservatives, moderates and leftists. At the same time, organizations such as the communist parties considered the new movements as indigenous versions of European fascism, while the populists tended to view the traditional left as competitors, that were extraneous and foreign to Latin American realities. Over half a century later, the pink tide included a large part of the organized left, who considered the reforms by Venezuela's Hugo Chávez or Bolivia's Evo Morales as the way towards a popular revolution.

This chapter posits that national and historical circumstances tend to define the relationship between the diverse populist movements and the left. At the same time, populism, as a political movement, remains sufficiently undefined, that it can be taken to mean different things to different people, and thus contrasts with the tendency of the left towards taxative ideological constructs and discussions.

Outside of Latin America, movements traditionally associated with populism, such as the Russian Narodniks, the French Poujadisme or the American Peoples' Party, are generally thought to have links to conservative perspectives, hark back to a mythical nation represented in "traditional" values and an "idyllic" peasant/farmer society. Instead, Latin American populism tends to be seen as a popular, multiclass, progressive reform movement, competing with the traditional left for the allegiance of workers, employees and peasants. At the same time, the Latin American left, in the 1930s, included sizeable communist and socialist parties, plus the remnants of a once powerful anarchist movement (in nations such as Uruguay it remained a considerable force), and smaller groups of left-leaning intellectuals.

Although the different movements and leaders never used the term itself, academics initially borrowed the term *populism* from the People's Party in the United States in the late nineteenth century and its appeal to a generic version of "the people". Actually what academics, and their opponents called populism, was termed "national movements" by its protagonists, as a way to describe early twentieth-century political developments in Latin America. The golden era for Latin American populism is usually cited as the 1930s to the 1960s, and is identified with such preeminent leaders as: Lázaro Cárdenas in Mexico (1934–40); Juan Perón in Argentina (1946–55); Getúlio Vargas in Brazil (1930–54); Luis Muñoz Marín in Puerto Rico (1948–64); José María Velasco Ibarra in Ecuador (1952–56); and Víctor Raúl Haya de la Torre in Peru and Jorge Eliécer Gaitán in Colombia (although neither reached the presidency). This initial populist period came to an end in the mid-1950s, through a combination of repressive market-oriented dictatorships and developmentalist governments. While it never disappeared as a mass movement (and in nations such as Argentina it reappeared with unusual strength in the late 1960s), it was reduced to a fraction of its initial appeal. However, at the end of the twentieth century, Latin America unexpectedly witnessed a new round of progressive governments (usually termed the "pink tide"), with an expansion of the possibilities for popular political participation. Many have considered these governments to be a modernized continuity of the movements from the 1930s and 1940s, and thus have termed them "populist", especially due to their appeal to "the people" and their emphasis on the state as a vehicle for popular demands.

The first wave of Latin American populism began at the start of the Great Depression in 1929. In various countries, politicians, who focused on the people and a series of reforms modelled on different aspects of the welfare state, were voted into office. At the same time, these new political leaders gave voice to an anti-imperialist discourse that claimed to represent national interests, in confrontation to those of powers such as Great Britain and the United States.

The second populist wave began in the final years of the twentieth century and continued into the twenty-first century. Like in the first wave, these governments relied on anti-imperialism, and a reinforcement of the state participation in social and economic matters. This "statism" was presented as a new type of socialism grounded, not on class, but on "the people", while respectful of what it termed "national capitalism" and the free market. It was Hugo Chávez in Venezuela and Brazil's Partido do Trabalhadores (Workers' Party) who coined the term, "twenty-first century socialism", while Evo Morales brought about reforms to establish a pluri-national state, anchored in the traditions of the indigenous people of Bolivia.

THE FIRST WAVE: POPULISM AND ITS COMPETITION WITH THE LEFT

As stated above, populism emerged in Latin America in the period between the 1929 crisis and the end of the Second World War. While European and American populism is thought to be a result of the destructuring of traditional societies during the Second Industrial Revolution (see Hofstadter 1960), the Latin American version arose out of a period of growth of the working classes, urbanization and small businesses which, in turn, arose from a post-Depression period of industrialization, through import substitution. For Latin America, the decades between 1929 and 1950 were a period of increased social conflict and political crisis, the rise of the middle and working classes, and the growth of the Marxist left, specifically of the various communist parties. This was the time of: the 1932 Socialist Republic of Marmaduke Grove in Chile; the 1932 Farabundo Martí uprising in El Salvador; Tenentismo and the Prestes Column in 1924 Brazil; the Bolivian 1952 Revolution; and the growth of communist-led unions in Argentina, Mexico and Uruguay.

At the same time, the 1929 crisis had a huge impact on Latin American society and economy, since it curtailed agricultural exports to industrialized nations such as Great Britain. The result was to generate changes with far-reaching effects. On the one hand, industrial imports had to be substituted with lower-quality local products, due to a reduction in foreign currencies available to acquire imports. The fall in agricultural exports, which local farmers grew, led to rural unemployment and migration towards the cities in search of jobs. One of the results of this migration was the growth of industrial unions and of the communist parties. Communists led large industrial unions that organized mostly the "new" migrant workers. The emergence of "Red" unions, the rise in the number of hard-fought strikes, and the danger of social upheaval was something that marked the worldview of populist leaders, such as Vargas and Perón. As Perón wrote in 1950:

> I spoke to them a bit in communism [*sic*]. Why? Because if I had spoken in any other language, they would have pelted me with oranges [...] Because they were men with forty years of Marxism and with Communist leaders [...] They wanted to go where they thought was convenient [...] They believed in class struggle [...] The people who followed me did not want to go where I was going; they wanted to go their own way. I did not tell them where to go; I started walking ahead of them in the direction they wanted to go. Eventually, as we travelled together, I started to turn and took them where I wanted to go. (Perón 1950: 290)

This was ratified by the Peruvian Víctor Haya de la Torre:

> A thousand times we have repeated this declaration: aprismo is not communism. And it is not communism, not because we say so. Our statement is based on Marx. The Peruvian Aprista Party has taken to heart, since its beginnings, the sincere invocation of José Carlos Mariátegui, who once upon a time belonged to APRA: 'Let us Peruanize Peru'. That is, we must nationalize it in an integral sense. (Haya de la Torre 1932: 217)

Perhaps because of what Perón had pointed out, and Haya de la Torre made clear, many of Latin America's populist leaders of the 1930s and 1940s appropriated many of the demands, the language and symbology of the traditional left while, at the same time, combatting it. They tended to enable a series of reforms, from the top down, that had been central to the left's demands and struggles. However, alongside these reforming programmes, each leader crafted a different response, with many unleashing a repressive wave towards the left.

The left itself, except in Mexico and Chile, branded the different populist movements as a Latin American version of fascism. This combined the political expediency of branding a competitor, with pointing out that populist leaders such as Perón, or Vargas, admitted their admiration for Mussolini. At the same time, the left (especially the various communist parties) were on more solid ground, when pointing up the repressive nature of many of these governments, the fact that they modelled their reforms along corporativist lines, and their emphasis on an alliance between the national bourgeoisie, the lower middle class and the labour movement leadership.

Despite their repression of dissent, especially that from the left, most populist leaders were pragmatic, playing the left and right wings of their movement against one another. As Perón would say: "I have a right hand because I have a left one" (James 2010). Many leaders' policies tended to be pendular, always supporting one faction against the other, to maintain leadership of the movement.

Thus, Perón reinforced the "Special Section" of the federal police, whose task was the "fight against Communism", and persecuted PCA members within the Labour Movement (see Kabat 2018; Cutillo 2018). Meanwhile, Getúlio Vargas passed the "Monstrous Act" and unleashed a violent persecution of Brazilian communists (see Levine 1970: 68) as masterfully described in Jorge Amado's trilogy, *The Bowels of Liberty* (*Os Subterrâneos da Liberdade*, 1954). The combination of support from labour, social reforms and progressive discourse generated a mystique that tended to obscure the less savoury aspects of the new political movements and their leaders.

Unlike in Argentina and Brazil, the coming to power of Lázaro Cárdenas in Mexico in 1934 implied a level of cooperation between the left and the populist leadership. Cárdenas gave refuge to Leon Trotsky; permitted Marxist Vicente Lombardo Toledano to become secretary general of the Mexican Labour Federation (CTM), which then joined the communist-led World Labour Federation (FSM); and established a wide-ranging education reform, called "Socialist Education". The Cárdenas government represented a paradigm shift within Mexican populism that included substantive changes in the ruling party (which would become the Institutional Revolutionary Party, PRI, in 1946). Unlike other populist leaders, including previous Mexican presidents, Cárdenas permitted the dissidence and organization of independent social movements, to contain the power of the official workers' and peasants' confederations. In this context, the Communist International recommended that the Mexican Communist Party (CPM) actively collaborate in Cardenista policy. The International believed that an active intervention by the CPM would eventually radicalize Cárdenas's nationalist policies, increasing communist social and political influence, and opening the way for the seizure of power. A former member of the party, Secretary Francisco José Múgica, was one of the ideologues of the Cárdenas government (González 1979; Hernández Chavez 1979).

Whatever populism's political inclinations, the Latin American left's fortunes were in decline by the 1950, as the lot of the average working person improved significantly. For instance, mass unionization and full employment meant that workers gained job stability and increases in real wages. Although the various communist parties remained important throughout Latin America, they had lost much of their revolutionary *élan* and working-class support. Many moved towards a strained conviviality with the different populist movements, especially as the 1960s ushered in market-oriented military dictatorships throughout Latin America. In the 1940s, the left had considered populism as a local version of fascism. By the 1960s, many leftists thought that populism's failure to deal with the alliance between the military and the great bourgeoisie, would radicalize the rank and file towards the left. As such, most leftists began a reinterpretation of populism, to be considered now as a progressive movement with revolutionary potential.

THE SECOND WAVE: POPULISM AND TWENTY-FIRST-CENTURY SOCIALISM

What are termed populist movements, after the break-up of the USSR and the rise of neoliberal social and economic policies, are quite distinct from the earlier manifestations. Although they retained a reliance on charismatic leaders and an emphasis on state-managed redistributionist policies, there were important differences. The main one centred on an acceptance of overall neoliberal economic policies, while maintaining a progressive discourse. In fact, it is worth considering whether these new movements were effectively populist or rather a new type of left. In addition, they cannot be seen as a uniform phenomenon. For instance, Venezuela's Hugo Chávez has called himself socialist, whereas Argentina's Cristina Kirchner has often disavowed any linkage to the left.

A crucial difference is that in the first period, the organized Marxist left had been a presence throughout Latin America, and a potential challenge to the new populist movements. In this latest edition, the left was a mere shadow of its former self. The various Latin American dictatorships of the 1960s and 1970s annihilated most of the organized left, including Marxist, Christian and nationalist groups. Thousands of activists were murdered, imprisoned, went into exile or "just disappeared". At the same time, the fall of "real socialism" had led to an overall crisis of the organized left, including those sectors that had been critical of Stalinism. In 1975, membership of the Argentine Communist Party (PCA) accounted for about 1 per cent of the population; 15 years later it had lost 90 per cent of its membership and had splintered into various groups. By 2019, many within the Argentine left, including former guerrillas, the remnants of the PCA, several Trotskyist splinters and the Maoist Revolutionary Communist Party (PCR) had joined the governing Kirchner coalition. The Mexican Communist Party, although not very big, had been an organized and combative presence in the labour, student and peasant movements, especially from 1930 to 1950. Subjected to increased repression after the 1968 Tlatelolco Massacre, it began a process of fusion with other progressive movements after 1981, until it disappeared into one of the new populist movements, the Cardenista Partido de la Revolución Democrática (PRD).[1] In other countries, such as Chile, Bolivia or Venezuela, many on the Marxist left, including former guerrillas from the 1960s and 1970s, joined various new progressive alternatives that, a mere three decades earlier, they would have considered "reformist". Others founded new left organizations that attempted to be consonant with the times, learning from earlier failures. Perhaps the most emblematic of these changes have been Brazil and Argentina.

In Brazil, in 1980, the Partido do Trabalhadores (PT) was organized by workers in the Sao Paulo ABC industrial area, whose main leader was Luiz Inácio Lula da Silva. The PT began as a new model for the post-USSR left, and then evolved into what can be considered as a new type of populist left movement. From its inception, it was organized from the bottom up, respecting the formation of tendencies within the party, and developing a lively and very democratic political life. That made it possible for a broad sector of the progressive community to participate in the PT. It was quickly joined by various Trotskyist groups, as well as social democratic politicians, Christian left activists, and former guerrillas, such as Dilma Rousseff and José Genoino. At the same time, the PT succeeded in proposing and enacting a series of innovative measures such as the "participative budget" (*orçamento participativo*) begun in the city of Porto Alegre in 1989. Taking a page from medieval traditions and from New England townships in the nineteenth century, the participative budget was a "town meeting" model, that is a form of direct democracy in which most, or all, of the members of a community come together to legislate policy and budgets for local government. By 1993, there were tensions between the pragmatic, more political sector and those who wanted to retain the original socialist principles. That year the resolution from the party's eighth National Meeting reaffirmed PT's "revolutionary and socialist character", condemned the "conspiracy" of the elites to subvert democracy, stated that the party advocated "radical agrarian reform and suspension of the external debt" and concluded that "capitalism and private

1. The PRD, or Democratic Revolution Party was founded in 1989 as an alliance between six traditional leftist parties and a split from the PRI called Corriente Democrática (Democratic Current). Its leader is Cuauhtémoc Cárdenas, son of President Lázaro Cárdenas. Although it is a member of the Socialist International, many of its policies hark back to those of the Cárdenas presidency.

property cannot provide a future for humanity". Until that time, the PT was considered as part of the new left and in no way populist. However, after Lula's 1994 presidential campaign loss, the pragmatic sector began to gain the upper hand. The process was gradual, full of contradictions and replete with intra-party tension. By 1997, the National Meeting resolution redefined PT's version of socialism as a "democratic revolution", emphasizing a political, rather than economic, vision of socialism that aimed to make the state "more transparent and socially accountable". In other words, it had abandoned the anti-capitalist perspective of its origins in exchange for a vision, where reform was preferred to revolution. A year later, in 1998, Lula's third presidential campaign platform removed all mention of socialist proposals, and even the mention of a transition to a socialist society (Weaver 2018).

This also started to change the internal organization of the PT and since the 1990s it has turned from a militant party, with the priority of organizing branches, to a party organized around elections, with professionalized campaigns, private financing, political consultants and an increased reliance on Lula's charisma. In a sense, this implied a transition from the new left to populism, albeit a twenty-first-century version of the latter. The tendency of moderating its platform to garner votes in the middle and upper classes accelerated, and in 2002, with a big businessman as his vice-presidential candidate, Lula was finally elected after making major concessions to the private sector (Mendes Loureiro & Filho 2019). At that point, the compromises and alliances that the PT had made would leave a definitive mark on its public policies, reforms and government programmes. As Steve Ellner wrote "some of these policies ran counter to the leftist positions defended by the same leaders prior to reaching power. The dynamic that gave way to pragmatic and populist policies has important implications" (Ellner 2019: 11).

On the other end of the pink tide political spectrum, and closer to the actions of a traditional populist leader, Néstor Kirchner proposed a new political movement in 2003, called *transversalidad*, meaning that people of different political orientations were welcome to participate. Former guerrillas, communists and Trotskyists, as well as right-wingers from the Guardia de Hierro (Iron Guard), Menemism and traditional Peronist *caudillos* were appointed to government posts. Critics from the left remembered that Perón had always said that "you get on the horse from the left, and off from the right" (actually, the phrase belonged to Peronist intellectual Arturo Jauretche); meaning that in Argentina you win elections by posing as a leftist and you govern as a conservative. They claimed that there was no substantive change between Menem's socioeconomic policies and those of the Kirchners. The Kirchners frequently insisted that they were not leftists but nationalist reformers, and that to be able to govern effectively, one had to compromise while making necessary changes. Old fashioned Peronists claimed that this approach had little in common with Perón's policies; the Trotskyist left insisted that the reforms were insufficient, while the liberal opposition regarded the Kirchners' style of governing as a form of authoritarianism. All the criticisms have elements of truth. But more importantly, there is agreement among the critics that, unlike Chávez, the early PT or Uruguay's José Mujica and the Frente Amplio, the Kirchners cannot be considered left in any way. And yet, they have enacted progressive new laws. And many former leftists have joined their government, including the rump Communist Party. Did these leftists join *kirchnerismo* so as not to become irrelevant in Argentine politics, or rather did they do so because they believe it might become a conduit for revolution? Who is right? Are the Kirchners a form of twenty-first-century Peronism, a neo-Peronism? Are they conservative populists? Or rather, are they the only possible reformism in the aftermath of the changes brought about by the fall of the USSR?

In fact, their reforms have been very limited, especially when compared to those of Evo Morales in Bolivia or Hugo Chávez in Venezuela. While employment and purchasing power improved from the time Kirchner became president in 2003 until 2011, other significant social changes meant that, by 2015 one in every four Argentines was either unemployed or had occasional employment; a third of all wage earners were employed "off the books" (*en negro*); job insecurity climbed to record levels; social welfare (*las obras sociales*) has all but disappeared for more than half of the population; trade union membership was at an all-time low of 35 per cent; a whole generation had never held a regular job; educational levels had dropped and illiteracy had increased, relative to 1989; and the gap between the richest and poorest 10 per cent had widened. President Cristina Fernández de Kirchner has stated, repeatedly, that business has never made a higher rate of profit. In fact, business in Argentina is heavily subsidized by the state, from private gas and light companies, all the way to racetracks and the restaurants in the *chic* district of Puerto Madero, Buenos Aires. These subsidies, begun under the Menem government, and blamed as one of the causes of the 2001 economic debacle, have continued unchanged. Argentine businessmen have been guaranteed a high rate of return, no matter how irrational the economic policies followed by the government: the mechanism of subsidies protects them from market downturns. The Argentine left has tended to be supportive of the Kirchners' policies, considering that the negative aspects are offset by the positive ones, and that they must be pragmatic, when the only other possible alternative is an overtly neoliberal government, such as the one headed by Mauricio Macri in 2015. In this process the left has been subsumed into the *kirchnerista* movement, losing many elements of its identity.

As with the case of the Kirchners, many of the pink tide leaders have tried to deal with the changes of the twenty-first century by passing new laws, campaigning for human, gay and women's rights, and taking on some sectors of the traditional establishment. Because of such laws and progressive policies, these leaders have been considered the "New Left" and have garnered the support of a large section of the more traditional left. The Trotskyist left has been an exception. In Brazil, several Trotskyist groups split from Lula's PT to form the Partido da Causa Operária, the Partido Socialista de los Trabajadores Unificado, and the Partido Socialismo y Libertad (PSOL). The PSOL has aligned itself with a variation of Heinz Dieterich Steffan's twenty-first-century socialism theory (see Steffan 2000), and garnered almost 3 per cent of the vote in 2018. In Argentina, several small Trotskyite parties formed the Frente de Izquierda y de los Trabajadores (FIT), receiving close to 7 per cent of the vote in 2021. Many of these leftist organizations have run into the problem of supporting several proposals of the pink tide movements, while trying to maintain an independent left identity. At the same time, the success of the pink tide movements, and their ability to co-opt a significant portion of the left, has influenced many of the more traditional left organizations to adopt proposals and a discourse more in tune with these populist movements. Specifically, many in the twenty-first-century Latin American left have replaced their working-class-oriented perspective, with identity politics and an appeal to "the people" and "the poor". As such, the differences between populist and left movements, so tangible and clear-cut in 1940, have become diffuse and sometimes quite indistinguishable.

Possibly this is the reason why, for many outside observers, these new populist movements in Latin America were seen as just a more modern, version of the left, that had finally abandoned foreign Marxist criteria, to ground itself more firmly in national realities and traditions. A similar problem emerges when we consider the "pink tide" governments. It is the case that both Kirchners, Lula, Chávez, Evo, Mujica, Correa, Ortega are all thought to be similar by outside observers. And yet numerous conflicts between them suggest differences – for instance those between Uruguay's Mujica and Bolivia's Evo Morales, on the one side, and the Kirchners on the other (Mujica often referred to Néstor Kirchner as a "one eyed crook"). The same can be said in terms of their policies and ideas. Chávez was a proponent of what he termed "twenty-first-century socialism", whereas Evo Morales insisted on the creation of a pluri-national society, with deep roots in indigenous traditions. Lula, on the other hand, began in an ideological position closer to Chávez, but became quite distant by the time of his alliance with Igreja Universal and PMDB.[2] Meanwhile, the Kirchners' have often repeated

2. The PMDB, or Partido del Movimento Democrático Brasileiro (Brazilian Democratic Movement Party) is a centre right political party that came into being as the acceptable opposition to the 1964 military dictatorship. Ideologically it was at the opposite end of the spectrum from the PT.

that they were not 'left' but rather represented a modernization of Peronism. These philosophical positions had an impact on government policies. For instance, Chávez took over Venezuela's petroleum corporation (PDVSA) and used its considerable income to develop various social programmes (albeit there seems to have been a lot of corruption). The Kirchners, in spite of their rhetoric, did nothing similar. Their nationalization of YPF, Argentina's petroleum corporation, implied becoming the majority stockholder by buying Spanish Repsol shares. As such, YPF remains a private corporation, driven by profit, paying dividends, and selling shares on Wall Street. The same can be said of Lula and Evo Morales. At least until 2010 Morales's policies implied a far-reaching redistribution of income, which differed significantly from the policy of government handouts implemented by Lula.

The differences in approach are telling, in terms of popular support. When Dilma Rousseff was overthrown in a parliamentary *coup d'état*, Lula and his PT were unable to mobilize any kind of a significant protest, bringing about the rise of Jair Bolsonaro. This was unlike Bolivia, where the coup orchestrated by Jeanine Áñez saw significant resistance and repression. It ended when Áñez accepted new elections, which were overwhelmingly won by Morales's Movimiento al Socialismo (Movement Towards Socialism),[3] albeit without Morales as candidate. In Argentina, the Kirchners' socioeconomic failures brought about their defeat in the 2015 election. For the first time in Argentine history, an overtly right-wing candidate was freely elected. Mauricio Macri also had the dubious honour to be the first presidential candidate who did not even bother to mask his neoliberal proposals.

What, if anything, did these governments have in common? First, they all became pragmatic to reach political power and, as such, drew back from questioning neoliberal premises, such as the importance of a market-regulated society. Second, they believed redistribution of income was a result of increased government subsidies, not something derived from job creation (especially full employment). Thus, unemployment tended to remain at levels close to those of the 1990s throughout Latin America. Third, they did not attempt to develop their economies integrally, breaking the export cycle. This meant that when the price of commodities fell after 2009, their situation became critical. And yet, they were clearly not all the same. Morales and Chávez were reformists in a more traditional social democratic sense; neither was a Marxist in any meaningful sense of the term. Lula, the Kirchners, Nicaragua's Daniel Ortega, and Ecuador's Rafael Correa are, at

3. The MAS is a political party that arose of a fusion between activists from the miner's federation (CSUTCB), the Confederation of Indigenous Peoples of Eastern Bolivia (CIDOB), several peasant federations and a split in the right-wing, neofascist Falange Socialista Boliviana.

best, neo-populists, or conservative populists. In fact, Ortega has a strong component of mysticism; it is no accident that Ortega's health policies during the Covid-19 pandemic were similar to those of Brazilian right-winger, Jair Bolsonaro, or that he has dismantled many of the original Sandinista reforms.

In the meantime, many in Latin America's left have been absorbed into the new populist movements, while those who retained their independence tend to have accepted similar pragmatic criteria to the populists. In a sense, Latin American politics suggests an anecdote by journalist Norberto Galasso. He recalled that once upon a time a foreign ambassador asked Perón to describe Argentine politics. Perón thought about it for a short while and, with a huge smile on his face, said:

> "Well, my friend, in Argentina, 30 percent are *Radicales*, another 30 percent are Conservatives, 20 percent are Socialists, 10 percent Communists, and there are 10 percent who really do not care about politics."
>
> "But that is 100 percent," responded a surprised ambassador. "What about the Perónists?"
>
> "Oh no, we are all Perónists," said Perón, laughing.[4]
>
> (Galasso 2005: 1096)

REFERENCES

Cutillo, I. 2018. *Historias Gorilas. Represión en la Argentina durante los años 1943–1955*. Buenos Aires: Editorial Prometeo.

Ellner, S. 2019. "Pink-tide governments: pragmatic and populist responses to challenges form the right". *Latin American Perspective* 46(1): 4–22.

Galasso, N. 2005. *Perón: Exilio, resistencia y muerte*. Buenos Aires: Editorial Colihue.

González, L. 1979. *Historia de la Revolución Mexicana: Período 1934–1940, Los artífices del cardenismo*. Mexico: El Colegio de México.

Haya de la Torre, V. 1932. *Repertorio Americano* 24(14): 217–19.

Hernández Chávez, A. 1979. *Historia de la Revolución Mexicana: Período 1934–1940, La mecánica cardenista*. Mexico: El Colegio de México.

Hofstadter, R. 1960. *The Age of Reform*. New York: Vintage Books.

James, D. 2010. Conferencia dictada el 6 de agosto de 2010 en la Cátedra de Historia Socioeconómica de América Latina y Argentina de la Facultad de Trabajo Social de la Universidad Nacional de La Plata.

4. In Argentina *radicales* are those people who are members of the Unión Cívica Radical (UCR) party, a centre-right, middle-class organization founded in 1890.

Kabat, M. 2018. *Perónleaks: Una relectura del Peronismo a partir de sus documentos secretos, 1943–1955.* Buenos Aires: Ediciones ryr.

Levine, R. 1970. *The Vargas Regime: The Critical Years, 1934–1938*. New York: Columbia University Press.

Martínez, T. 2015. *La novela de Perón*. Buenos Aires: Alfaguara.

Mendes Loureiro, P. & A. Filho 2019. "The limits of pragmatism: the rise and fall of the Brazilian Workers' Party (2002–2016)". *Latin American Perspective* 46(1): 66–84.

Perón, J. 1950. *Conducción Política*. Buenos Aires: Mundo Perónista.

Steffan, H. 2000. *La crisis de los intelectuales*. Buenos Aires: Editorial 21.

Weaver, A. 2018. "Putting Brazil in context: the fall of the Workers Party". https://blackrosefed.org/brazil-in-context-workers-party/.

AFTERWORD

A TALE OF TWO "PEOPLE": NATIONAL POPULAR AND TWENTY-FIRST-CENTURY LATIN AMERICAN POPULISMS

Francisco Panizza

As the purpose of this book is the study of populism in Latin America, it would be understandable to skip the debate about the conceptualization of the term. Yet, without conceptualization, debates are hollow. If we do not define populism, how can we agree whether Salvador Allende or Luiz Inácio Lula da Silva can be characterized as populists? And, how can we understand the relations between populism and other essentially contested concepts (Collier *et al.* 2006) such as democracy? Contributors to this book define populism in a variety of ways, which results in different answers to the many questions raised by the study of populism in the region. In this overview, I will first briefly outline my understanding of populism, a conceptualization that is grounded on Ernesto Laclau's influential writings on the topic, and which is also broadly in line with the one adopted by Ronaldo Munck in the introduction to this book.

Laclau's (1979, 2005a, 2005b) theory of populism centres on the priority that populism attributes to the constitution of "the people" as a political actor within an antagonistic relation, that pits the people against a certain *Other* (typically, the oligarchy, the political or economic elite, the establishment, etc.). According to this criterion, the sociopolitical field is structured as a dichotomous, antagonistic relation between two sociopolitical blocs: *Us* (the people, the underdogs, the oppressed) and *Them* (the oligarchy, neoliberalism, the partocracy, etc.). The criterion also implies that populist actors take sides, by claiming to represent the underdogs or, as Igor Goicovic (Chapter 3) puts it, "the social bloc of the oppressed".

The people, as a political actor, are the outcome of political identification, and not a pre-existing social category. As a signifier, "the people" is always something retroactively constituted, an empty signifier that needs to be invoked, a performative call that creates what it is supposed to be expressing.

In this approach, the signifier, "the people" operates as a *nodal point*, around which different, and often antithetical, signifiers are articulated to assert who are *the people* and who represents them. Moreover, the performative constitution of the people does not take place in a political vacuum, it faces political resistance. Articulatory practices around the signifier "the people" are thus the defining elements of hegemonic struggles, which seek to fix contested identities (Ostiguy *et al.* 2021).

What, if anything, is distinctive about "the people" in populist discourse? After all, every politician claims to represent the people. Laclau addresses the question by arguing that the presence of popular elements in a discourse is not sufficient to transform it into a populist one. As he puts it: "Populism starts at the point where popular democratic elements are presented as *an antagonistic option* against the ideology of the dominant bloc" (Laclau 2005a: 81, emphasis added). And he further adds: "In order to have the 'people', we need something more: we need a plebs who claims to be the only legitimate populus, that is partiality which wants to function as the totality of the community" (*ibid.*).

Laclau's politically centred theory of populism gives autonomy to the political in the constitution of populist identities. It dissociates identification from structural factors, such as models of economic development and the actors' socioeconomic and cultural roots, to make identification the contingent outcome of discursive appeals and hegemonic struggles. Yet, the contingency of populist identification makes it difficult to explain why certain populist appeals are more successful than others, why populism has widely different characteristics in different regions of the world and even within the same regions, and how populist appeals are facilitated or constrained by material circumstances.

To address these questions, it is necessary, as done by the contributors to this book, to reground the study of populism in the history, economy and institutions of Latin America and map its varieties and manifestations through the region's history. In this concluding overview I will draw on Laclau's theory of populism, and on the contributors' insights on populism in Latin America, to focus on the constitution of populist identities in the two populist waves of incorporation in the region; the first one that spanned broadly the period from the 1940s to the 1970s (henceforth "national-popular [Latin American] populism") and the second one that covered the first two decades of the present century (henceforth twenty-first-century populism). The purpose of this focus is to reflect on the specific characteristics of populism in Latin America, and on what the commonalities and differences between the two waves tell about broader questions regarding populism and its relations with models of development and democracy.

NATIONAL-POPULAR POPULISM

Two questions about national-popular, Latin American, populism are particularly relevant for this comparative analysis of populism. The first one refers to the relation between populism and models of economic development. The second one addresses the relations between populism and class. In his early seminal essay "Towards a Theory of Populism" (TTP), published in his book *Politics and Ideology in Marxist Theory*, Laclau (1979) distanced himself from the views of early scholars of Latin American populism, such as Francisco Weffort and Octavio Ianni, that characterized populism as the political superstructure of the economic model of Import Substitution Industrialization (ISI). Laclau argued that populism was not the *necessary* superstructure of any social or economic process (Laclau 1979: 177). Laclau's claim can be interpreted in two different ways. The first is that populism can emerge in the most varied socioeconomic environments. The second is that ISI was compatible with a variety of political regimes, some of which were populist and others not. It is difficult to disagree with either of these two claims, but their formulation does not exhaust the question of the relation of national-popular populism to ISI.

National-popular populism emerged in the 1930s and 1940s, in antagonism to both the laissez-faire liberalism of the time, dominated by landowning interests, and the liberal-oligarchic political order, hegemonized by self-perpetuating political elites. In this early version of populism, political and economic nationalism went hand in hand. In the discourse of populism, the people were the embodiment of the nation, denied political rights and social justice by domestic oligarchies, associated with foreign interests. Hence its characterization as "national-popular". In government, populist leaders sought to implement a nationalist economic model (ISI) based on state intervention, for the development of national industries, combined with trade protectionism and social welfare initiatives.

What was in place in Latin America between the 1930s and the 1960s was an economic-political matrix, that cannot be fully understood in separation from each other. ISI prompted the social changes, and provided the material resources that made possible the first wave of incorporation of the urban popular sectors. Industrialization created the social bases of the new political regimes and undermined the hegemony of the landed elites and of their political representatives. Protectionism, subsidies, public and private monopolies, moderate inflation, and the transfer of resources from the agro-exporting sector to the urban ones via exports and price controls and differential exchange rates, made it possible to set industrial wages above market equilibrium, and provided resources for social programmes and state clientelism that undermined the political hold of traditional urban and rural political machines.

National-popular populism constituted the institutional arrangements that gave political sustainability to the new model of development. The nation-state was at the centre of national-popular populist political and economic institutions. The centrality of the state in the new economic model gave the political forces that controlled the state economic and political leverage over the main economic and social actors, including workers and industrialists. The strongly personalistic relationship between charismatic leaders (Cárdenas, Perón, Vargas, Haya de la Torre, etc.) and the people went together with a systematic process of political organization and mobilization of the popular sectors that resulted in some of the most powerful popular movements of twentieth-century Latin America (Philip & Panizza 2011). When in government, populist leaders used state resources to both organize and control their followers in corporatist-style arrangements, and to repress dissent. Populism was not the necessary political superstructure of ISI, but it shaped its political contours, and provided the power resources, mechanisms of representation and control, and political institutions, characteristic of its state-led multi-class coalitions. If not one of base and superstructure, the relationship between ISI and national popular populism was one of elective affinities (Weber 2010).

Another issue concerns the role of class in the constitution of national popular identities. While apparently highly abstract, Laclau's theory of populism was grounded in the history and politics of Latin American populism, particularly of Argentina. In his early writings, Laclau kept theoretical and political distance from what he considered the Marxist left's class reductionism and political vanguardism. This derived political identities from the actors' insertion in the productive structure and regarded the working class (or rather the vanguard parties that self-attributed the representation of the working class) as the frontline of a revolutionary strategy, that was itself determined by the contradictions of capitalism. For Laclau (as well as for many other scholars of Latin America), the class structure of Latin America's dependent capitalism, strongly limited the working class's ability to spearhead radical change, in isolation from broader social sectors.

Yet, class was still central to the national-popular constitution of the people as a political actor, as it was, paradoxically, to Laclau's analysis of the period. "The people" of national-popular populism was a multiclass alliance, but the working class was at its core socially, economically and politically. For example, in Argentina, on 17 October 1945, industrial workers were the key actors in the mass mobilization that would elevate Juan Domingo Perón to the presidency and make him the dominant political leader of his country in the second half of the twentieth century. The first line of Perón's speech on that historical date stressed his identification with the workers: "Almost two years ago, from these same balconies, I said that I had three honours in my life: to be a soldier, to be a patriot and to be the first Argentinean worker" (my translation).[1]

During the years of Perón's rule (1946–55) and beyond, the workers' umbrella organization, the Confederación General del Trabajo (CGT), became the backbone of the Peronist movement, as did the Confederación de Trabajadores de México (CTM) in the long era of rule by the Partido Revolucionario Institucional (PRI) in Mexico. It could be argued that the centrality of the working class in the populist movements that ruled Argentina and Mexico is explained by the fact that the two countries were the most industrialized economies in the region at the time. Yet class was also at the centre of populist movements elsewhere across the region. Bolivia was the least developed and most rural country in the region. It also had the largest (mostly rural) indigenous population in South America. Yet, as Gustavo Bonifaz (n.d.) argues, in Bolivia, class became the dominant cleavage during the first era of rule by the Movimiento Nacional Revolucionario (MNR) (1952–64). During the debates of the Constitutional Convention of 1938, Wálter Guevara Arze, who later became a prominent leader of the MNR, rejected the hitherto dominant idea which saw, in the education of the *indio*, the answer to the so-called "*problema del indio*" ("the Indian problem"). According to Guevara: "it [was] because the *indio* ha[d] no land, that he [could not] be a citizen … [Therefore], the problem of the *indio* is an economic problem" (quoted in Bonifaz n.d.). Guevara proposed to avoid the word *indio* in the new constitution, since it was derogatory, leading a group promoting the incorporation in the new constitution of a section entitled: *On the Peasant* (*ibid.*). As other populist movements of the time, the MNR was a multiclass coalition led by middle-class, creole, political leaders. Yet, industrial workers (miners) and peasants' organizations constituted its social base. Led by the tin miners, the Central Obrera Boliviana (COB), founded in 1952, supported the government, while holding an informal power of veto over policy. To counterbalance the power of the COB, the MNR set up peasant trade unions under its control, leading to increasingly fractious compromises within the government's multiclass social coalition (*ibid.*).

The centrality of class in national-popular populism went beyond the importance of peasants' and workers' unions in the populist governments of the time. Its salience must be considered within the context of the political imaginary of the post-Second World War era, marked by the victory of the

1. Original, translated by autor: "*Trabajadores: hace casi dos años, desde estos mismos balcones, dije que tenía tres honras en mi vida: la de ser soldado, la de ser un patriota y la de ser el primer trabajador argentino.*"

Soviet Union over Nazi Germany and the worldwide resurgence of communist parties' political appeal. For both the left and the right, a communist-led revolution was regarded as a real possibility. Political leaders of the time sought to address the demands of the working class, as part of a strategy to prevent its radicalization. The following excerpt from Luis Batlle Berres's speech when he was sworn as president of Uruguay in August 1947 is representative of this strategy:

> I have had the opportunity of telling those who have come to see me in my office to find out something of what I am thinking – that it is impossible to ignore the fact that humankind is going through a violent social and political revolution which is shaking the whole world. Nobody should try to pretend that we can remain outside it, or simply condemn or reject it. What the time requires is for us to join this immense movement in order to guide its future course, even at the price of speeding up its evolution. (Batlle 1965: 56–7, my translation)

Historically, national-popular populism was regarded as a barrier to the advancement of the left in Latin America. Populist leaders sought to forestall the potential communist threat by incorporating the workers socially and politically, through a combination of recognition, redistribution, mobilization and repression. In turn, socialist and communist parties denounced national popular movements as quasi-fascist, bourgeois-led, class alliances that sought to repress and co-opt the working class and blunted the left's struggle for radical change (Munck, Chapter 1, this volume).

Scholars of national-popular populism have highlighted the role of populism in securing bourgeois hegemony. In Chapter 4 of this volume, Reinaldo Lindolfo Lohn and Silvia Maria Fávero Arend outline Francisco Weffort's classical take on the topic, with particular reference to Brazil under Getúlio Vargas. According to Weffort, populism represented the subordinated incorporation of the popular classes to the political system, in the context of the country's process of industrial development. He argued that the populist mode of incorporation prevented the masses from acting as a class, maintaining their political dependence on charismatic leaders. Weffort further argues that the absence of an autonomous party of the working class, and of trade union organizations committed to social change, characterized a Caesarist logic of direct relationship between the electorate and politicians, reproducing and expanding the scope of populism.

As the authors note, in Brazil these views were shared by the left and the right, with opposite political slants. For the left, populism was a political movement that negated agency to the working class. For the right, it represented the demagogic activation of the masses, a view associated with elitist forms of disqualifying the political participation of popular groups, culminating in support for the 1964 military coup against the populist threat. Right-wing contempt for popular participation was summarized in the statement of one of the country's military rulers of the 1980s, General João Baptista Figueiredo, that democratization was unfeasible because "a people that do not know even how to brush their teeth is not ready [to exercise the right to] vote".[2]

In contrast to this view, in *Towards a Theory of Populism*, Laclau turns on its head the negative notion of populism as backward class compromises. He argues that, for the dominated sectors, ideological struggles consist of the expansion of the antagonism, implicit in popular democratic interpellations, and in articulation with their own class discourses. He concludes that in this sense a "socialist populism" is not the most backward form of working-class ideology, but the most advanced one: "the moment when the working class has succeeded in condensing the ensemble of democratic ideology in a determinate social formation with its own ideology" (1979: 174).

It should be noted, however, that Laclau (1979) does not claim that populism is always revolutionary, or even progressive. He distinguishes between a populism of the dominant classes, in which an emerging fraction of the bourgeoisie activates the popular masses to gain hegemony over other bourgeois class fractions, and a populism of the dominated classes, led by the working class. The vindication of populism, as the royal road to socialism, is predicated on the assumption of the working class being the hegemonic fraction of the populist alliance, and on socialism being its ideological horizon, an assumption that is not sustainable if we abandon class as an analytical category in the study of populism.

The nature of populism (here in its national-popular version) as an anti-status quo strategy of antagonism and rupture with the oligarchical order, combined with the institutionalization and control of class conflicts, is reflected in the writings of several contributors to this book. Particularly relevant is Marcelo Raimundo's characterization of Peronism as a *passive revolution*, a concept he borrows from Gramsci. As Raimundo (Chapter 2) recalls, Gramsci defined passive revolutions as processes of change, in which the political initiative comes from above, born from powerful factions of the elite who are facing a situation of catastrophic equilibrium and who seek to organize an outcome that avoids the possibility of civil war, while acting as a collective capitalist force, faced by a potential crisis.

Raimundo elaborates on Gramsci's definition, noting that, while passive revolutions aim at overcoming a crisis of class domination, they unleash

2. *"Um povo que não sabe nem escovar os dentes não está preparado para votar."*

processes of activation from below that modify the pre-existing composition of forces, and become the matrix of new changes, not anticipated or desired by the dominant class. Raimundo argues that *Peronismo* combined the bureaucratization of the unions, with a strong level of organization at plant level, that opened opportunities for rank-and-file representation, a combination that had potentially disruptive effects over the political order. For him, the "revolutionary" aspect of Peronism is historically laid in that it produced a considerable change in the power relations between classes in the workplace, in favour of the workers. He concludes that the combination of political control and grassroots empowerment become two sides of the same coin, a duality which was not captured by the argument of class conciliation. I return to the question of populism as passive revolution in the conclusion to this chapter, but I now turn to twenty-first-century populism.

TWENTY-FIRST-CENTURY [LATIN AMERICAN] POPULISM

Twenty-first-century Latin American populism had its roots in its mid-twentieth-century national-popular tradition, but it emerged in a context in which political, social and economic changes prompted a reformulation of the relation between populism and models of development, in the way in which the people were performatively constructed by populist discourse and in the role of class in the populist coalitions.

Munck notes in the introduction to this book that the "progressive popular" governments post-2000s were born out of the crisis of the neoliberal matrix and the search for a post-neoliberal development strategy. To assess the nature and dimensions of the crisis, we need first to conceptualize neoliberalism. The definition of neoliberalism has parallels with that of populism, in that both are malleable concepts difficult to pin down. Both have traversed from the academic to the political domain, to become ill-defined weapons in the ideological struggles between the left and the right. In Latin America, the origins of neoliberalism were closely associated with the so-called Washington Consensus (WC), a term coined by the British-born economist John Williamson to embody what he claimed was the common wisdom, embraced by all serious economists of the time (Williamson 1994: 18). Williamson codified the WC in ten policy prescriptions, that ranged from fiscal discipline to trade liberalization, and from privatization to securing property rights. Williamson (2000) has disputed the identification of the WC with neoliberalism, yet there is little question that, under any conventional definition of neoliberalism, an economic programme that includes trade liberalization, privatization, deregulation and the liberalization of foreign direct investment should be considered part of the neoliberal model.

Neoliberalism, however, is more than a narrow set of market-centred economic policies. In its different iterations, it has drawn from political, cultural and social ideological elements, to articulate a broader worldview. In the context of the collapse of the Soviet Union, and the emergence of the United States as the world's only superpower in the late 1980s and early 1990s, it included, among others, a close association between free markets and liberal democracy.

Liberal democracy is, of course, compatible with different models of capitalism. But the elective affinity between neoliberalism and liberal democracy appeared to be particularly fitting for Latin America, which had experienced, in the 1980s and early 1990s, a double transition from dictatorship to democracy, and from ISI to neoliberalism. Perhaps, one of the moments in which the hegemony of the neoliberal matrix was most apparent was the first presidential Summit of the Americas, which took place in Miami in December 1994. In that meeting, the then democratically elected heads of state of the Americas (with the exception of Cuba) committed their countries to pursuing prosperity "through open markets, hemispheric integration and sustainable development". Reflecting on these times, Mark Peceny (1994: 188–9) claimed that there were indications that the Inter American System was becoming a Kantian pacific union of liberal states (Panizza 2009: 121).

Yet, even at its most hegemonic, the neoliberal matrix generated socio-economic dislocations and political opposition that undermined its hegemony. Market reforms polarized societies between a narrow social strata that had the education, social and financial capital and job opportunities to benefit from the economic opening, and a much larger social group that suffered from increasing inequalities and lacked economic protection from the force of the markets. The social impact of the neoliberal policies of privatization, de-regulation and liberalization manifested itself across the region in the shrinking of the industrial working class, the exponential rise of the informal sector and the increase in inequality in what was already the most unequal region of the world (Huber & Solt 2004).

The expansion of market relations also created new forms of individualization and consumption, that deepened the sociocultural gap between the economic elite and the globalized upper middle classes on the one hand, and the popular sectors on the other. The negative social impact of neoliberalism was compounded by weak economic growth, particularly in the "lost half decade" between 1998 and 2002, in which the growth of the early half of the 1990s effectively stalled, and by a succession of financial crises that reached its peak in the Argentinean financial crisis of 2001–02. By the year 2000, the percentage of people in Latin America living under the poverty line, although lower than in the 1990s, was larger than in 1980 (ECLAC 2004).

Politically, while national-popular populism emerged as an alternative to the crisis of the liberal oligarchical political order in the region, twenty-first-century populism emerged in Latin America some 20 years after the start of the longest wave of democratization in its history. Democracy opened spaces for electoral competition, as well as for the re-emergence of old social movements and the activation of new political identities along race, gender, ethnic and regional lines. But the pacted transitions of the 1980s, and the top-down introduction of stroke-of-a-pen free market reforms, as a response to the debt crisis of the second half of the 1980s, limited the scope for substantive democratization. For all the progress made in advancing civil and political rights, the democracies of the 1990s were low-quality democracies, in which the hegemony of neoliberalism offered little choice and the centrist consensus of the time offered only limited political options, while multiple inequalities undermined the substance of citizenship. The Mexican political scientist and politician, Jorge Castañeda (1993: 156), summarized the hegemony of the neoliberal matrix in the following terms:

> For any Latin American government, there are direct, often immediately and frequently dire, economic consequences of pursuing a policy contrary to Washington desires or interests [...]; the price of any departure from the tenants of free market orthodoxy is exorbitant [...] Nationalising natural resources, emphasising social policies or placing restrictions on foreign trade or investment, no longer necessarily invite invasion or destabilization, nor are they even likely to do so. They simply entice financial scarcity and economic ostracism.

However, the expansion of market relations to broader social domains, prompted a Polanyi (2001)-style double movement of popular resistance to marketization across different areas of society, that was capitalized upon by a new generation of populist leaders. Economic and political dislocations provided the political opportunity for the repoliticization of collective grievances, in antagonism to the neoliberal order and the parties that had dominated the political landscape for most of the 1990s. As Patricia Pensado Leglise puts it (Chapter 6), if it were possible to single out a common feature of the diverse forms of populism in the twenty-first century, this would be their origins, since all of them have emerged from social unrest against liberalism. In challenging the depoliticized democracies of the neoliberal matrix, twenty-first-century populists repoliticized economic policy, denounced corrupt political establishments, united fragmented popular identities; and mobilized the popular sectors (Philip & Panizza 2011: 76).

Neoliberalism became the constitutive outside of twenty-first-century populism when in opposition. Yet, as contributors to this book argue, once in office, twenty-first-century populists' economic policies were post-neoliberal, rather than anti-neoliberal. What is meant by post-neoliberalism, and whether it represented a break with neoliberalism or an accommodation with it are open to question. The economic dimension of post-neoliberalism can be defined, at its most basic, as an attempt to rebalance the direction of the economy away from the market and towards the state, and by the priority assigned to the reduction of poverty and inequality (Grugel & Riggirozzi 2012). Post neoliberal economic policies included (with significant variations from country to country): increasing state taxation and spending; selective rather than comprehensive forms of state intervention; the renationalization of some strategic industries; the imposition of selective price, exports and foreign investment controls; and the adoption of export duties or quotas (Grugel & Riggirozzi 2012; Levitsky & Roberts 2011).

Social policies included a massive expansion of the conditional cash transfers that were initiated by centre-right governments in the 1990s, as well as increases in other social benefits. Social benefits, such as non-contributory pensions and health coverage, reached historically excluded groups, such as domestic, rural and informal sector workers. There was also higher investment in education and an expansion in university access to underprivileged youths. Social policies were complemented with activist labour policies that promoted collective bargaining, labour rights and union recognition, as well as rises in the minimum wage (Levitsky & Roberts 2011).

Scholars differ on whether these policies represented a break with the neoliberal matrix. Grugel and Riggirozzi (2012) argue that, in practice, post-neoliberal governments tended to be surprisingly pragmatic, implementing policies that worked with the grain, rather than against the market-led model. Yet, Levitsky and Roberts (2011) are emphatic in arguing that, while the left governments of the time did not fully abandon the market-led model, they broke with neoliberalism by challenging the neoliberal orthodoxy and using state power to alter the distribution of income and economic opportunities in their societies. I agree with Levitsky and Roberts's claim that twenty-first-century populist governments marked a significant departure from neoliberalism. As detailed in the case studies, the economic, social and political gains for the popular sectors were real and non-trivial (Ferrero *et al.* 2021; Silva & Rossi 2018; ECLAC 2010). The mechanisms of social inclusion were broader than those of the first wave of incorporation and covered social sectors, such as informal workers, that did not benefit from social protection under ISI.

There were, of course, significant differences in the extent that the twenty-first-century populists sought alternative development models.

At the extreme, Chávez's twenty-first-century socialism project represented the most radical attempt at implementing an alternative to neoliberalism, including extensive nationalization and the setting up of worker-controlled enterprises. In his study of Venezuela under Chávez, Roberto López Sánchez (Chapter 7) argues that Chávez rethought the ideal of socialist revolution for the twenty-first century, linking it to the traditions of popular revolutionary struggle of the past century. In economic terms, the project was defined by the goal of overcoming oil dependence and its replacement by a neo-developmentalist policy, with strong state intervention in strategic areas. Ecuador, under Correa, also promoted an ambitious alternative development project that pioneered the recognition of the rights of nature and had the holistic goal of, materializing "the good way of living" (*sumak kawsay*). Policy instruments for achieving this goal included, among others, participatory planning, and an activist state that invested heavily in infrastructure. The Morales administration in Bolivia sought to advance similar principles and policies under the principles of Andean–Amazonian capitalism. Policies included support for small, so-called informal enterprises, new social programmes and the nationalization of hydrocarbon resources which, in practice, materialized in the renegotiation of the contracts with the oil companies, that led to a significant rise in royalties paid to the state (Chapter 8).

The principles underlying the different alternatives to neoliberalism were, in many ways, radical, and there were some innovative policies that sought to implement them in practice. Yet, none of them can be considered a successful development model. This is not so much the case because of continuity with some neoliberal policies; no model of development starts from ground zero. Rather, the fundamental failure of the post-neoliberal alternatives is, that they increased rather than reduced, commodity dependence and state rentierism. This is best summarized by Brown in Chapter 8:

> There was a clear movement toward a post-neoliberal model of development and democracy, and Morales and the MAS presented their project as a radical alternative to neoliberalism, involving a diversification of the economy away from primary export-based development, accompanied by a nationalization of Bolivia's natural resources. However, neither of these goals was fully achieved. Bolivia became more dependent on primary exports than before, with primary goods increasing from 89 per cent of total export value in 2005 to 95 per cent in 2012. (ECLAC 2013: 111)

When alternative principles, such as the preservation of the environment, collided with the governments' goal of extracting rents, they were set aside.

This was exemplified by the phrase of former President Rafael Correa, quoted by Pablo Dávalos in Chapter 9: 'We cannot be beggars sitting on a sack of gold.' In the case of Venezuela, hyper-dependency on oil rents was compounded by gross economic mismanagement, that led to hyperinflation and a fall in living standards that was without precedent in the history of the country.

In short, the commodity boom that was the result of the expansion of globalized capitalism to China, gave twenty-first-century populists more autonomy to deviate from neoliberal orthodoxy and resources to fund social policies. But this was at the cost of losing autonomy from international financial and commodity markets, over which they exercised little or no leverage. Increased commodity revenues lessened incentives for more radical reforms to the neoliberal economic model that could have diversified the economies, increased the value added of products, and generated the productivity gains necessary for the creation of more high-quality jobs and higher wages. The economic, social and political failure to reform became all too evident with the end of the commodity boom.

We need now to turn to the political dimension of the post-neoliberal matrix, as I have done with the state-centred and neoliberal ones. As noted by contributors to this book, twenty-first-century populism was part of a broader turn to the left in Latin America that had taken place by the turn of the century. The left turn comprised parties and movements that had significant political and ideological differences, and not all of whom can be regarded as populists. The divide between the populist and what scholars have labelled the social-democratic left (Panizza 2005) has been a matter of considerable debate. Among other criteria, a key determinant of the divide was the difference between the institutional path to office of the social democratic left and the more rupturist one of the populists.

So-called social democratic parties worked their way to office, through the liberal democratic political institutions of the 1990s, gaining power initially at local and state level, gradually increasing their parliamentary representation, and eventually winning presidential elections, often after several attempts. This was the path to government of the Frente Amplio in Uruguay and of the Partido dos Trabalhadores (PT) in Brazil. In both cases, presidential candidates represented long-established political parties of the left, with a mass social base, internal organization and an active militancy. Additionally, both parties had strong links with the working-class organizations of their countries, the Plenario Intersindical de Trabajadores – Convención Nacional de Trabajadores (PIT-CNT) in Uruguay and the Central Única dos Trabalhadores (CUT) in Brazil, as well as with other social movements. With regard to the economy, both left-of-centre governments maintained considerable lines of continuity with the free market model, moderating its excesses and substantially increasing social spending.

In contrast, the twenty-first-century populist route to office was marked by crises of representation, mass popular protests, a personalist leadership and a foundational political drive. Mass protests and crises of representation fed upon each other: in Argentina in 2001–02; in Bolivia in the "water" and "gas" wars of 2000 and 2003; and in Ecuador in the mass demonstrations that led to the resignation of three presidents between 1997 and 2005, culminating in the *forajido* movement, that preceded the electoral victory of Rafael Correa in 2006. In Venezuela, the crisis of the political system was evidenced by the Caracazo riots of 1989, and by the considerable popular support for the two failed military coups of 1992. Among the populist leaders, only Evo Morales was a leader of popular protest, while Hugo Chávez was the failed leader of the 1992 military coups. But whatever the leaders' relations with the protestors, populist leaders faced similar tasks: how to construct the people as political actors and refound the political order. The two political tasks were closely interrelated. In considering them, we need to re-examine the question of populism as the institutionalization of social conflict, as addressed by several contributors to this book. The question is posited by Munck in the introduction when he claims that: "whether it is Kirchnerism dealing with the unemployed movement of the *piqueteros*, or Lulismo dealing with the landless movement, we see a pattern of co-option and domestication of contestatory movements".

Theoretically, the relation between popular movements and populist leaders, parties and governments, concerns the horizontal and vertical dimensions of populist identification. Horizontal relations of identification are generated by everyday practices of association and struggle, such as those of the *piqueteros* in Argentina, the cocaleros in Bolivia or the people of the *barrios* in Venezuela (Ferrero 2014). Contestatory movements raise demands that, if failed to be addressed by governments, generate the dislocations that make possible counterhegemonic struggles. Laclau (2005b: 37) refers to this condition when he argues that a relation of solidarity can arise between demands on the negative basis that they all remain equally unsatisfied. However, considering mass protests as the privileged form of political struggle risks missing the importance of the vertical dimension of politics, that goes beyond historical moments of heightened popular mobilization (Mouffe 2018: 19). For Laclau, the vertical dimension of populist identification is a requirement for radical political change:

> The horizontal dimension of autonomy will be incapable, left to itself, of bringing about long-term historical change if it is not complemented by the vertical dimension of "hegemony" – that is, a radical transformation of the state. Autonomy, left to itself, leads, sooner or later, to the exhaustion and the dispersion of the movements of protest. (Laclau 2014: 9)

For Laclau, vertical identification is identification with the leader. According to him, the plurality of actors that constitute the people in populist identification are held together not just by their common antagonism to an oppressive *other*, but by their vertical identification with a leader, whose political persona becomes an empty signifier, symbolically unifying what are otherwise heterogeneous social identities. But, as Paul Cammack (2000: 52) notes, the moment of unmediated populist appeals to the people are short-lived. Laclau's emphasis on identification with the leader neglects the institutionalization of populism and its role in the restoration of political order.

Implicit in the populist anti-status quo appeal is the redemptive promise (Canovan 1999) that, once "the enemies of the people" are deprived of their institutional means of domination, a new institutional order will emerge, in which the people will have an unmediated, effective and lasting power This is what Gerardo Aboy Carlés (2013) means when he argues that populism comprises a double movement of rupture *and* of reconstitution of the political order, a balancing act that is in-built in the gap between the plebs (the underdogs), as a partiality that claims to be the only legitimate holders of sovereignty, and the populous (the citizens), as the embodiment of the entire community. When populism is in government, vertical identification with the leader becomes institutionalized in the leader's role as the head of the new institutional order, and in the relation between the people, the ruling party, and the machinery of the state. The institutionalization drive of populism, however, does not say much about the specific nature of the new institutional arrangements, nor about how institutions seek to reproduce popular identities.

The new constitutions of Venezuela, Ecuador and Bolivia, passed originally in 1999, 2008 and 2009 respectively, give an idea of the rhetorical foundations and legal architecture of the populist regimes and, in doing so, give an indication of who were regarded as "the people" (in its double acceptation of the plebs and the populous) of the new political orders. The three foundational texts evidence highly plural forms of conceiving "the people". The preamble of the Venezuelan constitution states that the aim of reshaping the republic is to establish a "multi-ethnical and multi-cultural" society.[3] Bolivia is defined in article 1 of the Constitution as a "pluri-national, inter-cultural state" and, in article 3 the nation is said to be formed by "all Bolivians" and "the native indigenous nations and peoples, and the inter-cultural and Afro-Bolivian communities".[4] The Ecuadorian state is defined as intercultural and multinational (article 1), and participation is based on "criteria of gender equity and parity,

3. The Constitution of the Bolivarian Republic of Venezuela; http://hrlibrary.umn.edu/research/venezuela-constitution.html.
4. Republic of Bolivia Constitution of 2009; https://pdba.georgetown.edu/Constitutions/Bolivia/bolivia09.html.

equal opportunities for persons with disabilities, and intergenerational participation" (article 61).[5] The three constitutions complement the statements of principles, with long and detailed enumerations of the political, social, economic and cultural rights of the different sections of the population that, together, constitute the people. It would be naïve to equate constitutional rhetoric and the enumeration of rights with their enforcement in practice, but this somehow misses the point. Constitutions have a performative, as well as a legal, dimension and, as such, they play a performative role in of the constitution of the people.

The constitutions' rhetorical construction of the plural people was complemented by the setting up of new institutional arrangements for direct popular participation. The new participatory institutions were in contrast with the more limited and top-down, corporatist-style mechanisms of political incorporation of national-popular populism. They were also aimed at deepening the limited forms of political representation of liberal democracy. To this purpose, the Venezuelan constitution created a fifth branch of power, the so-called "citizens' power" (*poder ciudadano*), which includes more than 70 articles promoting popular participation.[6] The most important participatory forum was the system of Communal Councils, created in 2006 with the goal of "allowing the organized people to directly exercise the management of public policies and projects, oriented to address the needs and aspirations of the communities for the construction of a fair and social, just society" (my translation). According to official figures, more than 45,000 councils were set up during Chávez's presidencies. Article 95 of the Constitution of Ecuador stipulates that, "the participation of citizens in all matters of public interests is a right, which shall be exercised by means of mechanisms of representative, direct and community democracy" and it adds that "participation shall be governed by the principles of equality, autonomy, public deliberation, respect for differences, monitoring by the public, solidarity and interculturalism". Meanwhile, article 11 of the Bolivian constitution states that "the Republic of Bolivia adopts a participatory, democratic, representative and communal form of government" and lists the mechanisms for the different forms of participation, such as referendums, citizens legislative initiatives, revocation of terms in office, assemblies and councils. There are also special mechanisms for the communal participation of the native indigenous nations and peoples.

The creation of mechanisms for popular participation in the new political orders set them at the intersection of participatory and populist

5. Republic of Ecuador Constitution of 2008; https://pdba.georgetown.edu/Constitutions/Ecuador/english08.html.
6. English translation of the Venezuelan Constitution; https://aceproject.org/ero-en/regions/americas/VE/venezuela-constitution-english-1999/view.

forms of democracy. On the one hand, they reflect at the institutional level bottom-up, participatory forms of democracy. Participatory institutions are also in line with populist notions of direct, unmediated exercise of popular sovereignty. Yet, as noted above, populism has also a vertical dimension, characterized by the embodiment of the people in the persona of the leader, now institutionalized in the presidency. While identification is always relational, vertical identification has a top-down dimension that is in tension with the bottom-up exercise of popular sovereignty. This tension was negotiated in different ways in different countries, but the case studies in this book evidence that the concentration of power in the executive that reflects the vertical, personalistic dimension of populism, as well as Latin America's tradition of hyper-presidentialism, together with mechanisms of co-optation, control and exclusion of popular organizations, significantly undermined the institutional spaces for bottom-up popular participation, making them largely inoperative in some cases, such as in Ecuador under the presidency of Rafael Correa.

CONCLUSIONS

Two questions arise from twenty-first-century populism's plural imagining of the people. The first one, of a theoretical nature, concerns the claim, mostly by European scholars of populism, that populism is anti-democratic because it has a homogeneous conception of the people (Müller 2016; Mudde 2007). While this may be true of right-wing European populism, based on ethnical homogeneity, the opposite is the case of twenty-first-century populism, in which the political construction of "the people" is ethnical, gender and culturally diverse, and inclusive.

The second question concerns the differences in the imagining of the people, between the national-popular and the twenty-first-century versions of populism. National-popular populism imagining of the people included a variety of popular actors and movements, such as women and youth organizations. But, as Silva and Rossi put it in relation to the twenty-first-century version, while it was a continuation of the first incorporation and displayed some similar features, other attributes were specific to this second process. These were mainly that it was not corporatist, but territorial, and that the central agents of transformation were not trade unions but the disincorporated popular sectors, comprising territorial, ethnic, race, gender and cultural markers of identity.

The reasons for this shift are both political and socioeconomic. Politically, the politicization of ethnic, racial, gender and other identities in the 1990s resulted in organizations, representing multiple socio-cultural cleavages, playing a significant role in the popular struggles against the established order, which set the ground for the rise of twenty-first-century populism. Economically, the process of de-industrialization and informalization of the 1990s weakened the trade unions and created a large, atomized, and heterogenous group of workers, with precarious links to the labour market and with weak organizational and mobilizing power. It is these people who were the main recipients of the targeted social programmes of twenty-first-century populism, in marked difference to the work-based welfare under national-popular populism.

Considered together, the activation of multiple popular struggles and the emergence of a large, precarious, mass of informal workers have significant implications for understanding the surge of populism, not just in Latin America, but also elsewhere. As Laclau (2005a: 150) put it, a globalized capitalism creates myriad points of rupture and antagonisms – ecological crises, imbalance between different sectors of the economy, massive unemployment, and so on. He further argues that, within this context, there is no reason why struggles taking place within relations of production, should be the privileged point of anti-capitalist struggle and it is impossible to determine a priori who will be the hegemonic actors in this struggle.

Laclau's arguments need to be analysed against the centrality of class identification in national-popular populism and its loss of centrality in twenty-first-century populism. As noted in the previous section, in his early works on the subject, Laclau used class as a key to distinguish between a populism of the dominant classes and a populism of the dominated ones, as does Gramsci to characterize passive revolutions. The diminishing importance of class as the strategically central actor in twenty-first-century populism, reflects the social and economic changes within the region in the past decades, and raises some significant theoretical and political questions about the nature of populist ruptures.

First, capitalism is a mode of production and neoliberalism a model of capitalism. As such, a rupture with neoliberalism would require a strategic role for the actors engaged in the relations of production, namely the workers, in challenging the neoliberal economic model. Second, the expansion of the field of popular struggles to sociocultural and territorial domains (ethnic, gender, ecological, etc.) is to be strongly welcomed. But, while a plurality of antagonisms potentially creates multiple points of rupture, it also opens the possibility for the differential absorption of demands by the established order, or for their co-optation by the populist state. Laclau (2005b: 46) captures this dimension when he argues that the regime resulting from a populist rupture risks becoming progressively institutionalized, so that the differential logic starts prevailing again and the equivalential popular identity increasingly becomes an inoperative *langue de bois*, governing less and less the actual workings of politics. The cases of Venezuela under the presidency of Nicolás Maduro (Chapter 7) and of Ecuador under Rafael Correa (Chapter 9) are examples of this process.

The construction of a radical alternative to the neoliberal order, in which class has not a leading role and there is no single point of rupture, requires the type of hegemony that Gramsci described as a war of positions, in which the horizontal dimension of identification plays a central role, not only in opposition to neoliberalism, but particularly when populist leaders and movements are in office. It also requires the reassessment of the role of class in the constitution of the populist people and its reconceptualization within the context of the political economy of twenty-first-century capitalism. As Mazzolini (cited by Munck in Chapter 1) puts it: "Populism can ensue in a new hegemonic order, but it is far from settled that it will. The question is what decides if it will" (Mazzolini 2020: 770).

REFERENCES

Aboy Carlés, G. 2013. "De los popular a lo populista o el incierto devenir de los *plebs*". In G. Carlés, S. Barros and J. Merlo (eds), *Las Brechas del Pueblo. Reflexiones sobre identidades populares y populismo*, 32–49. Los Polvorines, Provincia de Bueno Aires: Universidad Nacional de General Sarmiento.

Bonifaz, G. n.d. *Nationalism, Populism and Legitimation in Bolivia* (manuscript).

Batlle, L. 1965. *Pensamiento y Acción. Selección y notas por Santiago Rompani*. Montevideo: Editorial Alfa.

Cammack, P. 2000. "The resurgence of populism in Latin America". *Bulletin of Latin American Research* 19(2): 49–61.

Canovan, M. 1999. "Trust the people! Populism and the two faces of democracy". *Political Studies* 47(1): 2–16.

Castañeda, J. 1993. *Utopia Unarmed: The Latin American Left After the Cold War*. New York: Knopf.

Collier, D., F. Hidalgo & A. Maciuceanu 2006. "Essentially contested concepts: debates and applications". *Journal of Political Ideologies* 11(3): 211–46.

ECLAC 2004. *Social Panorama of Latin America*. Santiago: United Nations.

ECLAC 2010. *Social Panorama of Latin America*. Santiago: United Nations.

ECLAC 2013. *Statistical Yearbook for Latin America and the Caribbean*. Santiago: United Nations.

Ferrero, J. 2014. *Democracy Against Neoliberalism in Argentina and Brazil: A Move to the Left*. New York: Palgrave Macmillan.

Ferrero, J., R. Centeno & A. Roumpakis. 2021. "Transitions and non-transitions from neoliberalism in Latin America and Southern Europe". *Politics* 42(4): 524–39. https://doi.org/10.1177/02633957211048387.

Grugel, J. & P. Riggirozzi 2012. "Post-neoliberalism in Latin America: rebuilding and reclaiming the state after crisis". *Development and Change* 43(1): 1–21.

Hubert, E. and F. Solt 2004. "Successes and failures of neoliberalism". *Latin American Research Review* 39(3): 150–63.

Laclau, E. 1979. *Politics and Ideology in Marxist Theory*. London: Verso.

Laclau, E. 2005a. *On Populist Reason*. London: Verso.

Laclau, E. 2005b. "Populism: what's in a name?" In F. Panizza (ed.), *Populism and the Mirror of Democracy*, 32–49. London: Verso.

Laclau, E. 2014. *The Rhetorical Foundations of Society*. London: Verso.

Levitsky, S. & K. Roberts (eds.) 2011. "Introduction: Latin America's "left turn": a framework for analysis". In S. Levitsky and K. Roberts (eds), *The Resurgence of the Latin American Left*, 1–30. Baltimore, MD: Johns Hopkins University Press.

Mazzolini, S. 2020. "Populism is not hegemony: towards a re-gramscianization of Ernesto Laclau". *Theory & Event* 23(3): 765–86.

Mouffe, C. 2018. *For a Left Populism*. London: Verso.

Mudde, C. 2007. *Populist Radical Right Parties in Europe*. Cambridge: Cambridge University Press.

Müller, J.-W. 2016. *What is Populism?* Philadelphia: University of Pennsylvania Press.

Ostiguy, P., F. Panizza & B. Moffitt 2021. *Populism in Global Perspective: A Performative and Discursive Approach*. Abingdon: Routledge.

Panizza, F. 2005. "Unarmed utopia revisited: the resurgence of left of centre politics in Latin America" *Political Studies* 53(4): 716–34.

Panizza, F. 2009. *Contemporary Latin America: Development and Democracy Beyond the Washington Consensus*. London: Zed Books.

Peceny, M. 1994. "The Inter American System as a 'Liberal Pacific Union'?" *Latin American Research Review* 29(3): 188–201.

Philip, G. & F. Panizza. 2011. *The Triumph of Politics. The Return of the Left in Venezuela, Bolivia and Ecuador*. Cambridge: Polity Press.

Polanyi, K. 2001. *The Great Transformation: The Political and Economic Origins of Our Time*. Second edition. Boston, MA: Beacon Press.

Silva, E. & F. Rossi (eds). 2018. *Reshaping the Political Arena: From Resisting Neoliberalism to the Second Incorporation*. Pittsburgh, PA: Pittsburgh University Press.

Weber, M. 2010 [2005]. *The Protestant Ethic and the Spirit of Capitalism*. Oxford: Oxford University Press.

Williamson, J. 1994. "In search of a manual for technopols". In J. Williamson (ed.), *The Political Economy of Policy Reform*, 9–28. Washington, DC: Institute for International Economics.

Williamson, J. 2000. "What should the World Bank think about the Washington Consensus". *World Bank Research Observer* 15(2): 251–64.

CONTRIBUTORS

John Brown is a lecturer at the Centre for the Study of Politics, Maynooth University, Ireland. He is the author of *Deepening Democracy in Post-Neoliberal Bolivia and Venezuela: Advances and Setbacks* (2022). Recent journal publications include "Neoliberalization, de-democratization, and populist responses in Western Europe, the US, and Latin America" in *Critical Sociology* (2020) and "Party-base linkages and contestatory mobilization in Bolivia's El Alto: subduing the *Ciudad Rebelde*", in *Latin American Perspectives* (2020).

Barry Cannon (PhD, Dublin City University) lectures on politics in the Sociology Department of Maynooth University (Ireland). His research focuses on Latin American politics, especially the left and the right in the region and on populism as concept and practice. He has published in a number of key journals, including *Third World Quarterly, Latin American Politics and Society, Democratization* and *New Political Science.* His most recent book is *The Right in Latin America: Elite Power, Hegemony and the Struggle for the State* (2016).

Victor de Oliveira Pinto Coelho has a BA and MA in History from the Universidade Federal de Minas Gerais (Federal University of Minas Gerais, Brazil). He has a PhD in the Social History of Culture, from Pontifícia Universidade Católica do Rio de Janeiro (Pontifical Catholic University of Rio de Janeiro, Brazil). His thesis was on the subject of "Theory and Historiography". He works in the fields of modern and contemporary history, theory of history and political history. He has published *A técnica como totalidade: a mitologia política de Ernst Jünger no entreguerras* [recursos eletrônico] (2020).

Pablo Dávalos has a PhD in Economics from Grenoble-Alpes (France) and did a post-doctorate at Universidad Andina Simón Bolívar. He is a former vice-minister of economy (2005) of Ecuador. He is a professor-researcher at the National University of Chimborazo-Ecuador and visiting professor at the University of Grenoble-Alpes, France. He is coordinator of the CLACSO Working Group Indigenous Movements in Latin America. His most recent book is *Un Manifiesto para el Siglo XXI: de la Renta Básica Universal y otras utopías* (2020). He is a proponent of the project of the Universal Basic Income Law without Conditions for Ecuador and a founding member of the Foro de Economía Alternativa y Heterodoxa-Ecuador.

Silvia Maria Fávero Arend has a doctorate in history and is a full professor in the history department at the University of the State of Santa Catarina (UDESC), Brazil. She held a postdoctoral internship at the Fondation Nationale des Sciences Politiques (Sciences Po-Paris) and at the NOVA University, Lisbon. Her research has been concentrated in the following areas: history of childhood and youth; family history; and history of gender relations. Her most recent book is *Infâncias e Juventudes no século XX: Histórias Latino-Americanas* (co-edited with Esmeralda B. B. De Moura and Susana Sosenki, 2018).

Igor Goicovic is professor of history at the University of Santiago de Chile. He has a BA in history and geography from the Catholic University of Valparaiso, an MA in history from the University of Santiago de Chile and a PhD in history from the University of Murcia (Spain). His main areas of research have been in the study of conflict and social and political violence in Chile and Latin America with many books and scholarly articles in this area.

Reinaldo Lindolfo Lohn has a doctorate in History and did a post-doctoral fellowship at the Institute of Contemporary History at the NOVA University in Lisbon. Currently a Full Professor in the Department of History, at the University of the State of Santa Catarina (Brazil) he teaches at undergraduate level and in the Graduate Programme. His research is focused on the history of Brazil's Republic, mainly political history and history of the present time. His latest book is *Artífices do futuro: cultura política e a invenção do tempo presente de Florianópolis (1950–80)* (second edition, 2020).

Roberto López Sánchez is a professor at the University of Zulia (LUZ), Venezuela. He has a Master's in Venezuelan History and a PhD in Political Science. He currently teaches the subjects of Venezuelan history and universal history in the Bachelor's Degree Programme in Anthropology. He has been coordinator of the Academic Unit of Anthropology, the Diploma in Communal Councils, and the Diploma in Trade Union Training. His particular area of research is in social movements. He has published more than 50 scientific papers, is the author of more than 50 papers in scientific congresses and the organizer of more than 50 seminars and conferences of scientific dissemination.

Mariana Mastrángelo has a PhD in History (Universidad de Buenos Aires, 2010) and is an associate professor of History at the National University of Chilecito (Argentina), where she teaches Argentine history. She has published several books, including *Rojos en la Córdoba obrera, 1930–1940* (2011), *Desde las profundidades de la Historia Oral: Argentina, Brazil, Uruguay* (co-edited with Robson Laverdi) (2012) and *Anatomía de un Imperio* (co-edited with Valeria Carbone) (2019).

Ronaldo Munck is professor of sociology and director of the Centre for Engaged Research at Dublin City University (DCU) and a senior researcher at the Institute for Interdisciplinary Studies on Latin America (INDEAL), University of Buenos Aires. He was the first head of civic engagement at DCU. He has written widely on the impact of globalization on development, changing work patterns and migration. Recent works include *Migration, Precarity and Global Governance* (co-author, 2015); *Rethinking Global Labour: After Neoliberalism* and *Social Movements in Latin America: Mapping the Mosaic* (2020). He is on the board of journals *Globalizations, Global Social Policy, Global Discourse, Global Labour Journal, Latin American Perspectives* and *Review: Journal of the Fernand Braudel Center.* He is a lead author of Amartya Sen's International Panel on Social Progress Report, "Rethinking Society of the 21st Century" and a member of the Council of Europe Task Force on "The Local Democratic Mission of Higher Education".

Francisco Panizza is professor in Latin American and Comparative Politics in the Department of Government at the London School of Economics (LSE). He was born in Montevideo, Uruguay, where he studied law. He has an MA and a PhD in Politics from the University of Essex. From 1991 to 1995 he was a researcher in the Research Department of the International Secretariat of Amnesty International. He joined the Department of Government at the LSE in 1995. He is the co-editor of the Routledge series *Conceptualizing Comparative Politics.* He has written widely on populism including the acclaimed *Populism and the Mirror of Democracy* (2005) and (with others) the recent title *Populism in Global Perspective: A Performative and Discursive Approach* (2021).

Patricia Pensado Leglise is a researcher at the Dr José María Luis Mora Institute, Mexico. She has a PhD in Latin American Studies from the Universidad Nacional Autónoma de México and she is a member of the National Researchers System. She is a specialist in the history of Latin America and the Caribbean in the contemporary age. She has conducted oral history studies on the left in Mexico, from the second half on the twentieth century, and on the life stories of intellectuals and left militants. She is the founder of the Oral History Mexican Association and the Oral History Latin American Network. Her latest book is *Recorridos solidarios. Trayectorias individuales y montajes colectivos en la historia reciente* (co-author, 2020).

Pablo Pozzi has a PhD in History (1989) from New York's Stony Brook University (SUNY). He is retired and is a consulting professor at the Universidad of Buenos Aires, after having been a plenary full professor in the History Department, where he held the chair in United States history and taught the dissertation seminar on Argentine labour. Some of his works are *La oposición obrera a la dictadura (1976–1982)* (1988), *Los setentistas: Izquierda y clase obrera, 1969–1976* (2000), *Por la sendas argentinas: El PRT-ERP, la guerrilla marxista* (2001) and *Historical and Future Global Impacts of Armed Groups and Social Movements* (2020).

Marcelo Raimundo has a PhD in History (Universidad de Buenos Aires 2014) and has been full professor in the History Department of the Universidad Nacional de la Plata (UNLP), Argentina from 2006. He teaches on Argentine and United States labour history and on issues of history teaching, and use of computer technology in historical research and teaching. He specializes in contemporary social and political history, specifically post 1955 labour, and political-union militancy in Argentina. He is a researcher at Instituto de Investigaciones en Humanidades y Ciencias Sociales and has published numerous articles on political and ideological radicalization of Peronism and Argentine working-class history.

William I. Robinson is distinguished professor of Sociology, Global Studies, and Latin American Studies at the University of California at Santa Barbara. He worked as an advisor to the Nicaraguan foreign ministry in the 1980s and was affiliated faculty at the Central American University in Managua from 1994 to 2001. Among his many award-winning books are *Latin America and Global Capitalism* (2008), *Global Capitalism and the Crisis of Humanity* (2014) and *The Global Police State* (2020).

INDEX